The Dragon Doesn't Live Here Anymore

oving Fully
Living Freely

by *Alan Cohen*

Cover Portrait by	Photography by	Illustrations by
Jack McKiernan	Gene Dillman	Valerie Ginther

Alan Cohen

THE DRAGON DOESN'T LIVE HERE ANYMORE
Copyright ©1981 by Alan Cohen

ISBN 0-910367-30-2

Cover Art by Jack McKiernan.
Photography by Gene Dillman: pg. 3, 197, 217, 225, 249; Alan Cohen: pg. 93, 159, 167; Joel Friedman: pg. 309

For the reader's reference, these addresses are given for sources referred to by the author:

A Course in Miracles: Foundation for Inner Peace, P.O. Box 635, Tiburon, California 94920

The autobiography and writings of Paramahansa Yogananda: Self-Realization Fellowship, 3880 San Rafael Avenue, Los Angeles, California 90065.

To order *The Dragon Doesn't Live Here Anymore*:

Personal Orders:

For a free catalog of Alan Cohen's books, tapes and workshop schedule, write to:

Alan Cohen Publications and Workshops
P.O. Box 5658
Somerset, New Jersey 08875

Bookstore Orders:

New Leaf
5425 Tulane Drive S.W.
Atlanta, Georgia 30310-2323
(1-800) 241-3829
toll-free number for stores only

To Bless and to Heal,
The Godly purpose of all
who have dedicated themselves to
the love and service of humanity

Lay down your burden
Lay it all down
Pass the glass between you
Drink it up
Place the Light before you
Come through the door
The dragon doesn't live here anymore

Sing with the choirs that surround you
Dance to the music in your soul
Look into the eyes that really see you
Place all that you have into that bowl

O lay down your burden
Lay it all down
Pass the glass between you
Drink it up
Place the Light before you
Come through the door
The dragon doesn't live here anymore

— *"Lay Down Your Burden"* by Colleen Crangle

By Alan Cohen

BOOKS

The Healing of the Planet Earth

The Dragon Doesn't Live Here Anymore

Rising In Love

The Peace That You Seek

Have You Hugged a Monster Today?
with illustrations by Keith Kelly

Setting the Seen

Companions of the Heart

CASSETTE TAPES

Miracle Mountain

Peace
with music by Steven Halpern

Deep Relaxation
with music by Steven Halpern

I Believe in You
with songs & music by Stephen Longfellow Fiske

AUTHOR'S PREFACE

About two years ago, my good friend Barbara Cole went to well-known psychic Vincent Ragone for his counsel. As he was speaking to her about the path of her life, he stopped and said, "Tell Alan to write." This was quite surprising to her, since she had not mentioned my name or told him anything about me. His advice did not make much sense to me, either, as I was not interested in writing, and typing was one of my least favorite things to do. So I just filed away his suggestion in the back of my mind, in hopes that one day I would understand what he meant.

Then, one December morning a year later, I awoke to hear a gentle voice within me whisper, "Sit down and write." It was not a voice that spoke in words, but an intuitive prompting. As I sat down and began to record whatever ideas came to me, I was fascinated to see how thoughts that I have been considering for years came together with almost ancient memories to form themselves into integrated units with themes and direction. I continued with this process until somehow, without my ever planning it, a few hundred pages later I had a book in my hands.

There is more to the story. During the first few weeks that I was writing, I had a pleasant picture in my mind of doing this work in some quaint secluded cottage, surrounded by fragrant trees and the simple song of the birds. I set out to find such a place, but no matter what people I contacted, advertisements I posted, or affirmations I declared, such a place did not materialize, and I wrote off the idea as just a writer's romantic fantasy.

The weeks of writing turned into months, and it became clear to me that I would need to devote a full-time effort to bring the final form of the book into focus. Then, into my mind flashed the thought, "The Cenacle," the name of a spiritual retreat center staffed by a sisterhood of Catholic nuns. I had driven past the place literally thousands of times, but I knew next to nothing about it.

I telephoned the Cenacle and asked if they had a quiet room in their house where I could write for a few weeks. The director, Sister Barbara, told me, "I'm afraid we don't have such a place in our house, but we do have a little secluded cottage amid some trees . . . Would you like that?"

It was not long before this Sister Barbara was walking me down a winding path lined with delightfully scented spruce trees, to a cozy ivy-covered cottage on a hill overlooking a park and a river. As she opened the door, I could hardly believe my eyes. Before me was a wooden desk with paper and pencils laid out on top of it, a big comfortable easy chair, and almost exactly the room I had envisioned months before — plus a color TV and a little refrigerator. (God gave me my wish plus interest!) As Sister Barbara handed me the key to the cabin, so ended any doubts that I ever had about God's ability to perform the impossible. I figured that if He could get a Jewish guy named Cohen into a convent, He can do anything.

After working there a few days, I decided to take a break, and I went out to a local barn theatre to see a production of *Joseph and the Amazing Technicolor Dreamcoat*. As I was sitting in the lounge during intermission, I felt extremely comfortable in this place, and I wondered why. As I looked up at the low sloping ceiling with its century-old rough-hewn beams, I realized that this room reminded me of the Upper Room as it was portrayed in the movie *Jesus of Nazareth*. This was the room where Jesus gave the disciples His parting blessings, and where He returned to them after the resurrection to tell them, "I am always with you." This scene is one of the most powerful and touching I have ever experienced, and I have often thought how much I would love to be in that place, receiving the Master's Blessing and His charge to live for Love, Healing, and Service to all. The Upper Room has a special place in my heart.

The next day, I was sitting in the Cenacle garden with one of the nuns, sharing our ideas and aspirations, when I felt moved to ask her, "What does '*The Cenacle*' mean?"

"Oh, yes," she kindly explained, " '*Cenacle*' is the French word for 'The Upper Room.' "

It is experiences like these that make me feel that there is a great plan of Guidance and Direction working within our lives, a purpose deeper and more powerful than we usually recognize. I feel privileged to have participated in the process of this book, and its birth is a testimony to the Truth that God is everywhere, that He is constantly seeking to work with us and through us, and that He is always willing to share the miracle of Love with us, as we are willing to accept it and express it.

One P.S.: When the book was complete, it turned out to be a series of short lyrical essays, and I took it to my friend Barbara to share with her. As I did, she played for me the tape recording of her original interview with Vincent Ragone, one which I had never heard. When the tape came to the moment at which Vincent said, "Tell Alan to write," there was another statement which Barbara had not told me about. He said, "I think a series of short lyrical essays would be very good."

I hope that you will enjoy the book and that you find value in it.

Alan Cohen

There is a story about a man who left this earth and was taken on a tour of the inner realms. He was shown a room where he saw a large group of hungry people trying to eat dinner, but because the spoons that they were trying to eat with were longer than their arms, they remained frustrated. "This," his guide told him, "is hell." "That's terrible!" exclaimed the man; "Please show me Heaven!" "Very well," agreed the guide, and on they went. When they opened Heaven's door, the man was perplexed to see what looked very much like the same scene: there was a group of people with spoons longer than their arms. As he looked more closely, however, he saw happy faces and full tummies, for there was one important difference: the people in Heaven had learned to feed each other.

The coming together of this book has been a miracle at every step of the way. People, materials, and connections have all seemed to be in just the right place at just the right time. Most inspiring to me has been the Divine support and help I have received from my friends who have demonstrated themselves to be nothing other than selfless sisters and brothers. All of the words in this book could not express my appreciation for their support. I hope that this page will capture the thought of my gratefulness.

I would like to humbly acknowledge my mother and father, who have taught me the meaning of unconditional love, Hilda, who has shown me the Miracle of Grace, and B.C., who has given me the precious gift of friendship. I am equally grateful to my family on the Land, the sisters of The Cenacle, Valerie Ginther and Dorene Yonelunas, Jack McKiernan, Gene Dillman, The Roses, Karolyn Kempner, David Crismond, Jeff Woolley, and all of the many others who have contributed in many ways to this work. I wish to express, as well, my deep appreciation for the dedicated music of the Paul Winter Consort and the angelic voice of Susan Osborn, whose sincere offering of "Lay Down Your Burden" captures all the Love and Light this book is intended to express.

It is my further hope that all of the masters, saints, yogis, and loving teachers who have helped me in my own growth will be honored through the blessing of all who read these words. Truly God loves us through each other.

PART I:
THE JOURNEY

PART II:
THE HOMECOMING

PART I:
THE JOURNEY

"I want to learn to fly like that," Jonathan said, and a strange light glowed in his eyes. "Tell me what to do."

Chiang spoke slowly and watched the younger gull ever so carefully. "To fly as fast as thought, to anywhere that is," he said, "you must begin by knowing that you have already arrived . . ."

The trick, according to Chiang, was for Jonathan to stop seeing himself as trapped inside a limited body with a forty-two inch wingspan . . . The trick was to know that his true nature lived, as perfect as an unwritten number, everywhere at once across space and time.

— Richard Bach, *Jonathan Livingston Seagull*

Starting Points

ONE STORY

Love is the way I walk in gratitude.
— A Course in Miracles

At an early age, I remember saying to one of my Little League pals, "Gee, Johnny, wouldn't it be funny if we were all dead, and we were just dreaming that we are alive?" Then, as my childhood visions of playing centerfield for the Yankees were lost to a mad idea that dreams do not come true, I settled for a place in a world where the aspiration for love and freedom is written off as an impossible wish. Now, however, I have come full circle, and what I told Johnny is, ironically, pretty much what I believe now — that the life we live is something of a dream. The only difference is that now I believe that we are all alive, and dreaming that we can die.

When I was in second grade, I came down with pneumonia, and Doctor Bernie Friedenthal came to my house to tell my mother to sponge me down with cold water. As she continued to do this through the night, the thought occurred to me that I might die. I remember that at that time I did not fear death. The idea of dying seemed as matter-of-fact to me as the end of the school year. I asked my mom, "What will happen if I do not get better?" "Don't worry, honey," she told me comfortingly, "You'll be alright." But I was not asking out of fear — I was more curious than afraid.

Somehow, sometime after that, I learned to be afraid. I began to believe in a fearful and threatening world. I came to think that there were monsters out there, merciless dragons who could devour a helpless me. I forgot how to feel beautiful and I learned to feel ugly. Somewhere along the line, I traded in my sense of "O.K. Kid" for a self-image that seemed always to be somehow less than others. I was overweight, awkward, and the only Jewish kid in the neighborhood. I thought that there was something wrong with me, and that there was something I had to do (like be skinny, athletic, and Protestant) to be like the gang of popular kids.

Since that time, however, as I have gotten to know more and more of the popular kids, I have had a startling discovery: *they felt the same way*. They, too, felt that there was something different about them, and that they had to be popular and acknowledged to earn love. Just like me, they thought that there was an "in crowd," and they were out.

This gave me something very interesting to think about: if everyone felt out, who, then, was "in?" As it turns out, there never really was any "in crowd," except in the eyes of those who thought they were out — which was just about *all* of us.

And so we are not so different after all. As we begin to share our stories, it becomes clear that we all learned to fear and feel separate and alone. We can see, too, that it is only the details of our stories that are different, and that the heart of our separate stories is really the same. What we thought were different stories are really One Story — our story.

When I arrived at Miss Greenberger's kindergarten class at Washington School, I was quite self-conscious and embarrassed about my weight. More than anything in the world, I dreaded the event of having to go down to the nurse's office to get weighed with my class, because the nurse would call each weight out loud. As I would step onto the scales, a great hush would come over the spellbound class, as if it were the final drawing of the Irish Sweepstakes, and the moment my weight was announced, all the normal kids would go wild, and their eyes would bug out, and they would grab each other and say, "Wow! Did you hear that?" They had a blast. As for me, I just wanted to blast off into some remote corner of the universe.

Well, one day, the awful announcement came: it was time for us to all go down to the basement to be weighed. I wanted to run out the door and hide, but since I couldn't, I marched down the stairs with all the skinny kids, praying all the while that the nurse wouldn't say my weight out loud. It sounds funny now, but at the time, it was a horror story. When we got to the basement, an honest-to-goodness miracle happened: there, waiting for me were my mom and dad, with a big birthday cake with five candles, lots of ice cream, and party hats for everyone. The weighing story was just a ruse to get me downstairs for a surprise birthday party! (Talk about being saved in the nick of time!) I was glad they decided to surprise me, but they could have at least picked a more compassionate ploy! But they did not know the private hell I was going through, and it was really an act of love.

I tell this story now, as it has come to symbolize to me the story of our fears in life. We hold horrible catastrophic fantasies of what is to come — fears based on learned unworthiness and misunderstanding. When we are forced or choose to confront these fears, however, we learn that there was never anything to be afraid of, after all. The fear is like that of the boogeyman who supposedly lived in the basement, but who turned out to never really be there when we turned on the light.

There is a sequel to the story. Years later, when I was pledging a fraternity in college, we pledges were continuously warned about the ominous *Hell Night*. When I would pass some initiation test during the pledge period, the brothers would say, "That's pretty good, pledge, but just wait until Hell Night . . . Then we'll see who really makes it!" I couldn't imagine it being any worse than some of the stunts they had us do during pledging, such as the night we had to line up outside the basement door and be called downstairs, one by one, to face the weird brotherhood-at-large. As I sat there waiting my turn, all I heard were crazed and ghoulish screams from the depths below. During those minutes at the top of the basement stairs, every Vincent Price movie that I had ever seen flashed through my mind, and I was sure that they had hired him to conduct the evening's program. When I finally got down there, however, I found that it was just the brothers making those noises to scare us.

When Hell Night, the final trial-by-fire of the pledge period came, we were told to arrive at the fraternity house at 6 p.m. on Saturday with no money, no identification, and to tell no one where we were going. (Luckily, I was in a Jewish fraternity, and because I observed the Jewish sabbath, they were kind enough to postpone Hell until 7 p.m., after dark.) And I must confess that I cheated. I stashed a $5 bill in the sole of one of my penny loafers. (I must have had great faith to think that $5 could save me from Hell!) But please don't tell anyone, or they might take back my fraternity pin.

When I arrived, we were lined up and told that we would have to go through a series of dangerous adventures to prove ourselves worthy of the final test. The path to this test, we were told, was a cleverly designed scavenger hunt. Our pledge class was then divided into two groups and told to wish each other well, as there was no guarantee that we would ever see each other again.

Our first clue led us to a locker at a bus station, where we found one-way tickets to New York City. Then, behind a *Time* magazine billboard in Manhattan, we found an envelope with subway tokens, which took us to our next clue on the George Washington Bridge. And then to a restaurant in Chinatown, where a message was hidden in the duck sauce. And then we were directed to walk through Central Park and whistle a certain tune, which would draw to us our next instruction, delivered by a well-known prostitute (who was actually a very innocent coed drama major, put up to the job by the conniving brothers). Her message led us to a specific subway platform in Greenwich Village, where, emerging from another train coming from a different direction was: the other group of our pledge brothers! (All paths lead to the same place.) There we were met by a brother who gave us outlandish costumes and party hats and marched us through the streets to the front of the Fillmore East Theatre. Here we did not feel conspicuous in our silly outfits, since most of the people in line to get into the *Canned Heat* concert were dressed weirder than we were.

Then the Pledgemaster appeared. This was the one known for his uncompromising ruthlessness and sheer joy at seeing pledges cringe. He lined us up and told us: "You have successfully conquered your trials to this point. Your final test now stands before you. In a few minutes, you will be taken to a room in which a group of people will be waiting for you. There, you will be asked to perform an action that you have not previously experienced. If you want to be initiated into this fraternity, you must do anything that you are asked. You have the right at any time to withdraw your request to be a brother in this fraternity. Am I making myself clear?"

Too clear. We pledges looked each other in the eye like the Little Rascals on a windy night's camping trip. But we knew that we had gone this far, and we were not about to quit now. And so we were marched down the street, in our little party hats and funny costumes, wondering what diabolical scheme, extracted from the repressed subconscious of a crazed fraternity pledgemaster, was waiting for us. Then we were stopped and directed to enter into a certain bar, which, as we passed through the door, one of my pledge brothers whispered to me, was gay. I had no idea what to expect. My mind was going in circles, and the word "faith" took on new meaning for me.

We were ushered into a back room, and there, waiting for us, was indeed a group of people. It was all of our fraternity brothers, with big smiles on their faces, singing the fraternity song, and adding the verse, "and we are so happy to welcome you to our fraternity." That was it! The task that we had to do was to accept our welcome into the brotherhood! At that moment, my "big brother" in the fraternity came over to me, gave me a big handshake, and walked me over to the refreshment table, where I proceeded to enjoy one hell of a party. And I didn't even need to use the $5.

Sometimes, however, we have to wrestle with a paper tiger for a while before we realize that he is a fraud. By the time I was getting to be a teenager, my feelings about myself had dropped below freezing. I was six feet tall with a size twelve shoe, and I had to bring a birth certificate to get in to the movies for the children's price, since no ticket seller in her right mind would believe that I was a child. To make things worse, pimples were beginning to sprout on my cheeks and one morning I woke up with braces on my teeth. On top of it all, I became interested in girls, which seemed to magnify every pimple, oral twinkle, and extra pound.

Perhaps it was out of necessity that, when I was twelve years old, I undertook my first act of determination in this life: I put myself on a weight-loss program. I went on a strict diet of raisin bread and jelly. It was not exactly a regimen that Adelle Davis might go for, but it worked. Within a few months, my weight was normal, and with the pounds went an old idea of "me."

A few years (and a lot of raisin bread) later, I received in the mail an invitation to attend a Sunday morning brunch for teenagers at my synagogue. Though I put the letter aside, the event held a strange fascination for me. This fascination I later came to know as the loving Voice of God, gently prompting me to come home to His open arms. I call it the Voice of God because it led me to a teacher that would guide

9

me for a time on my path. Later, that very same voice was to draw me away from the forms of organized religion.

Out of what I believed to be curiosity, I went to this brunch. I had no rationale for going; in fact, after my Bar Mitzvah, I expected to steer clear of the synagogue forevermore. My parents were not affiliated with the temple, and there was no reason on earth for me to go — but there was a reason in Heaven.

When I got there, I met a man, Stuie, who was to become my spiritual guide for seven years. He was a dynamic, sincere, and open-hearted man, his life dedicated to the love of God. When he spoke that morning, his words touched a chord inside of me that had long been painfully silent. It was the chord of the awakening of my soul. My mind began to be intrigued with questions that I had long since put aside for lack of anyone to share them with, questions like "Why am I here?" and "Who is God?" More important, my heart flew open with the possibility of the reality of love and happiness and a purpose for life. I was on my way home.

Like a big brother, Stuie took me under his wing and gave me love and guidance in a way that I had not experienced in years. He respected me. He saw worth in me that no one else acknowledged. I felt accepted and whole, nurtured and good — feelings that I had nearly given up believing. My relationship with God was rekindled; I began to see positivity in life and wonder in the mysteries of the universe. I had stepped out of the loneliness of isolation and into the warm sun of a life worth living.

The years with Stuie and the temple youth group were ones of transformation and learning, and I shall always be grateful for them. I became very involved in Orthodox Judaism, strictly observing the sabbath, eating kosher food, and following the detailed laws and customs. Though I had to make some "sacrifices" in my outer life, such as quitting the track team and missing the Junior Prom, I did not care. I had found something within me that could not compare to that frightening outer world in which I had been struggling. I remember going to sleep one night wearing my prayer shawl, clutching its fringes, with such a love in my heart that I felt I was cradled in the arms of God Himself.

I decided to attend Yeshiva University, a college for Jewish studies, where I could continue my pursuit of God. There I had the good fortune to study with an exciting, inspired rabbi who made the

Bible more alive than anything else I was doing. He would come to class each morning and stand on the desk and literally yell about how wonderful is God! His love of Truth was so great that I felt drawn face to face with Abraham. There was something magical about the Truth brought to life. And there was something very warm and deep in the community of Judaism.

I would not be allowed to stagnate, though. After two years at the college, I no longer felt inspired. The laws and customs ceased to hold their magic for me, and I found myself performing rituals mechanically. I wanted to do other things; to live again in the world. I had extracted all that I could from Judaism, at that state of my evolution, and God had other plans for me.

There was a turning point. One holiday, a fast day, I found myself fasting and resenting it. I persevered and persevered, but it was not a perseverance of the heart — it was a clinging to a form that I had outgrown. I realized that I was fasting because I was afraid not to; I feared going off the path of Judaism (which I had been taught was a tragedy); I feared losing God's love and special favor; and I feared facing feelings of guilt and badness. At that moment I decided that fear was not a good enough reason to do a religious act, and it was certainly not a good enough reason to live a life, and I would rather take my chances in the world than live in fear. So I ate a piece of cake, and thus began the next stage in my unfoldment.

I transferred to a state college, joined my fraternity, and proceeded to whoop it up for two years. I lived out all the desires that I had repressed and missed during my Jewish years. Looking back on that time now, I see that I had to work through those desires and learn the ways of the world. Perhaps my evolution could have proceeded no further in a cloistered life. I certainly did not reason it out like this at the time; I was just busy having a good time; and that is exactly what I did. And I believe that in the long run the experience served my growth.

The summer after college, I went to Europe, and I had my nose rubbed in the world. A friend and I set out to have a two-month blast, but we soon found that life on earth is not always a fraternity party. Within one week of my trip, I had all of my belongings stolen, purely out of my own irresponsibility (I went to a rock festival and left my goods unattended), and this gave birth to a major lesson in my growing up.

11

I was not willing to accept responsibility for the world stealing from me. I felt the world owed it to me to make up the loss. So I decided to cash some travelers cheques and to fraudulently report them stolen. This way, American Express — and not me — would take the loss. I cashed several hundred dollars' worth of cheques with a sloppy signature to uphold the claim I would later make. The next step was for me to walk down the street to the American Express office to file the phony claim. But something stopped me. A quiet, but very real, still, small voice within me whispered, "No — don't do this — no good can come of it." This voice seemed new to me, yet astonishingly familiar. I stood in front of the door of the American Express office, thought quietly for a few moments, and then turned about and walked back to my hotel. I believe that then and there, in front of American Express, amid my raving desires and pounding emotions, I received grace from a guardian angel giving me gentle guidance to help me avoid further difficulties in the world, for, in truth, no good could have come of the act.

I returned to America to enter graduate school. How I got into the right graduate school is a miracle story, if ever there was one. I was pretty much a sleepwalker. Although I thought I was making choices, I now see that God was guiding me at every step of the way. What I thought were my reasons were really His Reasons. His Plan for me, you see, was much bigger than my little plan for my little self.

In college, I was a psychology major. Although I did not realize it, I was reaching out for a deeper understanding of the inner life. One night, at a local YMHA, I was hypnotized by an amateur hypnotist. I became intrigued with this process which led to another realm of experience and pointed to the possibility of states of consciousness beyond the one I usually experienced. Immediately I took up the study of hypnotism. I read all the books I could find on the subject; I mailed for pamphlets and began to hypnotize my friends; I entertained at fraternity parties, and had my fraternity brothers recite their Bar Mitzvah prayers, to the amusement of all.

I relate this now to show how the process of reaching out for God is one of homing in on target. At first it is gross and clumsy. In hypnotizing for fun, I was grasping on to a higher element of reality for which I yearned. At the time, it was the best — and the only — way that I knew how to touch God. Now I would not use mental power for entertainment, but then it was the best that I could do with what I knew or had.

Before long, I came upon the book *The Search for Bridey Murphy*, the true story of an amateur hypnotist who, through hypnotic age regression, took a woman into what she reported were a number of previous incarnations, for which documentation was later discovered. I became fascinated with the idea of reincarnation, and excited at the prospect of exploring it through hypnosis. It was not long before I was trying hypnotic regression to previous lives on any friend or student of mine who was game enough to try. I was obsessed with it. I even did it in some risky situations, such as with high school students when I was substitute teaching. I was crazy to do it as I did, but now I see that these experiments were really just attempts to know God. I was fortunate that I did not get into trouble over it. I like to believe, though, that my intentions were pure, and I was able to do what I did without harm of it.

Now, since I was also a finagler, I decided that I might as well get college credit for my treasure hunts into the subconscious. So I took a psychology senior research course and got to use the college laboratory for a hypnosis experiment which set out to verify the truth of hypnotic age regression. As it turned out, the study did not verify anything, but I did succeed in getting a pretty blonde coed to follow a post-hypnotic suggestion to call me up at midnight one night.

The professor of this senior research class was a very hip and transcendental sort of character. My first contact with him was an education in itself. I had just transferred from Yeshiva University, a very straight institution, as far as institutions go. When I came to Rutgers, I had to get my schedule approved by a certain Dr. Green, who, I was told, could be found in his office at the top of the stairs of an old house used as the psychology department. So I trod up a long stairway, knocked on the door, and heard a deep voice resonate, "Come on in!" There, sitting below a huge day-glow "Peace" poster, was this incredibly tall hippy with the longest arms and legs I have ever seen. His face was covered with a huge black beard and hair longer, it seemed, than his arms. He was sitting nonchalantly with his mile-long legs up on the desk, reading a magazine. He looked straight out of a *Fabulous Furry Freak Brothers* comic.

"Excuse me," I interrupted, "Could you tell me where I can find Dr. Green?"

"That's me, man . . . come on in!"
I had most definitely left Yeshiva University.

Dr. Green and I became good friends. I signed up for his
Psychology Seminar, in which he told about his LSD experiences,
threw around words like "karma," and assigned us to read Carlos
Castenada's *Teachings of Don Juan*. The first day of class, Dr. Green
wrote on the blackboard this quotation, which he told us was from
Don Juan:

> *Each man is different;*
> *Each man must find his own path.*
> *Each man is the same;*
> *Each man must find his own path.*

I was about to graduate from college, and the natural thing to do
seemed to be to go to graduate school. I must report that I never gave
a moment's thought to why I should go to graduate school, or whether
it was the best choice of action, and it never really occurred to me that
there might be something else to do, like join the Peace Corps or go to
work. I had gone to school all my life, and as long as there was more
school to go to, I guessed that I was supposed to go to it. On one level,
it was a very unconscious decision, my being seemingly pushed along
like a leaf floating on a river. But, as it turned out, there was a deeper
plan for me — a downright Divine plot — one which I never could
have guessed.

When I applied to graduate schools, there was no method to my
madness. I just mailed applications to whatever schools sounded
romantic or were well-known. It had very little to do with any reasoning. On my applications, where I was asked to state my career interests, I wrote down subjects like hypnosis, the placebo effect, and
dream therapy. I was not seriously interested in anything, but now, as
I consider what I wrote, they were all fields of inquiry that pointed
toward discovering the inner knowledge — the wisdom of the higher
self. My inner being was yearning for a deeper understanding of life,
and I was trying to get at it in the academic realm of psychology.

It was no wonder that I was rejected from eight of the nine
graduate schools that I applied to. And the one that did accept me, I
didn't want to go to. I just did not feel as if I had found my place.

14

Then a friend suggested that I try Montclair State College. I knew nothing about this school, except that it was a state teachers' college, and I certainly was not interested in teaching. But I felt attracted to it for some unknown reason, and so I decided to check it out. The moment I stepped on the campus, I felt at ease and very much at home. There was something that just felt right about it. At the time, I thought it was because there were lots of attractive girls on campus, but, as it turns out, the girl that was really attracting me was the Divine Mother.

I went into the admissions office and asked, "Do you think I can get into this school?"

The admissions officer asked me about two questions, and said, "Sure! — Would you like a scholarship?"

"Sure!" I replied, and about a month later, I received a letter in the mail telling me that my tuition was waived, and that I was now the Graduate Assistant to the Dean of Students and the recipient of a very generous salary. I have a feeling God wanted me in that school.

I entered the program for Guidance Counseling, which was not really what I wanted, but it was the best thing on the menu, and so I took it. In my first class, a short, grey-haired professor with smiling eyes walked into the room, plugged in a tape recorder, and announced, "This is my course in a nutshell." As the "play" button clicked, I heard Sammy Davis Jr. singing, "I Gotta Be Me." I sat there thinking, "This teacher's weird," and then I began to listen to the words of the song. What did he mean, "I gotta be me?"

The book for the course was Carl Rogers' *On Encounter Groups*. I knew about encounter groups only what I had read in *Newsweek* magazine. I thought it was interesting and kind of nice for people who liked to sit naked together and be honest and cry. "This is good for those with problems," I thought, "but I am already honest and open." Nothing could have been further from the truth. I was living a phony, closed, and uptight life. As I read through the book, even as I read the first paragraph, something marvelously thrilling happened inside of me. I felt as if a warm and wonderul sun was rising in my chest. The words went right into my heart. The spirit of the book appealed to a deeper and more satisfying level of my being than I had experienced since I was a little child. All Dr. Rogers was saying was that his life was much more satisfying when he was open, honest, accepting, trust-

15

ing, and loving. And that was all I needed to hear to remind me of a hunger in my soul for truth and simplicity, two of the very important elements of happiness that I had not known in many years. Even when I was in Judaism, I was so busy being Jewish that I forgot to be me. And now I was being offered the opportunity to once again know myself.

I responded with more enthusiasm than I have ever felt for anything in this life. In the book, Dr. Rogers spoke of "human relations laboratories," planned workshops for practicing trust, honesty, and communication. "God, would I like to find one of these," I thought. I would do anything to get involved in something like this.

All I had to do was to walk, the next day, through the college student center lounge, for there, to my astonishment, was a poster: "Human Relations Laboratory, October 4-7." I flew to the sign-up table and registered as fast as my little unconscious hand could write. There was nothing, I tell you, *nothing* that could keep me from that workshop. Don't ask me why. At the time, I couldn't really tell you. I just knew it was for me.

The workshop turned out to be all that I wanted, expected, and needed — and more. It was, if it is possible to say, the turning point of my life. For the first part of the weekend, I was uptight and phony. My ego, you see, was threatened. It knew it was about to die, for I would have to give up my old way of being, and that is something the ego does not easily relinquish — even if the old way of being is empty. In my heart of hearts, however, I knew that this death was but a birth into a new and more wonderful way of living.

Late one night, in our workshop group, someone confronted me. "Alan," she said, "You don't seem like you're really with us. How are you feeling?"

"Comfortable," I lied, "and confident." (Not only did I lie, but I swore to it.)

"That's funny," someone else commented, "you don't seem very comfortable or confident to me."

"Nor to me," another agreed. "I see you the same way," said another, and another, and yet another — all in a loving and supportive way.

At that moment, something happened inside of me that was perhaps the most profound experience of my life. It was as if a little light went on in my gut, or something like a door to a dark room being opened to admit morning sunlight. If I could give it a voice, it would have said, *"It's O.K., Alan. You can let go, now. It's O.K."* It was a moment so subtle and quiet that no one else could ever know it was happening, yet so spectacular that a new life sprang from it. It was nothing less than the transformation of a human being.

"Maybe you're right," I spoke, not believing that these words were coming out of my mouth. "I have not been feeling very confident; maybe I have been acting kind of phony."

When I finished these words, I felt as if a ten ton weight had been lifted off my shoulders. It was as if I could breathe again, as if the "me" that had been so long hidden under a burden of expectations and pressures had been freed to live once again in open daylight. I had found the key to unlock myself from a desolate tower of lonely isolation, and I began to dance down the stairs into a new world — a good world — in which I could allow other persons into my heart, and where I could share myself with them. I no longer had to be afraid of people, of my feelings, of opinions. I knew that I was alright, and that there was something wonderful in store for me if I could just make heart-to-heart contact with others. It was the end of my exile, and the beginning of a life that I could cherish.

I began to experience fantastic changes in my life. I literally threw away my contact lenses, for I knew I was loveable even *with* eyeglasses, and if someone would not have me with glasses, well, that was too bad for them. I began to write poetry and to be turned on by people. I could touch others, physically and emotionally. I spoke truth in my relationships. My life was evolving at a fantastic pace.

My old friends dropped away, as they had no idea what I was raving about. Some of them just stared at me and said, "That's nice," but I knew that they were just being polite, and our relationship was all but over. But new and more exciting and more fulfilling relationships blossomed in my life almost overnight. I just wanted to live, and to grow, and to experience this wonderful feeling of being that seemed brand new to me, and yet strangely familiar. I was in love with life, and life was in love with me. It was the very best kind of love affair.

Just around that time, I began to be interested in psychedelic drugs. When Dr. Green turned me on to Castenada and *Don Juan*, I became intrigued with the possibility that there were yet deeper realities. There was something temptingly mystical about Don Juan's teachings. It rekindled deep within my soul a memory of a realm of being in which *all* of life made sense. We were also assigned to read Aldous Huxley's *Doors of Perception*, in which he described his eye-opening experience with the drug mescaline. Huxley said that he became aware of a great "Mind at Large" — a universal intelligence which guides and knows and sees all things in wonder and delight. He had tuned in to God's Infinite Mind. That sounded pretty exciting to me. If this drug could reveal such a splendor, then I wanted to try it.

And so I did. A friend got me a small amount of mescaline, and I was in for quite an experience. I felt a tremendous surge of power pulsating through my body; not a physical power, but the release of a tremendous mind energy. It was wonderful, and frightening. At one point, I felt a great charge of love and peace, and all I could do was to smile at first, and then burst into uncontrollable laughter. Unfortunately, I and my friends were in a Chinese restaurant at the time. Fortunately, I was able to maintain some semblance of decorum, and I contained myself just long enough to retreat to the restroom, where the moment the door closed behind me, I burst into hysterical laughter. There I remained until this episode was over.

When I later "came down," the overall experience had had a jarring effect on my way of looking at the world. I had touched feelings and tapped energies that made the things that I had been taught to value seem empty. I had had a very brief taste of expanded consciousness, and after such a taste ("The first time the tiger tastes blood," described Claudio Naranjo), many of the activities that I was used to enjoying now seemed shallow and unfulfilling. I began to feel a little depressed and confused, for I did not know how to integrate my experience and new perceptions with my former way of life.

I felt a need for some kind of guidance, but I did not know anyone who could offer it. Then, a little voice inside of me kept gently repeating, "Go see Jim . . . Talk to Jim." Why it picked Jim, I had no idea. Jim was a strange and powerful man who had been in my wonderful, tranforming group on the human relations laboratory. I did not like him; his lifestyle, his manner, and his words seemed very foreign to me, and I felt threatened by him. I certainly did not understand him. There was something very unusual about him. When this little voice within me, a voice that I had never heard before, but that I trusted, told me to seek him out, I was perplexed. I put it off, and put it off, but my confusion was now being amplified by thoughts that I had lost my mind or gone crazy.

I had to talk to him. One evening I saw him at a workshop and I took him aside. "Jim," I asked reticently, "do you know anything about acid (psychedelic drugs)?" The moment he heard the question, his eyes begin to bulge, and I thought I saw mesmerizing whirlpool patterns begin to swirl in his eyes, the kind they show in the movies to indicate that someone is traveling through time into another dimension. "Acid?! . . . Did you say 'Acid'?!" (By this time I thought his eyes were going to pop out.) . . . "I *am* acid!!!" Boy, did I ask the sixty-four dollar question. I felt like Dorothy standing before the Wizard of Oz.

We sat down together, and Jim began to explain to me all of his understanding of acid. As you may have gathered, he was a little on the dramatic side. I wanted to be reassured that I was O.K., and that nothing horrible had happened to me as a result of taking this powerful drug. "Do you think I can go back to being happy doing the same things I've been used to doing?" I asked, half hoping that he would give me a simple "Sure," and that would be the end of it.

"Oh, no! You can't go back now!"

I was getting a little anxious, but I was magnetized to hear him out. "Do you know why?" he continued.

"Why, Jim?"

"Because now you are a *mutant!*" Chills of horror ran through my entire body. "Oh, no!" I thought, "I don't want to be a mutant . . . anything but that!"

"And do you know what else?" He didn't flinch one bit. (I could hardly wait to hear.) ". . . That's the best thing that could ever happen to you, because you are now a part of the next step in the evolution of mankind on the planet." I had no idea what he was talking about, but it was starting to sound good. He went on for a long time on the same theme. When he was done, I was still confused, perhaps even more so, but I was also encouraged and optimistic. I felt that there was a wonderous realm of understanding and a new awareness of life calling me. I had no idea what the next step would be; I only knew it would be exciting.

A few weeks passed. Then, one evening, Jim invited me to listen to what he described as an amazing tape that he had of a man named "Baba Ram Dass." The tape and the name had little appeal to me until Jim told me, "This guy knows a lot about acid." My ears perked up.

"You should really hear this tape . . . He gave four hits of acid to this guy in India, and nothing happened to him! . . . This guy was higher than acid!"

"Higher than acid? Wow!" I thought, "This guy must be *really* high!" I wanted to hear this tape.

So Jim and I got together and took some LSD and turned on this tape. The tape was four hours long, and it turned out to be the longest four hours of my life.

On the tape, Baba Ram Dass told the story of his spiritual awakening. He started out as a sort of neurotic high-achieving Jewish psychologist. I could identify with that. He got turned on to LSD, and he began to see the universe in a new way. I could identify with that. He went to India to find out what LSD was. I could identify with that, too.

By this time in the trip, I began to experience everything that Baba Ram Dass was saying as if it were literally the story of my own life. It was as if I had stepped right into his consciousness; I felt as if I was listening to *my* story being told by *my* voice on the tape. It was as if I knew everything he was going to say before he said it, like an ancient memory bank was made open for me.

The story came to when Ram Dass met his Guru, Neem Karoli Baba. After a long and depressing trip, Ram Dass found himself at the feet of Neem Karoli, who revealed to Ram Dass that he knew everything about Ram Dass' life. He told him facts that were known only to Ram Dass and God. "At that moment," told Ram Dass, "I let go completely . . . I fell at his feet and cried and cried and cried. The only way to describe the feeling was, 'I'm home.'"

At that moment, since I was totally identified with Ram Dass, I felt the exact same experience — and more. I felt that I had died — literally died; left my body; like my life was over. The thing that surprised me the most was that I was still here! Though I had died, I was still alive! The feeling of exhilaration and peace that I felt is not describable in words. What I saw was that death is not real; I had died, but yet I lived! Along with this ecstasy, I saw how ridiculous had been my fear of death. I looked back on my life and saw all the things that I had foolishly worried about, and I saw how silly I was to have ever feared anything. I saw the world as pure illusion. I saw death as illusion, and eternal life as real. I saw pain and suffering and starving children as illusion. It all seemed like a movie that had no substance. All I could do was to laugh and cry at the same time. I felt that I was home, and that the veils of ignorance had been lifted from my eyes. I saw that I never needed to ever worry about anything again, and I kept saying, dazzled and amazed, "There's nothing left to do now but to have a good time." I felt like I was in Heaven. Perhaps I was.

Well, this heaven lasted only a few hours, and then I went through the painful process of "crashing." Can you imagine entering the Holy Kingdom, and then being asked to leave? And then imagine not wanting to leave, but being compelled to. Christ told of this in the parable of the man who entered into the wedding feast without an invitation. "Bind him hand and foot and cast him into the outer darkness." I had crashed Heaven's party, but I had not earned the right to stay, and so back down I went.

The climax of the trip was over. The tape was over. Morning had come. Jim put on his jacket and left for his dentist's appointment. (How he could go to the dentist in that condition, I still do not understand.) But I was not the same person who turned on the tape player ten hours earlier. I called up a friend at seven o'clock in the morning and told her that I had just been to Heaven and that I had just seen God and that there is no death and that all is illusion. It was quite a wake-up story for her. She politely listened, but I began to see that I had been to a place that would be very difficult to describe.

Some kind of knowledge had been made available to me. It was as if some circuitry in my brain had been hooked up to a deep, deep memory bank, something like Aldous Huxley's "Mind at Large." That morning I went to the college cafeteria and had some coffee with a friend who was studying for an exam. Casually he asked me, "Do you know anything about Jung's *anima* and *animus*?" Somehow, my mouth opened and out came a discourse on the *anima* and *animus*, though I had but heard these two words and I knew next to nothing about them. Despite this, I gave him quite an explanation. My friend was amazed and he may have even taken notes. I don't remember. I was even more amazed than he was. Where I got the explanation from, I don't know. I don't know now what those words mean.

A few weeks later, I was substitute teaching for a seventh grade science class. Casually, I picked up a book on Einstein's theory of relativity. I understood exactly what he was talking about. I knew what his symbols meant. The equation made sense. "Of course he's right," I said to myself. E = MC² seemed like child's play to me. It just seemed so logical. "Old Albert was on the right track," I thought. Don't ask me now what it means. I couldn't tell you.

I was hooked. Not on LSD. On God. Yes, for a while I worshipped LSD, but I soon learned that the experience I had was possible without drugs, which can be dangerous. At the bottom line, it has to be us and God, with no intermediaries. More than anything else, I wanted that experience again. I wanted to see God. I wanted to feel Heaven. I wanted to know all the time that there is no death. I wanted to know that all is illusion. I was prepared to do anything for it. The tiger had tasted blood.

Jim became my mentor, my home-made Guru. Everything he said, I listened to with open ears. Everything he did, I did. I walked like he did. I talked like he did. I laughed like he did. I didn't have to, of course, but I idolized the guy; he was my connection to God. He and I developed our own language that no one else could understand. But we understood each other, and that was enough.

We decided to take a trip cross country. (Actually, he decided, and I went along, because I did everything he did.) It was a fun trip, a crazy one, and at times a grueling one. It was a pilgrimage. We went to the St. Louis Planetarium and looked at Venus with a troop of cub scouts. We went to the Indian caves and meditated on the moon. We went to Arizona and Jim lived out his life's fantasy of throwing a tennis ball into the Grand Canyon. It was quite an event for him.

Along the way, Jim taught me about the great philosophers, like Socrates, Hegel, and Marcus Aurelius. I had tremendous faith in this guy. Once, for example, while I was doing the driving through the mountains of Pennsylvania, I saw a hand reach over my shoulder from the back of Jim's '62 VW bus, and in it were about a dozen pills of assorted colors, shapes, sizes, and inscriptions. Along with the hand came Jim's voice: "Here, take these."

"What are they?" I had to ask.

"Vitamins! . . . They're really good for you."

So I took them. About five minutes later, I felt my face start to burn as if every cell had swallowed a handful of chili peppers; when I looked in the mirror, it was as red as a Pacific sunset. At the same time, I felt thousands of tingles prickling up and down my spine, and I had to look in the mirror again to see if my ears were shooting steam. I felt like one of those hot dogs that gets roasted from the inside out.

"Say, Jim," I nonchalantly asked (to seem cool), "what was that you gave me, anyway?"

"Oh, that was niacin . . . I take it every day . . . It really gets you cookin', doesn't it?"

Cookin' was not the word. Microwavin' was more like it. I thought for sure that we could make it to California just on the energy I was feeling between my ears. And so I just kept my eyes on the road, my hands on the wheel, and I kept driving. And I survived. For all of his craziness, Jim was a very pure soul with a very big heart, and he knew exactly what he was doing on the inside, no matter how weird he looked or acted on the outside.

One California morning, Jim asked me if I'd like to go to a Zen monastary, and although I knew nothing about Zen, I said, "Sure," and off we went. We traveled about four hours over treacherous hair-pin mountain roads, and finally we arrived at a most peaceful little community. Jim instructed me to say that we were experienced Zen students so we could get in for the student rate. What he didn't tell me was that as students we would have to do what the students did, which was meditate about three hours a day in lotus position. Now I had never meditated before in my life, and I didn't know much more about meditation than what I had seen on *Kung Fu* or heard on *Sergeant Peppers' Lonely Hearts Club Band*. Nevertheless, the next morning I found myself sitting at a cold 5:30 a.m., facing a grey wall and watching my breath for an hour and a half. You might say it was a crash course in meditation. We stayed there about four days, and by the time we left, I had learned a lot about how many thoughts the mind can think in an hour and a half, and a little about meditation. It was very good.

From there we went to Esalen Institute, where everyone walks around naked and acts real. At the desk, the receptionist asked us what program we wanted to sign up for. Jim explained, "We came for IT!"

"It?" she queried.

"Yes, you know, IT!" (Like I said, he was a little dramatic.)

"Well, which 'It' would you like to sign up for? We have encounter, and rolfing, and Gestalt, and . . ."

"You don't seem to understand," Jim politely explained. "Me and my friend here came for IT!"

Well, this went on for a few more rounds, and we soon found ourselves registered for a new program — Arica Training. It was a system of exercises, meditation, and philosophy brought back from a mentor in Chile. It was esoteric, mystical, and new age, and so Jim and I found ourselves quite comfortable in it. It really was "IT!"

There, I began to come into contact with people from all walks of life, people that I would never have met elsewhere. My roommates were a Guatemalan pianist who played chess and did Gestalt therapy on the side, and a retired Air Force Colonel. (I shall never forget the conversation in which I tried to convince the colonel that there is no real competition in nature.) There, too, I met a gay construction worker and an Egyptian psychiatrist, two personages I never would have come in contact with at Yeshiva. And it was at Esalen that I read for the first time the words of Jesus Christ. Someone handed me a Bible with the words of Christ in red, and, though I was Jewish (and orthodox at that), the words of Jesus seemed to jump off the page and burn in my heart like an eternal flame. Something wonderful was happening in my life. New doors were being opened to me daily. I was being shown realms of spiritual Light with incredible speed and intensity. I was given much grace. I can't think of anything I did to deserve it. I feel as if God was reaching out to me and kindly taking me by the hand into His Garden. I thank you, God, for this.

After Esalen, we headed back east, where it just seemed so strange to me that people walked around with clothes on. After a period of adjustment, though, I carried on with my life.

Now, I was still very much in love with and devoted to Ram Dass. I knew nothing about him, except what I had heard on his tapes and read in his book *Be Here Now*. The book became my Bible. I thought about Ram Dass, talked about him, dreamed about him, and more than anything else, yearned to make contact with him. I had no idea where he was or how to get in touch with him; all I knew was that I wanted to connect with him, for, to me, he meant God.

One evening, weeks after I returned from California, I went to a very coarse punk rock concert at an outdoor stadium. I won't even say what the concert was like. After the concert, there was a massive traffic jam in the parking lot. Cars were just not moving. I began to pop the buttons on my radio to see what was on. On one station, I heard a beautiful young woman's voice, a little like Judy Collins', and I liked the sweet words she was singing. Then a male voice came on the air, and it began to give a spiritual rap, using some of the words and expressions that Ram Dass used. "Hey," I thought, "this guy must be into Ram Dass." To my ecstasy, not only was he into Ram Dass, but he *was* Ram Dass. A few moments later, the announcer took the microphone and told, "We're here with Ram Dass for four nights from midnight to dawn."

I had pressed the right button at about five minutes past twelve on the first night of the four. In the parking lot of a raunchy concert. This remains to me a shining example of God's Grace. We are told that "the teacher will find you." He sure did. My dream had come true. I called out for God, and God answered.

The next four nights were something wonderful and enchanting to me, the kind of gift that one receives only at the bestowal of angels. I felt as if I had been waiting lifetimes for these moments. I listened keenly and absorbed as much as I possibly could. Those four nights changed my life. I was given many answers, not only in the words, but in the quietness and the love that Ram Dass gave to each of the listeners. I was being given a very beautiful *darshan* — the experience of sitting in the presence of a teacher of Truth. Nine years later, I am still assimilating what was offered on those four very special nights.

During the days, I was working at a Seven-Eleven kind of grocery store. Strange, someone with a recent Master's Degree would work as a clerk there, but that was the only job it felt right to take at that time. As a result of Ram Dass' talks, I wanted very much to learn more about meditation, but again, I did not know where or how. At the time, one of our customers was a pleasant young woman who came in regularly to buy honey. One day she asked me, "Do you know anyone who wants to learn meditation? I'm an instructor." Bull's eye. I didn't know how to make the connection, but God knew.

The final Grace I shall designate as the conclusion of this one episode of this one story. It is really the end of one era and the beginning of the next.

On Ram Dass' radio show, someone asked him if he knew where a lady named "Hilda" was. "Right here in the studio," he answered. Over the next few months, her name began to pop up again and again in my life. I was standing in the record department of Korvette's, for example, and I overheard from the other side of the rack a familiar voice talking about his visit to Hilda's class. Then I saw her name in a magazine that came my way. And then, at a party, another person would be talking about this "Hilda." Finally, as Grace and Destiny would have it, someone invited me to go to one of her classes. Curious, I went.

Walking into a homey back room of a church in Greenwich Village, filled wall-to-wall with people, my eyes fell on a pleasant, vibrant lady in a *sari*, which turned out to be Hilda. Next to her was a sweet looking girl singing some very beautiful songs. I recognized the voice from somewhere, but could not place it. Then, in a flash, I remembered: it was the voice I had heard on the Ram Dass radio show. Her name was Mirabai. I was in ecstasy. It seemed as if all the threads of my newly found spiritual life were being woven together into a very lovely tapestry.

That is the story of what I had gotten from life until I came to Hilda's class. What did I get from Hilda? The rest of this book is that story.

THE RIGHT PLACE

One morning, a friend and I decided to go to a concert of flute and harp music. It was only a few hours before the concert that we made up our minds to go, and we started late. We got caught in traffic, and then couldn't find a parking space. We arrived at the theatre quite a while after the concert began, and the only seats left were way up in the back of the balcony. As I took my seat, I found myself sitting next to a smiling little elderly Black man wearing wire-rimmed glasses. He seemed to be enjoying himself immensely, munching on handfuls of gumdrops that he kept picking out of a paper bag. As I was getting myself settled, it occurred to me that he, too, had probably just arrived. I turned to him and complained, "Gee, it's too bad we got stuck way back here." He just sort of twinkled back and replied, "Oh, it's absolutely perfect; we just get what we earn by right of consciousness! . . . Would you like a gumdrop?"

Yes, we were in our right place, one which we had earned. Though my friend and I knew about the concert for months, we vacillated in our decision to go. Our interest in the concert was uncertain, and so we got seats where our view of the concert was uncertain. Those who were sitting up front were certain that they wanted to be there; they had probably gotten their tickets well in advance.

The right of consciousness. It's something to think about. One of my favorite stories is that of Joseph and his brothers. Joseph's eleven brothers were jealous of him because he was having prophetic dreams and their father, Jacob, was especially fond of him. So they threw Joseph in a pit and sold him into the slave market, where he was bought in Egypt by Pharoah's chief advisor, Potiphar. Joseph did so well as a servant that Potiphar made him his top aide, until Mrs. Potiphar also took a liking to Joseph and attempted to seduce him. Although Joseph was guiltless, Potiphar had Joseph thrown in the dungeon, where he successfully interpreted two other prisoners' prophetic dreams. When Pharoah began to have some disturbing dreams of his own, he called in Joseph, who had developed something of a reputation by then. Joseph's counsel to Pharoah was borne true, and Joseph was made Prime Minister of Egypt.

On a superficial level, Joseph's story is an exciting drama with a happy ending. Upon closer inspection, it is an example of how we are where we are because of our consciousness. Joseph was obviously a very deep and wise soul. It was no accident that Jacob took a special liking to him. Nor was it chance that his dreams were threatening to his brothers: his spirituality challenged their belief system. And because Joseph had something going for him, he was attractive to Potiphar (and his wife!) as a ranking servant. Then it was Joseph's prophetic ability that got him out of the dungeon and won him the favor of Pharoah, who could have made any one of millions of people Prime Minister of the Egyptian dynasty. The teaching is especially powerful because Joseph kept working his way out of horrible predicaments, like Flash Gordon or the characters in *Star Wars*. He was in a pit, in slavery, and on death row — but it was always his consciousness that saved him and put him in the place that belonged to him.

We are all, right now, in the place that belongs to us — for it is the one that we have earned by our consciousness. It may seem like a good place, and it may seem like a bad place, but it is always the right place. Actually, it is always good, because we are in the right position to learn the lessons that we need to bring us to a new and more fulfilling stage of personal growth.

We can attempt to mock up (or mock down) where we would *like* to be, but because we cannot mock up our consciousness, we will always be returned to where we *belong*. When I was in college, it was very popular for students to march on and take over the administration building. The yippies and friends would put on old army shirts, break into the college president's office, turn over a few file cabinets, and then get their picture in the newspaper, showing them smoking pot with their feet up on the president's big wooden desk. Then they would issue proclamations about how they were now going to be the

University administration, and how they would initiate credit courses in The Grateful Dead, and so on. This would go on for a day, or two, or three, but sooner or later they would somehow be ejected, the regular president would regain his office, and things would go back to normal (— well, almost normal). Though the yippies tried to establish their place as the leaders of the university, they had not earned it, and so they lost it.

I remember, too, a man who wanted to earn some money heard of an opening as a department manager in a well-known chain store. Though he had no experience in the work, he told his interviewer that he had, and he "fudged" his references. He was given the job, but it was not long before he was overwhelmed because he just did not know what he was doing. His department was losing money and he was losing sleep. So he accepted a demotion to assistant manager, a position in which he could learn. He remained assistant manager for a year or so, and then he was promoted to manager in a related department, a position in which he is now doing well — because now he has earned it.

Neither can we minimize our consciousness. We cannot make believe that we are less than we are. There are many great yogis and gurus who attempt to avoid students, but, because the teacher has something very valuable, the students somehow find him or her. The great Nithyananda went off to the jungle to meditate, and people found him and built a city around him. I know, too, of a simple man who lives on a remote mountain and holds a humble job as a pipe welder. Though he does not seek students, many people are willing to drive through snowy mountain roads to receive his counsel. And Hilda, who has no desire for fame or recognition, receives requests from people (like Barbara Walters) who want to do TV shows and books and movies about her. She came back to this country from India with the intention of staying for just a few weeks, but friends began to ask for her help, and she decided to stay as long as people sought her support. That was fourteen years ago. She started out with one or two people coming to visit her in the living room where she was staying, and then they brought their friends, and they theirs, until now three or four hundred come to see her each week in the Cathedral of St. John the Divine. She has never solicited any students, advertised, or taken any payment for her work; in fact, she never even wanted to be a teacher. But she has no choice; she is where she is by right of her consciousness, or in this case — the responsibility of her consciousness.

Despite all the questions raised by our meandering minds, we *are* in our right place, doing exactly what we need to be doing, at exactly the right time. Because life is a school, we are always in the class that we have chosen to learn the lessons we need to master. Sometimes it is fun, and sometimes we have to work at it a bit, but is is always appropriate. I was speaking to a woman who was struggling with questions about the direction she should take in her life. When I shared with her my enthusiasm about the perfection of the right of consciousness, she looked at me with a combination of surprise and relief, and asked, "You mean I'm in my right place?" I chuckled and responded, "Where else could you be?"

"Because God is perfect and just, so is your position in life. This is the source of peace of mind, as fears of ill and error can find no home in a world seen through the eyes of Perfection.

Your place is assured. You cannot be other than where Love has placed you to learn its holy lessons. It is only the restless mind that seeks to impose disorder where there is alignment, and chaos where there is serenity. Because thoughts do not leave their source, thoughts of chaos come only of chaotic thinking, and the Vision of Tranquility is born of the quiet self.

Trust frees you to see the wisdom of the moment. The goodness of life is invincible, and in Justice is your assurance of success. The laws of consciousness work consistently for your highest good. They offer you consolation and guidance. You now embody the choice to earn your goal, which is at hand.

The rights that you once rigorously strove for are now replaced by the Right that has always belonged to you. When you accept your attunement, you accept Truth. Injustice has finally been replaced by awareness, and the end of all questioning is accomplished."

TAKE WHATCHA GOT AND MAKE WHATCHA WANT

A young Kansas City artist, struggling to realize his dream of drawing cartoons for a living, was turned away from every newspaper he approached for a job. "Forget it," the editors told him, "you have no talent . . . Find yourself another career." Rejection followed rejection, until one day he found himself holed up in an old, dilapidated, mice-infested garage, penniless, seemingly without a hope for success.

Having no shortage of time on his hands, he began to sketch the garage and the mice in it. He became fascinated with the little creatures, and he curiously developed a friendly relationship with them, especially one little fellow.

Little did the man realize at the time just how important this relationship would be for him. The man's name was Walt Disney. The mouse's name turned out to be "Mickey," and Walt and Mickey went on to become two of the most successful entertainers in the world, bringing happiness and joy to countless numbers of children.

If Walt had given up when the editors turned him away, he may have taken some other job, and his dream might have faded into a memory. But Walt had enough faith in himself to continue, and in so doing, he made an even greater discovery: God's infinite possibilities are *everywhere*, and success is always at hand — even at what seems to be the end of the road.

In a *Star Trek* adventure, Captain Kirk finds himself on an island planet, pitted against an especially creepy character — *the Gorn*. He is given the unenviable task of having to defeat this foe to save his life — and his ship. The challenge, he is told, is a test of creative ingenuity.

33

He is given no materials, but it is hinted that whatever he needs to save himself is available to him right on the planet. He must be clever enough to find what he needs and use it. The Captain suffers setback after setback, until he is battered and almost defeated, sprawled nearly helpless on the alien ground. Prospects look pretty dim for our hero.

At this critical moment, Kirk sniffs a familiar aroma — sulfur! Though he has seen it throughout his trials, he did not recognize it for how he could use it. Quickly he manufactures some rudimentary gunpowder, and (as you can guess) he soon overcomes the Gorn. Simply, the Captain took what he had, and made what he wanted.

One sage said, "*There is no invention — only discovery.*" The people who succeed are those who adapt, combine, create, and make the best use of what they have been given to work with. George Washington Carver, for example, was a God-inspired genius of the highest caliber. When most of us look at a peanut, we see a peanut. When he looked deep into the peanut, Dr. Carver, with the all-seeing eye of God, saw over 300 uses for the tiny legume, including washing powder, shaving cream, bleach, salve, paper, ink, synthetic rubber, axle grease, linoleum, shampoo, wood filler, coffee, and pickles. He also discovered 118 uses for the sweet potato. In short, he accepted what he was given, recognized its preciousness, and served the world through it. Dr. Carver put into action the maxim that "*What you are is God's gift to you; what you make of yourself is your gift to God.*"

Another one who made a gift of himself was St. Francis of Assisi. In his Divine simplicity, Francis was a misfit in a system of rigid religion. His heart yearned for the lofty freedom of the birds and the warm blessing of the sun. The inner voice whispered to him, "Francis, rebuild my church!" Symbolically, he took a small, abandoned, and unloved church, and, at first alone, place brick by brick, stone by stone, one upon another, bound together mostly by love. Before long, his sincerity and his purity attracted to him friends and followers in a new order of spirituality that has multiplied and gathered force for nearly one thousand years. The love of this gentle saint has won the hearts of millions, more books have been written about him than about any other saint, and he has recently been named the patron saint of the environment. St. Francis started right where he was, and God accepted him just as he was.

Just as we are now, each of us has all that we need to succeed.

TAKE WHATCHA GOT AND MAKE WHATCHA WANT

You and I are thoughts in the mind of God, and everything that we do, God does. God cannot be defeated. No matter what our past, our troubles, or our limitations, there is always a way for us to turn seemingly futile circumstances into splendid success, like the alchemist who knew how to transform lead into gold. There is, for example, a famous woman in Maine who lost use of her arms and legs — but she refused to be beaten. She put a paint brush in her mouth and began to draw the lovely country scenes she saw from her porch. Now she sells many of her beautiful paintings as Christmas cards. Her business is extremely successful — in more ways than one.

The aspect of human beings that sets us off from all other creatures is that of imaginative wisdom. Animals see things as they are, but we see them as they *can be*. We have been given the Divine ability to transform. I have never seen anything give a person as much energy as a vision that he or she is working to bring into reality. I have seen people forsake sleep, food, and comfort for the sake of a project that they love. There is something very holy about a human being dedicated to a purpose, something more precious than I can attempt to put into words. It is the miracle of creation.

It is exactly this miracle which enables us to transcend circumstances. Any circumstance is a good starting point for God. Dr. Carver was the child of slaves, and Francis was the son of a wealthy businessman; yet both of them found their way to God. The same energy that moved the Carvers, the Einsteins, and the Edisons to change the world, is within us. The alchemical power to activate Divinity is always speaking to us, if we are but willing to *listen* and *do*. It is none other than the Voice of God, beckoning to us to acknowledge the Divine Spark and to draw it into expression, that it may be shared by all.

"Genius is God's gift to all, though it is accepted by few. Within you lie riches and talents far greater than you have recognized and expressed.

The acknowledgement of your capabilities bears a double blessing. As you grow into your own evolution, you serve the world. The purposes of the individual are one with those of humanity, and the unfoldment of one marks the growth of all.

There is no limitation, Children, upon what you can do. God is incapable of containment or restriction. So, too, are you free, for you are Divine in nature.

Look at your lives with open eyes. If you see closed avenues, it is because you are looking with closed eyes. Do not be distracted by the small-mindedness of men. The child of man sees mountains where the Child of God sees skies. Choose your goal, and allow God to succeed through you."

ENOUGH IS ENOUGH

"There are three kinds of people," said the philosopher: "Those who complain, 'Too much! Too much!'; those who argue, 'Not enough! Not enough!'; and those who smile, 'Ah! Just right.' "

Really, these three symbolic groups can be distilled to two: *those who practice contentment*, and *those who do not*. Saying "Too much!" and saying "Not enough!" are really two sides of the same coin, for too much of what we don't want means not enough of what we do want. We are always practicing the Presence of God or His absence. No middle ground.

Contentment is an experience that we can cultivate through practice. Abraham Lincoln said that "most people are about as happy as they make up their mind to be." Like gratefulness and positivity, contentment is not usually handed to us as a gift, although it is always ours for the asking. We need only to align our thoughts with appreciation, for contentment is not so much a state of *affairs* as it is a state of *mind*.

If money could make us happy, millionaires would rest complete after their first million. If sex could fulfill us, those who enter relationships or marriages based upon sex would roam no further. If power were the source of peace, heads of state would be the happiest people in the world. But we all know that persons with much money, sex, or power are not the happiest; in fact they are often among the most unhappy. Why? Because anyone in a state of *seeking* can never be happy. Only those who are constantly *finding* are fulfilled. And finding is not something that happens to us — it is something we *do*.

For the past few years, I have been practicing a very powerful mantra: "Perfect!" It is not the kind of mantra that is to be said sitting with eyes closed, although we certainly can do that. Instead, it is a mantra for daily life. It is a mantra that turns troubles into blessings. It is a mantra that gives encouragement and support. It is a word that heals. It is a statement of the truth.

Not long ago, I went to a concert by an elementary school band. As the director raised his baton, I sat back and for some reason expected to hear a beautiful symphony. To my surprise, I heard, instead, a horrid cacophony of squeaks, honks, upbeat notes on the downbeat, and a march that sounded like a 45 r.p.m. record played at 33. "This is terrible!" I thought, as I shriveled inside. And then I heard a gentle voice speak within me: *"These are children; they are learning; they are doing very well."* The voice, of course, spoke truth. I was judging them according to my expectations, not accepting that they were all expressing according to their ability. At that moment, the music became so lovely to me. I sat back and thoroughly enjoyed every remaining moment of the concert, and I think I cheered the loudest at its finale.

When we see life in clear focus, it is always giving us enough. We have to get our minds tuned into contentment, even work at it a little bit, to win at the game of living. One evening, for example, I had a pot luck dinner, and everyone brought a main dish. Desserts were conspicuously absent. "Perfect!" we decided. "Here is our chance to cut calories and lose some weight." Several weeks later, everyone brought only dessert. "Perfect!" we declared, "This is our opportunity to celebrate!" Celebrate what? I don't exactly remember. We just celebrated.

It's not so much what we do that counts, but *what we think* about what we do. We can take any seeming failure, and find some way to turn it into a success. There was a man in South Africa who sold his farm for a pittance because the earth was too rocky and hard to till. Those who bought the property examined the land more deeply, and today it is the famous Kimberly diamond mine.

When we dig deeply enough into our own lot, we find that we are well taken care of. We must learn to distinguish between *needs* and *desires*. I often hear an "I want" masquerading as "I need." Our needs are so simple. St. Francis said, "I watch the sparrow enjoy just a little sip of water. How free are the birds who need so little and yet soar so high!" It is only when we think that we need more than we do that we lose sight of our aspirations.

A student went to his guru and asked to be enlightened. "Very well," said the teacher, "find yourself a nice cave, sit naked, and meditate. Then you will surely attain your goal." "That sounds fine," thought the student, and off he went. He decided, however, to take with him just one possession — a small loincloth.

The young yogi set out easily enough on his venture. He found a good cave and began to experience deep meditation. His loincloth, however, required occasional washing, after which he would hang it on a tree to dry. One day he noticed that mice had nibbled some holes in it, so he went into town to ask what to do. A kind lady advised him, "What you need is a cat to keep the mice away," and (since she just happened to have a litter of kittens) she gave him one.

Things went along nicely, until the yogi realized that the cat required milk. So he returned to town and begged for milk until the townspeople got fed up and told him, "Why don't you buy yourself a cow? That would provide for all your needs." So he took a few weeks off from his meditation to earn some money to buy a cow.

As it turns out, cows need grassy land on which to graze. So he left his cave for a longer period, this time to buy a small patch of pasture. Now, of course, he had to feed the cow and tend to its needs, so he took a wife who could care for the animals while he practiced being enlightened. (This was in pre-liberation days.) With marriage came children, and within a few years he had a *bona fide* family to support. As you can imagine, he soon found himself the busy manager of a small farm, and he just couldn't seem to find the time for even a moment's meditation.

One day years later, the guru happened to be passing through town, and finding the yogi's cave deserted, he ironically came to the man's house to inquire if anyone knew what had become of the yogi.

"That yogi was *me!*" the farmer told the teacher.

"What happened?" asked the guru.

"I took a loincloth with me," was the explanation.

We have ideas, concepts, and opinions about how things would be better if we had this or that, or if we were there instead of here. Often, however, our ticket to satisfaction is in mastering the job at hand. If we do well with what we have, we do not need to figure out how to advance; God, the best Manager of all, will take care of us. Martin Luther King, Jr., in a stirring address called "Remaining Awake During a Great Revolution," told the people:

> *It does not matter what you do. What does matter is that you do it the best. If you are a street sweeper, then be the best street sweeper that there ever was. Do your work with pride, and do it with dignity, and in so doing it, you will be doing it with greatness!*

This lesson was proven to me when I worked as a cook in a health foods restaurant. While I found the job very rewarding, some people did not think it was a very important job to do. (One fellow called me aside one day and asked, "So, Alan, what do you do in real life?") But because I saw God in that place, I used it to practice love, positivity, and mastery, and in so doing, I found great enthusiasm and commitment for the work. It was there that I was shown the principle of advancement through right use. Although the store was financially ailing and the owner turned down the other employees' requests for raises, he approached me one day to tell me that he was giving me a raise — one that I did not even ask for!

"There is enough of everything for everyone," explained Patricia Sun. It is only when we begin to *fear* lack that we *create* it. Wars, famines, and shortages occur only when someone feels afraid that he or she will not have enough, and a person, or a group, or a nation begins to act out of fear. God and Mother Earth (God's symbol for Abundance) have never withheld sustenance. Famines do not occur by happenstance or Divine Decree. They are always a result of war, economic turmoil, and political unrest — all created by us *people*. I learned that in the Bengla Desh famine there were shiploads of food that rotted in the ports because political bickering in the war-torn country held up the process of delivering it to the starving people for whom it was earmarked. We cannot blame God for withholding providence from us; it is *we* who must be prepared to *accept* it. If we can just hold on long enough not to act on fear of lack, abundance on earth would be manifest in the fullness that was originally intended.

Thoughts of "too much" are also out of the flow of life. In our struggle to realize the true meaning of spiritual living, we sometimes confuse non-attachment with unnecessary self-denial. In the early stages of treading the path, some seekers believe it is spiritual to shun money, or to denounce possessions, or not to bathe, or to starve, in the name of renunciation. Real renunciation is being able to take it or leave it, according to what is necessary. (The great Paramahansa Yogananda said, "*What comes of itself, let it come.*") I used to avoid money, gifts, experiences, and people, in fear of being selfish or attached. My mistake was that I was attached to not being attached.

I don't believe that God sent us here in exile. I think He sent us here for education. If a wealthy father sent his son to a boarding school, would he not send with him clothing, money for food and transportation, and even some "pin money" for an occasional movie or ice cream soda? Of course he would. Our Heavenly Father is no different. In fact, He is even more compassionate than most earthly fathers would be. You see, it is *we* who have chosen to run away from home to attend a school in a far country, and even in light of our rebelliousness, God lovingly provides for us as if He had sent us Himself.

One evening Hilda told us, "Take care of God's business and He'll take care of yours." That same night, a friend asked me for a ride home, quite a bit out of my way. This was during a gas shortage, and I knew that if I took her home, I would have to find an open gas station for me to make it home myself. But since she needed a ride, I decided to take care of God's business. As I dropped her off, the needle on the fuel gauge was leaning on the bottom of the big red "E." I knew that I would have to find an open station before I turned onto the Garden State Parkway. It was after midnight as I drove down Bloomfield Avenue, and every single station that I passed was closed. I was down to just a few blocks before the parkway. Then, on the very corner where I had to turn, there was an open station. Very late at night. Very unusual in a gas shortage. Yet there was no shortage of God. His tanks were full.

"Children of Plenty, you are heirs to the riches of the universe. It is God's good pleasure to give you His good gifts.

Thoughts of lack are empty musings, expressive not of the Truth, but of a limited consciousness which you have outgrown. Hold fearlessly to thoughts of fullness, and so shall your experience be confirmed as whole.

Remember that you are worthy of abundance. Know your spiritual riches, and material good shall be yours as well. There is a right amount for you. Trust the Creator to uphold and support you in your material life. He will not abandon you. This is the promise proven by your willingness to trust.

Stand with open arms to receive His riches. Extend your hands, as well, to allow blessings to flow forth in service to a waiting world. Be a comforter to your brethren. Uphold not thoughts of emptiness, but hold fast to your meditation upon the source of all. When you see all as full, you see all as God created it.''

IF NOT NOW, WHEN?

Dr. Leo Buscaglia tells a sad story of two college students who were unexpectedly killed while walking across their campus. They were young, vibrant, in the mainstream of life, with many unfulfilled dreams. They had no idea they would be cut off so soon. "This," tells Dr. Buscaglia, "led me to realize that every moment of life is precious." He went back to his very unique "Love" class and asked the students to write an essay on what they would really like to do if they had the time. Some wrote, "I would take a long walk on the beach at sunset." Others wrote of shining aspirations: "I would leave college and devote all my time to playing music," and yet others wrote, "I would call up my Dad and resolve our strained relationship." In big red letters, across the bottom of their papers, Dr. Buscaglia wrote, "WELL, WHAT ARE YOU WAITING FOR? WHAT ARE YOU DOING HERE? WHY DON'T YOU DO IT NOW?" He says, "If you don't like what you are doing, then get out — quick — and fulfill your dream now."

We never really know how much time we have to do what we want to do. We act as if we have a hundred years, when we may have but a minute. If we ponder on these sobering thoughts, they must lead us to but one conclusion: *Now is our only moment to live.*

A few years ago, I attended a conference on the predictions of earth changes that have been prophesied to occur in the coming years. A diversified group of psychics, scientists, and spiritual teachers told of earthquakes, food shortages, economic and political collapse, and all kinds of holocausts, which they all agreed would culminate in a

43

new era of peace and unity on earth. The peace and unity sounded great to me, but the holocaust predictions were rather unnerving, especially when all of the speakers concurred that a large portion of the earth's population would be wiped out. The thought occurred to me that I might be one of those who went down, and I lost my cool. I wrestled with this fear for several days, trying to figure out how to escape and save myself. Then, one morning I woke up and my fear had vanished; I was resigned to my death. I just felt that it would not be so terrible if I did go down, for I knew that God would take care of me anyway. So I took the attitude that I had just a few months or years to live, and I began to look at life from this point of view.

I think that the few months that I held that outlook were the freest and most joyous in my life. I didn't worry or care about anything. All of the foolish little concerns that had occupied my attention became meaningless to me, and I saw that they really didn't matter after all. My meditations were the deepest and most powerful that they had ever been, and I found new appreciation to enjoy my friends. The teaching was that in learning how to die, I learned how to live.

There are many similar stories of persons who are diagnosed as having terminal illness, who confute their diagnoses by learning to live in the present. I have heard of a number of people, who, upon being told that they have just a few months or a year to live, let go of their businesses, boxes, and burdens, and go out to enjoy all the things that they have been putting off until retirement. They take the camping trip to the mountains that they've been dreaming of; they hop into the car late in the evening and drive to Friendly's for that hot fudge sundae they've been denying themselves; and they spend the money that they've been fearfully saving for some unknown need. The result is that they have such a good time enjoying life in freedom and ease that the dis-ease disappears, and they live long and fruitful lives. They learn to *live in the moment*, and in so doing, they learn to *live*.

There are three expressions which I have learned not to believe: "I will *try* to be there"; "*Maybe* I will do it"; and "I will do it *later*." All are polite but irresponsible ways of saying "No" or "I don't want to." "I will do it later" is especially seductive because we use time as an excuse to avoid making a stand in the present. This is sad because, as anyone who has ever dieted or stopped smoking knows, *there is no later*.

The ancient Jewish *Ethics of the Fathers* puts it very succinctly:

*If I am not for myself, who will be for me? If I am only for
myself, what good am I? If not now, when?*

Harvey Freeman tells the story of Joe, a man who is familiar to all
of us. Joe is a pretty regular fellow, never really quite satisfied. In high
school, he knows that he will be happy just as soon as he gets his
driver's license. He gets it, but now he needs to get into a certain college to feel really fulfilled. Well, he is accepted, but now he very much
wants to marry a special classmate. And so on. Then it's a child that
will really do it, and then he just needs to be promoted to vice-
president of the company. And then Joe begins to live vicariously
through the children. And then he is just waiting for grandchildren,
and then he begins to count the years until retirement, when he can
really relax. Finally, Joe retires and sets out on his long-planned dream
fishing trip in the Smokies. Joe rows out into the middle of the lake,
casts out his line, and keels over, dead. Joe's moment of happiness
never came; it was always just around the next bend.

Jesus spoke of the present. "Take no thought or worry for tomorrow," he instructed. "Look at the lilies of the field; they neither spin
nor toil, and I tell you that Solomon, in all his glory, was not arrayed
like one of these. If God takes care of the grass, which is here one day
and gone the next, will He not all the more care for you, His
Children?" The Master also explained, "The evil of the day is sufficient
unto itself." In other words, just do what you need to do for today,
and tomorrow will take care of itself.

Ram Dass, in *Be Here Now*, describes his training with a yogi
who taught him the meaning of living freely in the moment. Ram Dass
would ask, "Say, did I ever tell you about the time that I saw white
light?" and the yogi would respond, "Don't talk about the past — just
be here now." And then Ram Dass would ask, "When do you think
we'll get to Madras?" and the teacher would interrupt, "Don't worry
about the future — just be here now." The message was this, explains
Ram Dass: "If you can live fully in the Now, when 'then' becomes
'now,' you will be perfectly taken care of and know exactly what to
do."

Stephen Gaskin put it in another way. He said, "The here and
now is always heavy (full and complete). If it's not heavy, you're not
tuned in."

The process of this writing has been, for me, an education in living in the moment. At first, I planned only to write a short pamphlet on stress reduction and relaxation for the workshops that I conduct. This, I thought, would have to be a very scientific document that would appeal to professionals. As I began to write it, I noticed that I was staying away from "spiritual" topics, and especially avoiding the word "God." I knew in my heart, though, that I really wanted to write something that would express my deepest beliefs, which most certainly are God and the spiritual life. So I decided to write two separate works — first the secular stress reduction pamphlet, and then something about God. I got about two pages into the stress pamphlet, and I thought, "Wait a minute! What am I doing? What I really feel and want to do is to write something that expresses *all* of me, not a diluted version of me. Why am I putting second that which is first in my heart? How can I write about living in the moment when I am postponing my dream? I will write what I feel. If some people do not read it because it is too spiritually oriented, I cannot worry about that. At least I will be able to sleep at night, knowing that I have been true to myself and to God. I am not writing to please people; I am writing to express God." With that, I sat down to write a few chapters, and of those seedlings grew a book. I don't know if it will be a best seller, but my heart is satisfied, and that, to me, is the best seller of all.

Too many dreams are cast by the wayside in deference to opinion and tradition. Too many ambitions have been postponed for the wrong reasons. Too many lives have been lived for a tomorrow which never came. Ask yourself now, "If I had only a few months to live, what would I be doing?" Do not dwell on the fear, but consider your opportunities! Then do it. Can any of us afford to throw away one moment of life?

One of my favorite times in this life was the late 1960's, the early years of what is called the Age of Aquarius. It was a time when people from many different lifestyles were awakening to new and exciting possibilities of what life on earth can be about. It was a time when the Beatles took the world by the hand and led it from *"Money"* to *"A Little Help From My Friends,"* and when Peace became more than just a catchword. It was a time that gave permission to young people to give away flowers on the street corners of San Francisco, and when young and old became one in an action to stop a war which just not enough people believed in. It was a time when a new wave of spiritual understanding began to sweep the planet in the seed-lights of new age com-munities and appreciation for the sacredness of our home, the earth.

Now I sometimes hear people make fun of that era. (The other day someone accused me of being a flower child — but I took it as a compliment.) Perhaps the brightness of those days has become over-shadowed as we have moved into a time which requires more concrete social action. This is a serious time on earth, and I am willing to be serious to face it, but those days of the late 60's have a special place in my heart, and I refuse to compromise my appreciation for their wonder. In fact, I believe that that time was a taste of things to come; perhaps now we have to earn it.

I share this with you now because during that era, one early sum-mer day I found myself in a little crafts shop in Denver. I remember the place for the bright rainbow painted over its faded brick wall fac-ing an empty lot. In that shop was a poster with a caption which I shall never forget, one which has become my mantra for life:

TOUCH EVERY MOMENT OF LOVE

"Dear ones, live for all that you would live for. Search your heart for your purest ideals, and set your life around your noblest vision. In the years to come, when the institutions that you know crumble around you, only your deepest aspirations will carry you through outer change. Live now for your heart's ambition.

Think, beloveds, and think clearly. What do you truly want from your life? Why, in all earnestness, have you come to earth? Who do you now live for? Are you beholden to the misdirected vanities of the world, or do you respect your inclinations from a source resonating deep within your Self? Answer these questions for yourself, beloveds, and live the answers you find.

Time has been given you for a purpose. Learn to use it for your benefit, but do not be a slave to it. Make it work for you. In your awareness of the purpose of time is your mastery of it.

Set your priorities. Do not delay that which is most important. You can know God now, but you can never know Him tomorrow. Your enlightenment is the one thing that you cannot postpone. God is now."

Overcoming Limitations

BREAKING MOLDS

"It just makes me so mad when my husband squeezes the toothpaste from the middle of the tube!" reported a woman in one of my classes. ". . . Everybody knows you're supposed to squeeze it from the end!" Just for the fun of it, we took a class survey to see whether, in fact, everybody *does* know that you're supposed to squeeze it from the end. As it turned out, about half of the class knew that you're supposed to squeeze it from the end, and the other half knew that you're supposed to squeeze it from the middle.

The truth is, of course, that you're not supposed to squeeze it from any particular place; what you're supposed to do is get the toothpaste onto the brush, and it doesn't really matter how it gets there. If it matters, then it is a matter that we have created with our mind.

To live — to really be alive — we must allow ourselves to flow with the people and events around us. We cannot afford to confine ourselves to any rigid picture of who we are, or how things should be done. An oriental sage said that the secret of happiness is to "cease to cherish opinions."

Hilda calls these set ways of acting "molds." "We stuff ourselves into little habitual ways of doing things in a certain way," she explains, "and then if we do not get to do it our way, or if someone comes along who wants to do it a little differently, we get irritable and we become a nuisance to ourselves and those around us."

When I have shared the idea of "molds" with my yoga classes, the students have confessed to some delightfully zany molds. One woman would get upset if she found the toilet paper put on the roller in the "wrong" way. She liked it when the paper rolled from the wall side of the roll. Another person had to get "his" exact parking space when he left his car at the train station each morning. If someone else took that spot, he would think, "I am just going to have a terrible day." And another man would get irritable if his jogging socks were not folded in a certain way.

"The way to really be free, kids," explained Hilda, "is to find out what your molds are, and then break them: drive to work by way of a different street one day; wear a new hairstyle; rearrange the furniture in your room; do anything you can to keep from getting stagnant."

I suggested to the man who thought he had to have a certain parking space that he try, for one day or one week, purposely parking in a different spot, and see what happened. The next week he came to class smiling and beaming. "I tried what you suggested," he reported, "and I even had some great days! I see now that I was binding myself with my own thoughts. Now I am free to park wherever I like!"

I remember when I first discovered the power of breaking molds. I had a mold of a cereal bowl. Every morning I would take the same blue bowl and make myself the same breakfast of granola, milk, and one banana. This was my routine and my mold. One day, I went to take "my" blue bowl from the cabinet, and it was not there. A dilemma! When I looked and saw that someone else was using it for their breakfast, I got annoyed. "How dare he take *my* cereal bowl for *his* breakfast!" I thought. I had become the slave of a blue bowl. (If that is not selling out my freedom, I don't know what is.) Fortunately, I remembered Hilda's lesson and I thought, "O.K., this is my chance to get free of a binding mold . . . I can just as easily use another bowl." I did, and to my amazement I enjoyed my breakfast just as thoroughly as if I had that old blue bowl. After that, I was free of bondage to a bowl.

We are all free spirits and we are not bound to anything unless we think we are. We are all free to park wherever there is a space and to enjoy our granola out of any bowl. There was an old Three Stooges routine in which Larry would cry out to Moe, "I can't see! I can't see!" Moe would rush to Larry's aid, asking "Why not?" Larry would then smile and proclaim, "Cause I got my eyes closed!" (And then, of course, Moe would bop him on the head.) It is sometimes a good idea to think about what it is that we are not seeing because we have our eyes closed (before we get bopped on the head). We need to consider whether it is life that is penning us in, or *we* who confine ourselves with small thinking. Our happy realization is that we cannot be tied to anything, and that the only way we can be bound is with our own thoughts.

There is a relationship between freedom from molds and being young. I am not speaking of a number of years, but of the vitality, exuberance, and aliveness in a person's way of being and growing. Childhood lasts as long as we allow ourselves to think expansively, act freely, and be new. The secret of youth is open and adaptive thinking. We are eagles.

Scott and Helen Nearing left their city life in the 1930's and moved to the Green Mountains of Vermont, where they built a homestead of stone houses, made a lush garden out of soil that would at first yield only radishes, and became popular and beloved folk heroes. After about thirty years in Vermont, they decided to escape the growing commercialism, and the two started all over again in Maine, where they built more stone houses, set up a sun-heated greenhouse, and established a completely new self-sufficient farmstead. Scott is now about 98 years old, and Helen in her late 70's. I had the great privilege to meet them a few years ago, and they are two of the youngest people I have ever met. Helen said, "Flexibility increases with experience."

When I first saw Hilda, she appeared to be an older woman. After spending about five minutes in her presence, however, I felt no sense of age in her at all. She is as fresh and young as a little child. Someone gave an affirmation that perfectly describes Hilda: "I am as old as God, and as young as the morning." When Satya Sai Baba (a revered saint in India) would ask her, "How old are you, Hilda?" she would answer brightly, "I was never born and I shall never die!" This pleased Baba to no end. She is a beautiful and fascinating person to look at. Though she has spent a good number of years on earth, there are none of the lines or wrinkles in her face that tell of worry or resistance. In one of her lectures, Hilda was speaking of trends of years ago. She started to say ". . . but that was in my time," when she caught herself, stopped, thought for a moment, and explained, "I can't really say 'That was my time,' kids; my time is *now*."

The time for all of us is, of course, now. There is no need for anyone to wither in an unfulfilling and mechanical pattern of life. Routines cannot bind us unless we believe in them. Patterns were given to serve us — not for us to live for them. The Fountain of Youth is not a mysterious hidden well in Florida, but an ever-invigorating, ever-refreshing stream of life that is constantly flowing through us, bubbling up to renew us when we are but willing to make space for it and drink of it.

Behold the turtle, who makes progress only when he sticks his neck out.

"You are a Child of the Living God, and it is only your awareness of your True Identity that sustains, nourishes, and heals you.

Restriction and age are human inventions. They are born of limited seeing, and so bear fruits of like nature. You who would aspire to express your immortal heritage must remain free of narrowness. Those who would be grandiose must be grandiose. Those who would live must accept life. Those who would be immortal must love what is eternal.

Habits have been given for your strengthening, but they cease to be purposeful when you become subservient to them. Be masterful in approaching your activities. Consciously decide for free ways of being. No one is a master who is a slave to his own inventions.

We guide you to your next stage of evolution. The transition requires a surrender of the tools which served you in your earlier work. No more can you rely on forms for your strength. The time has come for you to rely on God and God alone."

FISHBOWL TO BATHTUB

If you wish to live in freedom, you've just got to become Divine.

— David and Jamil

One morning, Eve decided it was time to clean her fishbowl. Unable to find a container in which to put her two goldfish, Yin and Yang, while the bowl was being cleaned, Eve let about two inches of water into her bathtub, and lovingly placed the little creatures there. When she finished scrubbing the bowl and putting the ceramic deep-sea diver in a new position, Eve returned to find Yin and Yang engaged in a very thought-provoking behavior: the two goldfish were swimming around in one little corner of the bathtub, in a circle no bigger than the fishbowl!

In many ways, we humans are like the goldfish. We develop our patterns, our habits, and our taught lifestyles (which we have adopted from families, friends, and television commercials), and then, when we have the chance to go beyond them to discover a new and freer dimension, we prefer to remain in our tiny corner of the world, though it offers us little joy, a lot of anxiety, and no expansiveness.

Most people are sleepwalking. Many wander through life in a sort of semiconscious state, having some idea of what they do, but not really sure why they are doing it. Mostly, we do what other people do, for we have made gods of popular opinions, beliefs, and actions. We worship the masses instead of the mass. For a long time, I depended on the world to tell me who I was and what to do. After wandering through my life like this for years, I realized that this kind of unchosen living just doesn't work.

When we live in attempt to fulfill the dreams and desires of others, we may (for a while) succeed in convincing ourselves that we are happy, but sooner or later we must admit that we have our own calling in life. I know a young man who suffered through medical school because his parents wanted him to be a doctor, and they had almost convinced him that was what he wanted, too. He stayed in medical school for a while, mostly out of guilt and fear, for his father had taken out a second mortgage on their house in order to buy his son's way into an accredited school. But, alas, how long can one live a lie? The young man eventually became ill, quit the school, and got a job teaching science in the Virgin Islands, a position in which he now feels comfortable and fulfilled.

My friend's story reminded me of that of Zumbach the Tailor, which symbolizes the predicament in which many of us have found ourselves. A man went to Zumbach the Tailor to be fitted for a new suit. When the suit was ready, he stood before the mirror with the tailor, for final alterations. The man noticed that the right sleeve was just a bit short. "I think the sleeve is a little too short for my arm," he told Zumbach; "You may have to lengthen it."

"The sleeve is not too short," answered the tailor. "Your arm is too long. Just draw your arm up into the sleeve a bit, and it will look fine."

Reluctantly, the man did so, but this threw the collar of the jacket into disarray. "Now the sleeve looks alright, but look at the big gap between my neck and the jacket!"

"There is nothing wrong with the jacket," Zumbach defended. "What you need to do is raise your left shoulder a few inches."

The man again complied, but now the rear of the jacket was lifted far above his posterior. When he showed the tailor this misalignment, he was instructed to "lower your head and lean forward, and there will be no problem!"

Finally, the man walked out of the shop, convinced of its proper fit. (Unfortunately, he had to walk in a most contorted and uncomfortable position.)

He stepped onto a bus, and the man next to him laughed, "I'll bet you got that suit from Zumbach the Tailor!"

"How did you know that?" asked our friend with the suit.

"Because only Zumbach the Tailor could fit a man as crippled as you!"

God did not intend for any of us to be crippled. It is we who cripple ourselves with small thinking, ideas of limitation, and fear. Let's consider for a few moments what the average person might believe is stifling or preventing him or her from being all that he or she wants to be: lack of skill . . . lack of money . . . too much or too little age . . . too many or too few people . . . not enough physical energy . . . bad luck. These are not reasons for failure; they are the excuses that many people hold to justify a "victim" position that they are not even aware they are holding.

Not one of these circumstances has any power to withhold our highest good from any of us. This was an idea that took me a long time to accept, but I have now seen too many people break through these mirage barriers for me to believe in them any longer.

Let us take lack of skill, for example. I know a girl who was failing ninth grade; her counselors told her she was not school material, and so she dropped out. She worked for a while, traveled, and two years later passed a high school equivalency test, entered college, and completed her freshman year of college before her former classmates graduated high school.

Neither can the physical body bind us, unless we let it. Lack of physical energy is a lack of mental enthusiasm. I used to believe that I needed eight hours of sleep every night to be rested and effective. When I began this writing, however, I had so much enthusiasm for what I was doing that I would sleep for four hours or less, and awake fresh and energetic.

Nor has money ever stopped anyone from doing anything. If our intention is clear and our faith strong, the money will come. Howard Johnson started out with a tiny ice cream stand in Brooklyn. John Kraft and his wife sold cheese out of a pushcart. Louise Berlez had a dream to go to France, but not a penny. She made up her mind that she would be in Paris in six months. Five and a half months passed, and there was no sign of any trip. Then, unexpectedly, her supervisor called her into his office and asked her if she would like to go to Paris on business, all expenses paid. And so she did.

Faith is a magnetic force that draws to us as much good as we are open to accept. A few years ago, a friend and I took a vacation to Puerto Rico. Just before we were about to leave, our return airplane tickets were stolen. Although I thought that we could have them reissued at the airport, when we got there the ticket agent told us, "I'm sorry; you'll have to apply for replacements. Here are the forms; it takes only about thirty days." Thirty days! Well, that did not quite suit us, as our flight was scheduled to leave at 7 a.m. the next morning. My friend became very upset and worried, but I was not. I said, "I just know that we are going to be on that plane at seven tomorrow . . . I can just see those clouds below us, now!" I didn't know how; I just knew. Several hours later, two friends — people that we had met only a few days earlier — gave us their plane tickets (worth hundreds of dollars and their way home), trusting us to wire them new tickets. Their kindness was a twinkle in God's eye and our safe arrival His wink.

Confidence in God's ability to meet our needs is returned with Providence that laughs at chance. Eric Butterworth, the insightful and prolific Unity minister, tells that once, while he was on a cross-country airplane trip, the plane was forced to land for repairs. The passengers were sent into the terminal and told that there would be a twelve or more hour delay before another plane would be available. Nearly all the passengers became angry, grumbling and complaining to the airline personnel. Dr. Butterworth, however, realizing that disappointment is Hisappointment, remained relaxed and was attracted to the one other passenger who was serene and unruffled, a man who sat calmly looking through a picture magazine. The two men got together and were enjoying a pleasant conversation when an announcement came over the loudspeaker: "Attention passengers of flight 721 to New York: a replacement flight is now available. The substitute airplane is, however, smaller than your original one, and only a limited number of passengers will be able to leave immediately. These passengers will be selected by lottery." A hush came over the crowd as the names were about to be chosen. The first two names announced were those of Dr. Butterworth and his friend.

I often remember these two airplane stories when my faith starts to waver. They remind me that there is a much bigger scheme to life than most people see from the ground floor of the airport. We must observe our departures and arrivals from the control tower, and not the waiting room. We must listen with our hearts, and not our ears. We must have confidence in our Self.

A while back, I quit a well-paying government job with a certain

amount of power and prestige, and I took a job in the Magic Garden
Health Food restaurant. One day, while shopping in Foodtown, I ran
into Mrs. Rothman (an old friend of my mother), somewhere between
the cauliflower and the eggplant. When I told her of my job change,
she asked me, "So, are you happy now?" "I am, Mrs. Rothman," I
reported sincerely. "I love my work; I feel creative and alive; I enjoy
the people I work with; I'm free of the pressures of working for the
government; I'm happier than I've ever been!"

"Don't worry, dear," she told me, with a consoling look on her
brow — "you'll find yourself."

The irony, of course, was that I was already found. And we are
all already found, but it is each of us that must find our own self, and
it is only within our own heart that we can know it. Once we align
ourselves with a direction from within, no one in the world can convince us otherwise, for our Source of acknowledgement is far more
powerful than any that the world could offer or any challenge the
world could pose.

There was a cartoon about a fairyland that was oppressed by a
dark tyrant called the "Shadow." All the fairies, elves, and animals in
the kingdom fled in terror of the Shadow, until he was about to turn
the entire kingdom into one huge shadow, and light would never
again be seen. There was but one day of light left before darkness
would rule completely. One brave little boy, armed with nothing but
one single candle, decided to challenge the Shadow by heading
straight for the evil one's lair. Unafraid, he entered the Shadow's
chamber and lit the candle. That was the end of the Shadow, for, you
see, the moment the light shined, it revealed that the Shadow had no
substance.

Our learned limitations are our shadows, and, like the little boy
in the story, we can rid ourselves of them only by facing them with a
little light. Each of us must ultimately conquer our own shadows. Until then, our Divine Self remains penned in a little corner of a frightening world while we are acting happy, but really knowing that there is
more, for we are more. Once we begin to see that we can be anything
we want to be, our limits reveal themselves to be as illusory as the
glass of a fishbowl that doesn't exist.

"You now stand on the brink of a vast realm of unlimited, eternal, and infinite space. You are free to enter it and to recognize the purpose for which you were created, a recognition which has too long lain covered with unsubstantiated thoughts of forms with empty powers.

For too long have you wandered through the mazes of narrow thinking and hopeless hopes. You have drawn your own boundaries and then given them homage as if they were Divinely ordained. You have made your own hell and resigned yourself to it.

Now before you is the answer to the dreams that you have denied as fantasy, but which your memory of the Divine has fanned and kept alive like an inextinguishable ember. Here is your moment, Children of Light. Here is found the long-lost portal to your ancient Home. Here is your Self.

Step forward, free of fear or hesitation. Your Heritage of Spirit must offer you more than you could ever offer yourself. It would gladly take from you your sufferings and disappointments, and lovingly replace them with living dreams that cannot be shattered by the vicious winds of

ephemeral chaos. Here, beloveds, is your dream, offered to you freely, recognizable only by the absence of conditions or guilt bargains for its return. It is given to you without barter, for it has always been yours for the asking, held in trust for you by an all-forgiving Father who is incapable of the kind of judgement that you have created to justify your learned guilt.

Here is the Answer to the questions that you learned to ask, but never fully believed. Here is the resolution to the problems that you were taught to worship, but never truly suffered. Here is the goal that you came to seek, but never really needed. Here is God.

Would you turn your back on All, for the sake of some? Would you trade your Heritage for hell? Would you remain in prison when the gate stands open?

Your taste of the Divine has ensured your acceptance of its blessings, and has so undone any need for fear. You cannot fail. In this happy fact is the assurance of your success, and the redemption of every soul that is carried into the Light because you are.''

THROWING AWAY CRUTCHES

Quietly sitting in the glow of a crackling campfire overlooking a peaceful mountain valley, I told the teacher what was bothering me. Two friends of mine had undergone a parting of the ways. They had been working together for spiritual service, but for reasons which I did not understand, they dissolved their partnership and set off on different paths. I told the teacher, "I am feeling a lot of pain about this separation."

"Come sit near me," he invited, with a strength in his voice that could come only of deep understanding. He gently placed his hand on my shoulder and explained, "What kind of happiness is that? You have let their actions determine your happiness. They were together, and you were happy. Now they are apart, and you are unhappy. What will you do if they get together again? . . . Be happy? Do not invest your happiness in the outside world, which is constantly changing and can never bring you real peace. Why not place your happiness in God, the unchanging, Who will never let you down?"

Although I had heard these ideas before (and had mouthed them myself many times), at that moment they rung in my heart like a mighty bell. I knew the truth of his thoughtful counsel, and my pain was resolved, never to disturb me again.

Another student, a paralytic, came to another teacher for healing. "Take up your bed and walk!" commanded the Master, and the man was healed. There is great grace in this lesson. Jesus was speaking not only to the paralytic, but to each one of *us*. Though we may not be physically paralyzed, we paralyze ourselves with mad ideas of experiences, people, and objects that we believe we need to keep us happy, and then we "lean out" on them in a false dependence that only keeps us sedated into believing that we are less than We Are.

We return to earth time and time again, we are told, to fulfill desires — thoughts that there is something "out there" that will satisfy our soul. We believe that a man, a woman, a cigarette, or a job will be the end of our seeking. The irony, or the joke, is that our soul is already satisfied, except for the *thought* that we need something else to fill us in. We must live out our desires in a painful evolution of disappointment until we realize that we are — and always have been — whole.

This process of disillusionment may sound callous and be difficult to accept, but life on earth is callous. No one in the world can escape the bumps and bruises of life. (Even Hilda was given a $50 summons for letting her dog off its leash for just a few moments.) Buddha said, "All life has in it the potential to bring suffering; when we give up craving, or attachment, then and only then does the pain stop." A woman came to Buddha with an appeal to restore her dead father to life. The Buddha gave her an empty cup and told her, "Fill this cup with sugar from a house where there has been no death, and I will restore your father's life." The woman eagerly went from door to door, but alas, there was not one person who was free of the pain which she sought to avoid. Buddha was not negative or cynical; he is called "The Compassionate Buddha" (Enlightened One). He knew that in the momentary pleasure of passing sense-objects, there is the possibility of pain when the object is lost.

We must be brutally honest with ourselves in assessing what brings happiness and what brings sadness in our lives. We must clearly discern between *fleeting* happiness and *real* happiness. People, objects, and experiences can make us "high," but the high is not whole, because we believe that it is the thing that has given it to us. We would give God's power to a thing. Satya Sai Baba says that drug experiences are "false grapes"; they look just like the real thing, but the moment we bite into them, we realize that they are imposters. The problem is not in the experience of a high, for we were made to be high; the error is in the association between the thing and the high. Believing that something can take us to Heaven means that we have left Heaven, and the only way we have left Heaven is in consciousness, and not in Truth. Because we are the Children of God, we carry God within us. If we believe that someone or something can give us God from outside, we have denied that She is already inside. No one can sell you the Brooklyn Bridge. If you live in New York City, you already own it. Buying it from someone means that you agree that it is not already yours and that someone else has the right to sell it to you.

I recently read that scientists believe they have found the cure for the common cold. Unfortunately, it is a rare enzyme from the stomach of a whale that can only be found in certain Arctic waters at a particular time of the year. This would mean that the Creator is so cruel, and that He so hated His creations, that He would plague them with a disease and then hide its cure in a remote and inaccessible place!

I prefer to think of the story of mankind, instead, as that of the musk deer, who searches the earth for the source of a beautiful aroma, only to find it emanating from within its own body. We tend to live on the periphery of our beings, seeking outside solutions for *inside* problems. When we believe that a degree, a raise, or a house can clinch our security, we sooner or later find that there is no more — or less — security outside than there is inside. And we see, too, that disillusionment is the best thing that could happen to us, for disillusionment means that illusion is over, and Reality is obvious.

Most of the dramas that we create over things in our lives are disguised attempts to feel spiritual peace; we have confused things with Spirit, and mistakenly equated acts with Love. But because we are spiritual beings, nothing less than spirit will satisfy us. I once sat through a long, drawn out court case of a woman who made a complaint against her next door neighbor, who had cut down a branch that was hanging onto her property from a tree that the plaintiff claimed belonged to her. The judge and lawyers argued the principles of the case in such microscopic detail that the judge finally decided to adjourn court and to have all the parties involved (including himself) go to the tree to see who was the rightful owner of the branch! The issue, of course, had nothing to do with trees and branches — it had to do with *people*. Before the incident, the two neighbors had been bickering for a time over some insulting things that one of them had supposedly said, which touched off a series of tit-for-tats, separation, and divisiveness, which led to the legal complaint over a broken branch. As I saw it, it was more of an issue of broken hearts than broken branches. People were feeling hurt and unloved, and the physical world of trees, branches, and fences was used as a means to

THE DRAGON DOESN'T LIVE HERE ANYMORE

manifest these hurt feelings. What I heard these women saying — screaming — in disguised ways was "I want to be loved! I want to be acknowledged! I want to feel connected!" All else, sadly, is the commentary of unskillful attempts to feel love.

Spiritual practices can be misused as crutches, too. We can become so attached to a teacher, to meditation, or to a diet that we lose sight of the fact that it is really *God* that we want, and not a habit. A teacher or a discipline ceases to serve its purpose if it becomes a dead end of devotion to a form. Stopping at vegetarianism or a particular form of meditation is like hanging out on Boardwalk and forgetting to pass "*Go*." In the end, all forms must go.

When necessary, however, it can be very helpful to accept the support of a discipline, a person, or a group that can further our spiritual growth. If a man injures his leg, a crutch is very much in order, and a great blessing, at that. When the leg has healed, though, the crutch must be relinquished. At a stage of the journey, it may be very valuable to become attached to a teacher, to a physical practice (such as yoga, tai chi, or a good diet), or to a spiritual community. These positive crutches give us the momentum to free ourselves of old, destructive habits such as smoking, laziness, or negative company. These spiritual crutches are habits that lead to *no* habits, which is our real destination.

The reward of the adventure of life is freedom. The irony of the adventure is that we were free before we set out, but we needed to learn that freedom was not to be found where we fantasized it to be. We needed to learn, like our old friend Dorothy from Kansas, that there's no place like home, because there is no place *but* Home. When we learn that God is everywhere, that Love fills all space, and that Truth is the very Ground of our Being, we may surely release the little to embrace the All.

> *To be free, to be able to stand up and leave* **everything** *behind — without looking back. To say "Yes" —*
> —*Dag Hammarskjold*

"You can — and must — stand firm and whole as you are. Nothing in form can offer you more than what has already been given. That which is whole can never be made complete by addition to it. You only burden yourselves with thoughts of emptiness. Dwell in fullness, and providence is proven.

How long can you search the outer world for fool's gold? Do you not realize by now that the world is a house of mirrors with no foundation? Are you not weary of hunting for fulfillment in a land where none is to be found?

We remind you of choice. There is no choice as to the outcome, but you may realize your goal quickly by your own willingness to be complete. We ask you to release only that which brings you pain, for your freedom is without cost. We have no conditions for peace, for we know ourselves to be Peace. Surrender your crutches, and see that you never, in Truth, had any need for them.

You are close to the end of your journey. Were you not, you would not be drawn to these words. Allow God to offer you His final — and only — gift. You know the outcome of your journey. So close to the summit, who here would tarry? Accept guidance, and light shall the way be made. It is easy to release all when you have already released much.

Take up your bed of self-created sorrow, and walk. This is not a command, but a promise of the Divine possibility for yourself that you are now just beginning to see. The full Reality of that vision is your right and your promise."

ARTICHOKES AND ROCKS

The best form in which to worship God is every form.

—Neem Karoli Baba

One day, an African tribesman was sitting on a rock by a stream, eating an artichoke and enjoying the dance of the sunlight through the green leaves of the forest. Suddenly, as if a flash of lightning burst forth in his brain, he saw the truth, the wonder, and the glory of creation. He realized that he was born of God; he saw the marvelous perfection of the great plan of the universe; and he was filled with a sense of peace that made him complete right down to his toes.

He returned to the village to tell of his wondrous insight, and before long, crowds of his fellow tribesmen began to gather around him. They realized that he knew something great that they, too, yearned to know. When he told them of their wholeness and their perfection, someone asked him, "How did you find this wonderful knowledge that makes your face so bright and your heart so full?"

"I'm not exactly sure," he admitted. "All I know is that one morning I was just sitting on a rock by the stream, eating an artichoke, and all of a sudden the Truth was revealed to me!"

The next morning, this wise man awoke to find the village empty. Puzzled, he began to search for his brothers and sisters, but they were nowhere to be found. After hours of looking in huts and calling their names, he gave up his search and decided to rest for a while down by the stream. There, to his amazement, he found the whole tribe, huddled together on that rock, all eating artichokes!

We too often mistake the form of an experience for its essence. We worship the physical manifestation of the Holy Spirit, and not the Spirit itself. The tribesmen had confused the circumstances of one man's enlightenment with enlightenment itself. If they truly understood his message, they could have gone about their business and left the rock and the artichoke to their one brother, for it was *his* destiny to awaken in that spot, and not theirs.

Enlightenment is not something that we can acquire through an action. It is a deep inner knowing from which successful action proceeds. Rituals, which are very powerful and necessary, can also be misunderstood, and function as a distraction. For a long time, I had a long list of rituals that I believed I had to do before I could make contact with God. I thought I had to get up at a certain time in the morning, take a cold shower, do a certain number of yoga postures and breathing exercises, perform a certain preparation for meditation, and then (I believed) I could go within and experience my inner peace. And it worked. I grew tremendously from this practice — but there was a flaw in the way I was doing it. My mistake was that if I was occasionally unable to perform my rituals, I would feel frustrated and unfulfilled. I felt as if I was not prepared for the day, as if I had missed something. I had the mistaken notion that my happiness depended on these exercises. I believed that God is something that could be accomplished, when it is a Presence that needs only to be recognized.

On certain days, however, something very interesting would happen. I would have only ten minutes to meditate, and I would say a little prayer or affirmation to myself, like "O.K., God, I only have ten minutes to be with You now, so I will really concentrate and just dive right in to my Source." Then I would imagine that I had done all of my rituals and preparations, and I would go into a lovely state of meditation. And it worked. This led me to the important realization that all the ceremonies were not necessary to do all of the time — my intention and concentration were more important.

This lesson was made obvious to me on the tennis court. My partner and I would bike up to a court in a lovely spot overlooking a valley of patchwork farmland and play for a few hours. For the most part, our volleys would last three or four returns. Toward the end of the session, I or my partner would say, "Let's just play out these last three balls and then go home." At that point, an amazing phenomenon occurred: our volleys would go on for ten, fifteen, or more returns! Our skill level increased about two hundred percent! I would think, "Well, I have just a few minutes left; I'll really pay attention to what I am doing and see how well I can do." One day it occurred to me that I could probably do that well *all the time* if I would just concentrate, and that I certainly did not need to wait until the last five minutes to begin to play up to my potential!

We all have a potential for succeeding at the game of finding inner peace; we need only to let go of the idea that there is something that we need to do first to be peaceful. The way to be peaceful is to be peaceful. We can never find peace through war or strife; it just doesn't work that way. The only way it works is to start out where we want to end up, to begin by knowing that we've already arrived, and to recognize all as wholly Divine.

When we realize that God is everywhere, it becomes easy to see and love Her in all that we do. Every word becomes a prayer, every action a spiritual ceremony, and every morning a holi(Holy)day. We can read Her words in the funny papers and experience communion through Fig Newtons. Hilda tells how some of her house guests began to scrutinize a box of cookies that she offered them, to see if there were any eggs in the ingredients. "I don't eat eggs," she once told a large audience, "but I'm not afraid of them, either!"

Hilda also tells of a time when she climbed to the top of a mountain in the Himalayas to find a remote ashram (retreat) for yogis who had renounced the world. As she approached the monastary, she heard (to her amazement), "Give me my pillow!" with another voice retorting, "No! — it's *my* pillow!" The first voice came back: "That's the pillow that I use for meditation!" Second voice: "Well, I'm using it now!" and so on, into the night. These yogis had supposedly renounced everything in the world. Perhaps all they owned was a loincloth, if that. Yet the seeds of attachment to a form lay within them, sprouting at the first opportunity. They gave their power to enter the Kingdom of Heaven to a pillow.

You might like to take a few moments to ponder if there are any forms with which you bind yourself. Are there any spiritual rituals, practices, ceremonies, or disciplines which, if you were interrupted from performing by, let's say, a friend in need, would leave you angry, annoyed, or frustrated? If there are, you are perhaps confusing your priorities. Reconsider the importance of your practices and see whether or not you are giving them power over your happiness.

There are very few people in the world who think originally. Most people act like puppets, mimmicking the latest trends in fashion, voicing the popular opinions, and catching the same diseases, thinking, at the slightest sniffle, "I must be coming down with the flu that's going around." The few people who do think originally and have the courage to act on their inspiration are hailed as geniuses, trend setters, and saints. We are all geniuses, through God's wisdom. We can each set a trend toward God in our own lives, even if no other person ever follows (and probably they will follow if we are sincere in our own striving). And a saint, as Hilda has said, is "nothing other than an ordinary person, living the life that God intended." Saints, I believe, have no special dispensation; their portion of God is no greater than yours or mine. They just recognize the God within, and live it without.

There is a lovely story from the Jewish Hasidic tradition that I would like to share with you. Rabbi Zusya, a pious and revered sage, was lying on his deathbed, weeping. His students stood by him, perplexed.

"Rabbi, why do you weep?" one of them ventured to ask. "Surely, if anyone is assured a place in the Kingdom of Heaven, it is you."

The sage turned his head toward his beloved students and began to speak softly: "If, my children, when I stand before the Heavenly court, I am asked, 'Zusya, why were you not a Moses?,' I shall have no hesitation in affirming, 'I was not born a Moses.' If they ask me, 'Why, then, were you not an Elijah?' I shall speak with confidence, 'Neither am I Elijah.' I weep, friends, because there is only one question that I fear to be asked; 'Why were you not a Zusya?' "

"Know ye, Children of Light, that each of you is dear to God in a unique and individual way. To follow the path of another is a fruitless search in the thicket of shadows. God dwells within your very heart, and you need never look outside yourself to find Light.

Honor the words of those who have remembered their Divine Heritage, for, as your heart understands, they speak the very Truth. It is more important that you follow the example of their Love than the personality of their mannerisms.

You are created in the image and likeness of God. You are creators, according to your lineage. The hallmark of creativity is freshness and aliveness, not stagnation or imitation. Those who follow the path of forms are rewarded in their own way, for they are expressing according to their right evolution. Those who can hold lightly the way of forms are free to hold all forms with equal appreciation. We invite you to discover your own God Self in the way that most pleases your heart, for your joy is God's fulfillment. God holds no limitation over you.

Your path, Children, is one of ever-expanding freedom. Tarry not in modes and practices. Ceremony has been given to you as a stepping stone to communion. Let it be as such. The Light welcomes those who stand beyond the stricture of ritual. Be not afraid to come freely, for it is in freedom that you are accepted. Acknowledge yourselves in the selfsame awareness, and you will clearly understand the role of form in your journey into God."

THE EXCEPTION

We live in a world that is based upon *agreement*. If enough people agree on something, it seems to be true. We then act as if it were true, and our experience tends to recreate itself as true. This will occur even if what we agreed upon is not true, and it will continue until someone demonstrates the fiction of the original idea. Then everyone will agree to a new idea, whether or not it is true. *"As ye think, so shall it be."*

Consider, for example, the notion that the world is flat. Everyone agreed that this was so, and since everyone believed that if you set off toward the horizon, you would fall off the edge of the earth into space, nobody tried it. Everyone lived a lie, for that was the experience that they created with their thoughts. They all agreed, and that made it *practically* true.

Then along came Columbus (or perhaps, as some say, someone before him), who did *not* agree. This was a very rash and bold thing to do — not to agree with what everyone else believed. Very threatening. Downright heresy, some would say. Well, you know the story from there. He challenged the agreement, proved that the agreement was fiction, and now everyone agrees that the world is round. Maybe it is. Maybe it isn't. But we all agree that it is, and that seems to be good enough for most of us.

It only takes one demonstration of one freedom-thought to break agreement. This is very important to know, because all of our thoughts of limitation are upheld only through *absence of challenge*. In order to discern Truth from limitation, we must challenge the agreements we believe in, to which we add power through mass thinking.

THE DRAGON DOESN'T LIVE HERE ANYMORE

For many years, to run a mile under four minutes was considered impossible — beyond the capability of a mortal man. It was simply unheard of — basically, because it was *unthought* of. Then, one day in May, 1954, one man, Roger Bannister, did it. He just went out and ran a mile in three minutes and fifty nine point four seconds. Basically, because he did not agree that it was impossible. He was one person who did not subscribe to mass thinking. Now it is fairly commonplace for good runners to run the mile in under four minutes. Roger Bannister trampled down the weeds of limitation, and everyone ran down the path behind him.

Jesus demonstrated the possibility for the fullness of humankind. He showed us who we can be — and are — when we cease to think of ourselves as small and limited. "Even greater things than I, shall ye do," He said. While most people in the western culture are not aware of it, there are many yogis and mystics in the East who have performed "miracles" such as walking on water or raising the dead, like Jesus. They would not call them miracles, however; they simply describe them as the intelligent use of the natural powers of mind that God gave to all men and women. More important than the miracles, however, is the force of love and forgiveness that Christ released on earth. He shattered the agreement that we must take "an eye for an eye and a tooth for a tooth." He demonstrated that it is possible to be crucified and to forgive at the same time. That is breaking a very big agreement that humans commonly hold to be true — that we cannot forgive. But He did it — He really did it. And we can all do it.

Agreement is safe. It is comfortable. It is easy to continue, for when we agree to limitations we fit right into the mold of mass thought and action. All that it takes is one original thinker — of which there are few — to change or reverse a whole trend of culture. When the Beatles first emerged in the early 1960's, they were mocked for their long hair. They were considered by some to be freaks and heretics. Before that time, I would be reprimanded if my hair was even slightly longer than "it should have been." Within just a few years, however, long hair — and even very long hair — became stylish, and anyone sporting short hair was considered to be an oddball. Now the pendulum has swung in the opposite direction, and shorter hair is in fashion. All arbitrary. All agreement.

We have got to challenge the agreements that we hold to be true.

We must boldly ask, "Do I believe this because I really believe this, or because everyone else does?" I am amazed to find out how much of our belief systems are unfounded, adopted from the norms of others. So often I see children taking on the beliefs, values, and expectations of their parents or some figure that they idolize. They are living out someone else's thoughts. This usually brings reinforcement from the world, for other people just love for us to do what they do. Challenge them in the slightest, and see their friendship fade. A true friend is one who supports you in standing for what *your* heart tells you is True.

If you have an inspiration for a project that seems to fly in the face of agreed-upon reality, then test it! Those who laugh at you or criticize you do so only out of misunderstanding or a sense of threat; you may demonstrate the fragile nature of the values which they hold dear. Assume that God Himself is showing you a new possibility, and if He is, your venture will be borne out. Who ever heard of a burning bush talking, anyway?

"To know the Truth, you must extricate your consciousness from trends of thought. Too often, you mistake the power of popular belief for the power of Truth.

When the student of Truth sets out on his venture to discover what is Real, he may at first be met by opposition, derision, and loneliness. This challenge is, however, temporary. The spirit of Truth will nourish you far more deeply than any comfort that is offered you by the agreement of the world. In the end, only Truth stands triumphant.

There are wayshowers — those who would mark the path for those who would follow. You, My Children, must accept the responsibility of showing the way for others, for, beloveds, if you do not do it, who will? Know your Source, and know your Destiny.

Set your foot firmly upon the path of all that you wish to be, for in Reality your aspirations are but a memory of that which you already are. He will light your way. Tremble not, dear ones, for this is the path to your very Home. You must turn your back upon that which you have called home, for it is already disintegrating in a world of confusion.

At the edge of the woods is light. This is the Light of our Love for you, the all-encompassing Joy of the Father, who would have His Children live happily in the Home He makes for them. Turn away from the agreement of men and know the Love of the Father, which bears no need for agreement. Dare to live as a true Child of the One, and all of your inspirations will be upheld by the ranks of all the beings of loving kindness that guide you ever homeward."

THE MARGIN OF GREATNESS

What makes someone great in the eyes of the world? Are our heroes supermen and women who have come from another planet with exceptional powers? Or are they human beings, like ourselves, who have used just a bit more of the potential for greatness that is shared by all?

I was very surprised to learn that many of the saints had rather ordinary childhoods. St. Theresa of Lisieux, for example, describes herself as a terror of a child; her mother had to tie her in bed to keep her from throwing tantrums. Yet, as she grew into God, she learned to master her emotions through little acts of humility and positive thinking. Once, when a fellow nun returned a pitcher that St. Theresa had loaned her — Theresa's only valued possession — with a crack in it, St. Theresa was overjoyed. "Thank you, God," she thought, "Now I have no more ties to things!"

Swami Satchidananda, one of the most poised and one-pointed men that I have encountered, has a similar story. I used to think that this eloquent and accomplished yogi emerged from the womb six feet tall, in flowing orange robes and a long white beard. But this was not the case. Swamiji started like the rest of us: he had a family, he was an auto mechanic, and he smoked cigarettes. Little by little he used his life to develop mastery, self-control, and peace. He tells this story:

I used to meditate and pray a little, but my mind was on the market and the cinema. I used to go to the Himalayas, sit in front of the Ganges, close my eyes, and start

> *meditating, but I would be meditating on the cinemas of New Delhi. I would be sitting in a cave but my mind was in the city. I repeated all the prayers correctly, and people who heard them said they sounded wonderful. They admired how I would sit quietly for hours and hours in meditation. But nothing came to my heart. I didn't feel or realize anything... Then I learned to pray for the sake of prayer and not for anything else. I would not be satisfied with anything but God. If our prayers are that sincere and our interest is only in God and nothing else, then God cannot sit quietly somewhere. He has to run to us. If we need help, it is always waiting. All we need to do is ask sincerely.* *

The swami's story inspired me to work a little harder. I had a yoga teacher who told our class, "*You can always do a little more than you think you can.*" I have experimented with this principle, and I have found it to be true. In fact, we must continually apply this truth, or else we cease to be alive and grow. Accept limitations, and they confirm themselves. Challenge them, and they disappear.

Let's take a contemporary example of the margin of greatness, a very insightful one, told by Eric Butterworth. In professional baseball, most batters hit for an average of about .250, which means that they get one hit for every four times at bat. This is considered a respectable average, and if a hitter is also a good fielder, he can expect to enjoy a secure career in the major leagues.

Anyone who hits .300 — three hits out of ten at bats — is considered a star. By the end of the season, there are only perhaps a dozen players (out of hundreds in the leagues) that have maintained a .300 average, and these hitters are honored as the great ones. They get the big contracts, the acclaim, and the shaving cream commercials.

What is the difference between the greats and the ordinaries? *One hit out of twenty!* A .250 hitter gets five hits out of twenty, and a .300 hitter gets six hits out of twenty. In the world of baseball, one hit out of twenty is the margin of greatness! To me, this seems miniscule.

This slim margin of greatness symbolizes the dynamics of greatness in life. When we actualize just a tiny bit more of our potential — a miniscule amount — we become outstanding human beings.

*Swami Satchidananda, *Beyond Words*, Holt, Reinhart and Winston, New York, 1977.

The purpose of being outstanding is not to win acclaim or glory, but to be more of what we can be — and until we live up to all that we are, we shall never be satisfied.

It takes so little to make a difference in our lives and in the world. We humans are very easily influenced creatures. One day, for example, I was feeling a little grumpy and someone called on the telephone for one of my housemates. As I took his message, he spoke in such a sincere and polite way that it changed my whole attitude. He did not tell me that I was wonderful, or that he loved me, and he did not offer me a million dollars. He just spoke with a little kindness in his words, and that, to me, made a big difference.

I remember, too, when a friend once called me up to give me a suggestion on how I could improve my singing. She didn't have to do it. It was even a toll call for her. But those five minutes were precious to me. It was a real act of friendship on her part, and I shall not forget it. And it seems that wherever I go there is one person whose smile is just a little brighter, or whose welcome is just a little warmer, or whose hug is just a little more genuine than the others. These are the people that I really appreciate, who inspire me to try a little harder to give a little more and to make a difference in the lives of the people around me. Their extra effort makes me want to be like them, and to pass along what I have received.

It is the "little" acts such as these that have given me the encouragement to carry on when the path seemed steep. Many of these kindnesses are actions which most people would overlook, but which my heart remembers. I am sorry to say that I have not always acknowledged these kind deeds, but I hope that these words will be a source of encouragement to those who do not always see the fruits of their given love.

These quiet and unacclaimed acts are, to me, the real margin of greatness. Greatness is not in popularity, wealth, or long life, as most people believe. Real greatness is in simplicity and supportive words. It is in firm encouragement and gentle patience. It is in finding God in the midst of the turmoil of the marketplace, and remembering His goodness during hardship. No, greatness is not always found in those whom the world calls its heroes, but in the unheard of saints who unselfishly serve their families, lend a kind ear to a friend in despair, and lovingly see the Best in those who have become too accustomed to seeing themselves as mediocre.

"You, within whom greatness lies dormant like a sleeping saint, arise to your hidden spendor! We do not ask you to be world leaders or heroes, but to do what you have been given to do, with loving care and your best ability. There is much, much more that you may know, that you may do, and that you may be. Seek out your highest calling and respond with your all. Do a little, if you wish, but do it well.

Seek not greatness in the eyes of the world, for the world loves its own, and would have you be a part of it. When you serve God, you serve the world, for the world knows not how to serve itself. It believes it can serve itself, but only encumbers itself with thicker delusion. Seek worth in the eyes of God, who would have you be great through humility. Meekness is the refuge of the mighty which the arrogant cannot enter.

Be not deluded and blinded by the small thinking of men. Their goals are as foolish as the paths they take to reach them. You are living in a world of erroneous thinking. You must break out of the patterns of thought that bind men to themselves. Begin your liberation with a few small changes in thought, and you mark for yourselves the right to walk the entire Kingdom."

DETERMINATION

"A saint is a sinner who never gave up," said Paramahansa Yogananda. This potent statement is, to me, a promise of the power of determination to make our dreams come true. We must push on relentlessly toward our goal, no matter what thoughts of unworthiness or failure attempt to dissuade us.

Let us consider the original apostles that Jesus chose to spread His message of Love and Light. There was a tax gatherer, some fishermen, a prostitute, and a doubter, among others. We are told, as well, that Jesus spent a good deal of time preaching in the taverns. Surely these, chosen by Jesus, are not our idea of saintly beings. They were, however, human beings who *grew* into sainthood. They did not descend on a silver cloud from Heaven; they rose from the dust of the earth. Jesus paid no attention to their outer garb of sin. He saw within them the Divine spark of greatness that He could fan into splendor, that those in the world might recognize their own Divine potential.

One of the early companions of St. Francis asked him, "Why you, Francis? Why you? Why did God choose you as a lighthouse to bless the world? You are not learned, you are not handsome, and neither are you wealthy. One would think that He would choose one who is attractive and successful to be exalted for His work. But you are none of these. Why you?" St. Francis smiled and replied, "Why me? I'll tell you why me. Because there could hardly be anyone who has made as many mistakes as I have! I have done and been everything you can think of that is abhorrent and unholy. I have absolutely nothing to offer to the world. That is precisely why God chose to glorify me! — to give hope to people who feel they have nothing to give, for if the Holy Spirit can work through me, it can work through anyone!"

These examples have given me the courage to keep going in the face of failure, to persevere in the absence of recognition, and to remain true to my Goal even when I seem to have fallen. Never allow yourself to feel that your spiritual work, your striving, or your discipline is not paying off. Even if you do not see the results immediately, or if you are not acknowledged by others, your actions are never for nought. If you are chopping down a tree, you may hack away for hundreds of blows and not see the tree move a millimeter. It is only when you make the final cut that the tree falls. Although you saw no apparent progress, each and every one of those blows was equally necessary to accomplish your goal.

There is no one who is so far from God that she or he cannot succeed. Star Daily was a convicted murderer and a criminal of the toughest order. He was so arrogant that the warden threw him in "the hole" — solitary confinement — to break him. He did not break, though, and he was near death when Christ appeared to him in a glorious Light and filled him with the Spirit of Peace. He walked out of that "hole" a new man, not broken by the warden, but transformed by the Grace of God.

Sometimes things come easily in life, and sometimes they don't. Sometimes we are given the gift of growth, and sometimes we have to work for it and earn it. There is a marvelous motto that encourages me to keep on keeping on when things do not seem to be flowing my way: "When the wind is not blowing — row!"

The people who succeed are the ones who are willing to hold steadfast to their dream, even in the face of apparent or temporary failure. When I first took a job as a coordinator of an agency, I met with several other men who were in similar positions. One of them gave me priceless advice: "There are going to be rewarding days and there are going to be days when you just want to quit. They are all part of the job. On the tough days, just keep plugging away." I never forgot his words. He was quite correct. Whenever I had a rough day I remembered his advice, and I gained the confidence of looking at the job from a broader perspective — and that made all the difference.

It is said that "Character is the ability to follow through on a *project long after the mood has passed."* Often, we must stick to a task even if the goal does not seem to be at hand. Thomas Edison put up with over nine hundred failures in his effort to produce an electric light, before he hit on the right formula. He had quit school at the age of eight, after only three months of education; his teacher labeled him "backward." Ronald Clark, Edison's biographer, tells us, too, that "Leonardo da Vinci, Hans Christian Anderson, and Niels Bohr were all singled out in their youth as cases of retarded development; Newton was considered a dunce; Einstein's headmaster was to warn that the boy would never amount to anything."* But deep within their souls was engrained a spirit and a confidence to persevere, a faith that carried them over all obstacles to achievement.

Like these successful men, when we make an inner commitment to realize a clear-cut goal, a great force of Will wells up within us. It is a Will bigger and stronger than our little will; it is like a wind from the great Will of God that comes to fill the sails of the ship of determination, the mast of which we have hoisted with our commitment to succeed. We can do nothing by ourselves, but when we declare our firm intention to accomplish a task and we ask for support from God, we are given the strength, the wisdom, and the means to succeed.

One summer, years ago, I travelled cross country with a friend who was extremely determined and positive. I was driving through the Texan desert late one night when I noticed that we were very close to being out of gas. I began to feel anxious about running out of gas in the middle of nowhere. We came to a gas station, closed for the night. I decided to just pull into the gas station and wait until it opened the next morning. My friend, who was sleeping in the back seat, woke up and asked, "What's happening?" I explained my plan to him. With a masterful combination of will and compassion, he urged, "Oh, come on, we'll find a station that's open!" Sure enough, not far down the road, we did.

The force that opposes determination is *inertia*. Inertia is not a static thing; it is a *dynamic force*. Like any force, it tends to magnify itself and gain momentum until or unless it is superceded by another force stronger than itself. If you jog every day, and then stop for a day, and then two days, and then three, the momentum of inertia will

---

*Ronald Clark, *Edison — the Man Who Made the Future*, G.P. Putnam & Sons, 1978

make it more and more difficult for you to re-initiate your practice. This is how we can get sidetracked from our dreams. We slip into the undertow of inertia, and then forsake our commitment. It takes a strong will to buck inertia, but overcome it we must. When we refuse to be intimidated by unchosen habit, and we do just one act of our practice again, the momentum of the *practice* will increase, and it will be easier and easier, and not harder and harder, to continue. It's all a matter of vectors and dynamic momentum.

The secret to maintaining a disciplined practice, I have found, is to always continue to do *at least a little bit*, even when I don't feel like it. When pushing a car, the hardest part is to get the car rolling, for an object at rest tends to remain at rest unless acted upon by an outside force. Once the car is moving, it is easier to keep it moving than it was to start it, for an object in *motion* tends to remain *in motion* until it is acted upon by another force. So, if I don't feel like doing a lot of exercises one day, I just do one or two, which keeps the discipline alive and, in a sense, keeps the door open for further practice. And sometimes those one or two exercises feel so good that I want to continue and do more.

To mobilize will and determination requires practice. Hilda has taught us a "1,2,3" method for developing will. "If, in the morning, you do not feel like getting out of bed, but know that you must, say to yourself, 'I am going to count to 3, and when I reach 3, I will get out of bed. '1' . . . '2' . . . '3!' and then you get out of bed!" You have to. There are no two ways about it. Your whole life depends on it. It really does.

As we make determination our own, there is yet a more subtle teaching that calls for our mastery. We must be determined, but not *headstrong*. We must have faith that God will help us reach our goal, but we must hold a greater faith that if we have chosen a goal that is not in our best interest, there will be a good reason for our not accomplishing it. We must take the attitude of high school shop students: our teacher will give us all the materials and methods for improving our skills, but if he sees us heading for an accident, he will turn off the electricity at the master switch. We must hold firmly to determination, but be ready at any moment to let go of our goal if we discover that our plan is not God's Plan. Our challenge is to distinguish between inner guidance and outer thoughts of limitation.

Hilda illustrates this distinction with two stories. Once, she was traveling with a yogi, on their way to visit a sick person. They had car trouble and Hilda remarked, "Maybe this is God's way of telling us that He doesn't want us to go." The yogi admonished her, "Don't be silly! We will go!" Off they went, and the person who was ill was healed.

On another night, Hilda was driving up into a mountain canyon when she got a flat tire. As she repaired it, she felt as if the flat was given as Divine guidance and she turned around to go home. Just at that moment, out of the canyon emerged a gang of sinister-looking men. Her setback was a blessing in disguise, and she chose well in not bucking it. Intuition and inertia, you see, wear the same garb; it is for us to distinguish between the two.

Determination is the very opposite of "chance." When we practice determination, we take our destiny into our hands. The determined person refuses to surrender to the random winds of circumstance. Determination is mastery, and chance slavery. If we rest our fate in the hands of fortune, sometimes we shall succeed, and sometimes we shall fail, but always shall we be weak. When we practice determination, we live up to our identity as masters of destiny. In so taking charge of our fate we shall succeed most of the time and fail some of the time, but we shall always be strong. We shall have no regrets about our life, for we know that we gave it all we had to give.

George Bernard Shaw said,

> I want to be thoroughly used up when I die, for the harder I work, the more I live. I rejoice in life for its own sake. Life is no "brief candle" to me. It is a sort of splendid torch which I have got hold of for a moment, and I want to make it burn as brightly as possible before handing it on to future generations.

Be determined. Be tough. There was a sign that I saw in a gym: "When the going gets tough, the tough get going." Seize on opportunities to practice mastery and determination. Meet your tests with enthusiasm, knowing that through conquering your challenges you are bound to become stronger. Remember that you will never be faced with a challenge that you cannot overcome, and that you and God are a majority.

91

''There is a special place in our hearts for you who are determined to succeed. The force of God rushes to your support with enthusiasm and encouragement. While there are few gifts that you can offer to God, determination is one of them. It is the soul's way of demonstrating sincerity of aspiration.

Hold fast to your dreams, Children, for they are the stepping stones to the success for which you yearn. Do not make a distinction between determination to succeed in the world, and that to succeed in God, for it is the quality of steadfastness that is to be developed, more than the object of determination.

Know, as you strive, that there are and will be resting points - oases - where you may replenish your strength. Do not seek them or wait for them, but in the midst of your disciplines, know that when you have need of them, they will be shown to you.

We urge you to continue with your will to grow. No effort, however small, goes unnoticed or unrewarded. Call upon the higher forces within you, and they shall most certainly give you their blessings in great measure. Your faith will carry you through your travails. Your commitment to God is answered with His commitment to you.''

The Mind

THOUGHTS ARE THINGS

"I was meditating on Love," explained a woman after she shared in a group meditation, "and I saw a rich, vibrant rose as a symbol. I held that lovely image in my mind, and soon my whole field of mental vision was filled with red roses."

"That explains it!" exclaimed the woman sitting next to her, with a broad smile of surprise. "I was meditating on Light when, all of a sudden, a bouquet of red roses appeared in my mind. They were beautiful, but I could not understand where they were coming from. Your roses came into my meditation!"

Thoughts are, most assuredly, things. They are conceived in the mind and they travel through time and space like ripples in a pond, affecting all that they touch. Thoughts are the building blocks of our experience; the world that we see is the one that we have created with our thoughts. Edgar Cayce said, "Mind is the builder." We think a thought, attach a feeling to it, and a circumstance in our life is attracted to it. If we want to see how we got to be where we are in life, we need only to trace our experience back to our thoughts.

Hilda once told this story: "I went to the country last weekend, and as we drove up a hill, I looked down at all the cars driving to and fro on the highways. What do you think was driving those cars, kids?" No one knew. "Thoughts! That's what was driving them! Someone woke up that morning and had a thought, 'Let's go see grandma today,' and off the family went. Or, 'I have to go fix my country house before winter,' or 'I'm gonna have a real good time fishing,' or some other thought of like nature. Each car was being led by a thought. You thought gasoline was powering the cars, but gasoline was only serving a thought!"

Everything we see, in fact, is serving — is a result of — thoughts. *"Your body is your thoughts in a form you can see,"* said Jonathan Livingston Seagull. This is easy to understand if we use a house as an example. Every house came only after an idea for it. Can you imagine a house being built before someone had a thought to construct it? No, houses always come from blueprints; never the reverse. In the same way, our circumstances are always a result of the mental blueprints — thoughts — that preceed them.

When Swami Satchidananda came to America, he was asked by his students to pose for a book of photographs of yoga postures. Although he had not done this kind of physical yoga in fifteen years (I am told), he went into the most difficult positions with ease. It was explained to me that his physical body had no tightness in it because his mind remained fresh and easy going. A calm mind pictured a relaxed body.

If there is any stress, resistance, or limitation in the mind, it will be manifested in the body. In yoga classes, for example, I see that most of the people who cannot do the headstand are prevented not by their body, but by their *mind* and by their emotions. Most of them are physically capable, but one little thought of "I can't" dams up the whole river of physical power. That little imp of a thought drags with it the emotion "I'm afraid" and the two together form a deadly duo that can effectively immobilize a muscular two hundred pound man. I could do the headstand only when I ceased to *think* of myself as "someone who cannot do a headstand" and began to *think* of myself as "someone who can."

To demonstrate this relationship between thoughts and the body, I did a simple muscle testing experiment in one of my classes. I asked a strong fellow to resist my pressing down on his outstretched arm while he thought of a stressful situation in his life. His arm became so weak that I was able to press it down easily, though he was trying hard to keep it up. I then asked him to think about his most refreshing and enjoyable vacation while I pressed on his arm again. This time the arm was so strong I could hardly move it. His mental stress had weakened his physical body, and his mental ease strengthened it. His body was a mirror of his thoughts.

There is more to our story of thoughts. Because they are things that are constantly, dynamically emanating from us, they create a subtle environment around us, like a force field or even a weather pattern. Although thoughts are not visible to the physical eye, we are always aware, on a subtle level, of the thought fields, or auras, of those around us. If I come into contact with someone who has just experienced emotional upset, for example, I feel or sense some kind of disturbance about them, even if there are no obvious physical signs. We all sense these kinds of energies. You may have had the experience of walking into a room where two people have just been arguing, and even though the people may have left the room, the air or atmosphere feels turbulent or muddy. By contrast, if you are in a room when a positive, happy person enters, you may begin to feel light, clear, and effervescent. I think we all know someone who makes us feel good just to be in their presence. Such a person is radiating thoughts of strength and positivity, and when we are near them we receive the benefit of their dynamic thought energy.

The reality of thoughts and the power they have to create and to change the world around us brings with it a supremely important realization: *we can bless and we can heal.* Blessing and healing are not mystical secret powers reserved for a special few. They are the God-given right — and responsibility — of every single human being, and as soon as we admit to ourselves that we can really be instruments for God's healing Love, we can begin to make the kind of changes in our lives and in the world that we always wanted to make, but did not feel that we were worthy or capable of offering.

A friend of mine arrived early to work one day, and while waiting for the store owner to arrive to open up, he decided to silently send out thoughts of good will to each person who passed by him on the street. After he was doing this for a few minutes, a shabbily dressed man walked up to him and told him, "What you're doing with your mind is good."

Such is the reality of thoughts. We must respect the power of thoughts, for they can make us or break us. We do not create our lives from nothing, but we certainly set into motion the events that create circumstances. By the time we see a circumstance, we are seeing the effect of a series of events that began with a thought long ago. This is why it is so ineffectual to attempt to improve life by manipulating circumstances. Any change in circumstances is due only to a change in the way we think. If we want to change our circumstances, we must change the way we think. We cannot allow ourselves the luxury of an "idle" thought, for there is no such thing. Every thought is a seed. What we plant in our mental garden will grow. This is the Law of Mind.

> *Sow a thought, reap a word;*
> *Sow a word, reap a deed;*
> *Sow a deed, reap a habit;*
> *Sow a habit, reap a character;*
> *Sow a character, reap a Destiny.*

"You have been endowed with a great and marvelous gift. Your thoughts are the key to your freedom. You who would reclaim your Divine Inheritance must do so through your thoughts, for it is only in thought that you have strayed from the path, and only through thought that you regain it.

The power to change the destiny of humankind is in your hands. There is no nobler charge that is given you than that of the salvation of the world. And there is no lesser task that is worthy of your participation.

Attune your consciousness with the Good, the Beautiful, and the True. Be a light to your sisters and brothers. Your Love is more powerful than any negation. Your faith can overcome all doubts. Your Divinity will awaken Itself in your brethren. You will certainly beautify the world, for those who know the miracle of thought know the secret of blessing."

THE LAW OF ATTRACTION

A young woman burst into my office one afternoon and pleaded, "You've got to talk to my brother — he's going to kill himself!" I went out to her car and I sat down with the young man, who did not particularly want any counsel. After a long conversation, it was clear to me that his intention to take his life was strong. I attempted to work with him in the clearest way that I knew, but it seemed that there was nothing that I could say that would change his mind. We parted, and I knew that prayer was our only chance.

That night at Hilda's class, I told Hilda, who interrupted the class to pray for him. We all sent him our love and our intention that he would choose to continue to live. When I next saw his sister several days later, I eagerly asked what had happened. "He's in the hospital," she reported. I was disheartened. "Could it be that our prayers failed?" I thought. "But it was not from attempting suicide," she went on. "The most amazing thing happened: That night, though his plan seemed set, he suddenly changed his mind and decided not to go through with it. A few days later, though, he slipped in the shower and hurt himself seriously."

This, to me, is a strikingly clear demonstration of the Law of Attraction. We attract to us that which we think. If we think and see goodness and prosperity, they shall come to us. If we dwell upon negativity and suffering, that is what we will find. Although this man renounced his foolish plan, he had to reap the results of his morbid thoughts of self-harm, in the form of experience.

"As ye sow, so shall ye reap," said the Master. "Cast your bread upon the water and it shall return to you." The man's fall in the shower was no accident, nor did he purposely do it. He was simply facing his own thoughts in a form that he could see.

Every thought is a prayer. Each thought that we think is like an order that we place with God, who is prepared to give us all that we ask for in the form of our thoughts. The more we dwell on any thought, the more likely we are to see that thought manifested in our experience. We can make this principle work for us by focusing our minds on the thoughts that we would like to see turn into events and experiences. Hilda put it in plain language: "If you keep after God enough, He'll get so tired of your bellyaching that He says, "Let's give that one what she wants, and shut her up, already!" She once told someone, "If I had a goal like that, I'd pound the ethers until it came to pass!"

Actually, we do not need to talk God into anything She doesn't want to do, because there is no difference between our will and Hers. Resolution comes when we realize that there is no will outside of the one that God gave us to use. We are "co-creators" with God. We point the bow, and She shoots the arrow. A beautiful young boy once asked his father, "Daddy, who loves me more, you or God?" The father thought for a moment and answered, "God loves you *through* me, sweetheart."

We are encouraged by shampoo, deodorant, and handcream advertisements to be attractive. Actually, we are already as attractive as could be! We are constantly attracting to us people and conditions that mirror exactly our patterns of thought. There is no getting around it. Every element of our lives is where it is through very lawful placement. *We may see the events in our lives as being unlawful, but that is only because we do not yet understand the laws of mind that are operating behind the scenes of our daily dramas.* Once the laws are clear to us, we can see that "random" or "accidental" events are actually the result of a very intelligently designed system of justified relationships. What we think is what we get.

I saw this principle strikingly illustrated in a film that I saw on the laws of sound. A handful of iron filings was placed on a thin sheet of metal, and a certain musical tone was played near the sheet. Wonderously, the filings arranged themselves into the form of a snowflake! They were conforming to the vibrational pattern of the tone that was being played. Another tone was sounded, and the filings rearranged their formation, this time into a star pattern! Every sound had its own pattern, and the visible filings demonstrated the invisible pattern of the sound.

Our thoughts are like the sound, and the circumstances in our lives the iron filings. The filings had no volition or will of their own. They simply fell into the vibrational pattern of the sound. In the same way, automobiles, money, food, jobs, and relationships have no particular will of their own. Their nature is to follow the direction of the waves of thoughts that we send out.

Some say, "Look what I created!" but another way to say it is, "Look what I *attracted*." The word *circumstance* neatly depicts the process: *circum*, around, *stance*, stand. Circumstances are the conditions that stand around us, magnetized to us by the central core of our thought-forms. Change the thoughts at the center of the magnetic field, and you change the conditions that stand around you.

This ability to draw conditions to us has tremendous practical implications. It means that we can use our thoughts to make our life. It means that we can really change for the better. It means that *things no longer hold power over us*, for we realize that they are *just the expression of our thoughts*, and nothing more. Our bodies, for example, look just like we have made them with our thoughts. They have no mind of their own; they depend on our mind for direction. One yogi said, "Your physical body is made up of pizza pie and ice cream . . . Pizza pie has never made anyone overweight — but *thoughts* have. It is the mind that says, 'I need pizza with double cheese . . . Hand, pick up the pizza . . . Mouth, chew it!' The mind is the general and the hand and the mouth are the privates in the corps — or the *corpus*!"

"By their fruits shall ye know them" is a teaching that we usually take to describe the effects of a spiritual teacher or path. A pure teacher will bring about peacefulness in the hearts of his or her disciples, and an impure teacher will give rise to troubles. Perhaps there is yet a deeper meaning to Jesus' words, as I believe there always is. The Master spoke in parables because they describe the *inner dynamics* of life as well as the outer events. The "fruits" can mean the events and conditions in our lives. The "them" is our thoughts. To paraphrase, "By the events shall ye know the thoughts." If you want to know what is the nature of someone's thought patterns, just look at the conditions in his or her life.

Harmonious living tells of harmonious thinking. A turbulent life reveals some kind of inner turmoil or lack of resolution. We may believe that we are positive, settled people, but if we notice troubles or conflicts in our outer conditions, we must look *within* to see what inner negativity is bubbling, or bubbled at some earlier time. If you want to know what's in your subconscious, you don't have to go to a psychiatrist or a psychic. Just look at the condition of your bedroom, your car, your house, your health, and your relationships. They are photographs of your subconscious. *Outer events are simply the skin and bones of inner thoughts, and to really take control of our lives, we must treat them as one.*

This is why we cannot be a "victim of circumstances," for it is none other than *we* who have brought about the circumstances in our lives upon which we would like to blame our unhappiness. We have attacted to us, for better or for worse, the conditions that were born of our very thoughts. When I was seventeen years old I drove my car through an unmarked intersection and collided with another car. I cannot blame my car or the other driver, nor could I sue the city for not having marked the intersection. I can only hold myself responsible for being careless and not proceeding with caution. My car, you see, looked like my consciousess at that time — a little battered and misshapen. Before the "accident," I had had a mental and emotional collision with a girlfriend. The car was repaired, but my consciousness was not. Two months later, I had the *exact* same "accident" in the parking lot of a department store thirty-five miles away. My car was damaged in *exactly* the same spot, this time with slightly less damage, by a smaller car. (You can imagine the look on my father's face when he came home and saw the car in the garage, damaged again!) Let's face it: I was in collision consciousness. The universe taught me, through two very solid collisions, to proceed with caution. An expensive lesson, but a valuable one.

The principles of attraction work between like-thinking people, as well as within each person. We are attracted, in deeper ways and through more subtle channels than we may be aware of, to persons who vibrate in harmony with us. Last year a friend of mine invited me to accompany her on a long ride that she had to make to a remote town in the mountains of Pennsylvania, where she was going for a job interview. I had no idea how I would occupy myself for the few days that she had to be there, but I felt that it might be nice to go with her.

When we arrived on a Sunday afternoon in the middle of winter, we felt like taking a ride to a nearby college that she thought she might like to attend if she took the job. It was a blustery, below zero day, and there was hardly anyone on the frozen campus. Hardly anyone, that is, except a dark-skinned man walking just ahead of our car, a man conspicuous only by the orange robe rippling in the wind just below the hem of his overcoat.

"I must find out who this man is!" I told my friend, and we pulled over to ask him.

"My name is *Gunaratana*," he told us. His eyes were deep set and they spoke of tranquility. "I am here to lead a meditation retreat. Would you like to join us tomorrow?"

And so, the next morning, when my friend went to her interviews, I took her car and went to meditate with Gunaratana, who I learned was not only a very advanced yogi, but the teacher of two of my very dear friends in New York. There is no way I could have planned that one — but the Law of Attraction knew a way.

At another time, I received a letter from a friend of mine in New England, who had just returned from a convention in Canada, where she met a man named Stan, who was looking for someone to teach yoga in his program in New Jersey. My friend wrote me that she thought he and I might work well together, and she suggested that I contact him. He and I discussed the idea through a few letters, but his program was a little too far from my home, and our correspondence ended. Several months later, I went to a psychology conference in Atlantic City. In the first workshop of the program I met a man with whom I felt a strong connection. As this was a non-verbal workshop, we did not speak, but there was an unspoken bond between the two of us. We saw each other in passing during the weekend, but simply exchanged a warm hello.

The last workshop of the conference was a very dramatic and powerful one. Those who chose this workshop were asked to role play the successive stages of a human life. We were to act out and experience birth, youth, growth, clustering in families, maturity, and death. Toward the end of the workshop, we were told to choose families in which we would feel comfortable "dying." I went from group to group, interacting with many different individuals and clusters of "families," but none felt like home. I met, for example, two friendly women who invited me to be a part of their family, but my intuition told me not to stay. Though I very much wanted to find a place, there was none that seemed right for me. I began to feel lonely, and a bit of panic set in, for I feared dying alone and unsupported. All the others were with families, and I had no one. At that exact moment, on the verge of despair, I looked up — and there, walking toward me, also by himself without a family, was the very man with whom I had established such a strong connection in the first workshop. It seemed as if we were the only two people without a family in a workshop of a hundred or more persons. He, dramatizing the part of an old, crippled man, limped toward me with open arms, tears streaming down his cheeks. I felt a great wave of love well up within me as I approached him. We embraced each other like two ancient kindred spirits, and there, in each others' arms, we "died," our family — and our intuition — fulfilled. It was a very moving scene.

After the workshop, we introduced ourselves. His name was Stan. He was the very man about whom my friend had written me, and with whom I had corresponded about working with him. My friend was from Vermont, she met him in Canada, and I met him in Atlantic City. Attraction.

And the two women who had invited me to be a part of their family? Months later I met them again at Hilda's class. A year later they bought a house, and a few months after that, I moved in. In the end, I accepted their invitation to join their "family" — two years after they offered it — but the Law of Attraction is not always concerned about time — just results.

These lessons of attraction demonstrate that our thoughts *do* make a difference in how our life turns out. Where we are now is always a result of what we have thought, and where we will be will be a result of what we think now. If we wish to find ourself in a state of success, it will not be by accident; it will be only by our drawing success to us by thinking success-thoughts. By the same rule, we can condemn ourself to failure by concentrating now on what is wrong. The way of conditions is prepared by ideas.

This is why we must take care to think and attract to ourselves only that which is in harmony with our highest aspirations. If we think on or pray for something that is a passing desire, we may be forced to face the object of our desire long after the thought that spawned it has faded into obsolescence. Hilda has said, "Be careful what you ask for, kids, because you just might get it . . . You pray and pray and beseech God for a certain person or experience, and then when it comes to pass, you wish God wouldn't have listened to you!"

The *"Fantasy Island"* television show is very much about this teaching. There was an episode in which a man who always wanted a lot of money came to Fantasy Island with his wife, and there learned that he had just inherited one million dollars. Immediately all of his friends began to use him for his money, and he became very insensitive to his wife. He got caught up in a vicious cycle of inflated self-importance and decreased depth of his relationships, until he had no real friends and his wife was ready to leave him. Finally, his life was such a mess that all he wanted to do was to get rid of his money and return to his simple, peaceful lifestyle. Fortunately, Ricardo Montalban arranged for his inheritance to be discontinued, and the man and his wife left Fantasy Island with one more breath of happiness and one less fantasy.

I can think of jobs, relationships, and automobiles that I yearned and prayed for (through dwelling on them in my thoughts) that came to me long after I ceased to want them. I then had to deal with them. If I was strong, I would let go and say "No" when they came. If I was weak, I would accept them, living in a sort of dream world of memories that had outlived the desires that created them, until I would be forced to admit that the object of my desire was more a part of my past than my present.

As some persons begin to discover the relationship between thoughts and events, they begin to be afraid of thinking negative thoughts, worrying, "Oh no! I just had a thought of something bad happening to me . . . That means I will attract it!" This anxiety comes from an incomplete understanding of how thoughts attract events. There is no need to be concerned about stray thoughts of disaster or failure. They have no power unless we feed them with fear. We are thinking many, many thoughts per second (Buddha said trillions) and we are also catching the thoughts of those around us. Occasional thoughts of negativity or failure may creep into our consciousness, but if we "throw them off" before we indulge in them, they cannot harm us. It is thought *habits* that count. Continually dwelling on the same thoughts, feelings, and mental pictures begets conditions. Keep your thought *patterns* positive, and little negativities shall have no power to penetrate your established force field of positivity. We are told that there are many little disease germs in our bodies, but our overall health and strength of resistance holds them at bay.

If you now have negative circumstances in your life, cease to dwell on them mentally, and they will leave you. The best way to get rid of an unwelcome guest who lingers at your home is to empty the refrigerator. He'll be forced to seek refuge elsewhere. When we stop feeding our bad habits and conditions with thought and feeling energy, they will drop off like an old scab. If we pull out the plug from an electromagnet, all of the scraps of junk metal that cling to it fall off instantly. Refuse to water a weed, and die it must. Negative circumstances cannot survive when we refuse to sustain them with emotional energy.

Simply put, we are undeniably responsible for our lives. Wed to this responsibility is the freedom to use the laws of life in whatever way we choose. We can create Heaven or hell for ourselves through our thoughts and our actions. Do not wait for the world to stop "socking it to you." Start generating as many positive thoughts as you can, and you will bear witness to miraculous changes in your life. Think love, success, and happiness, and sooner or later these blessings are sure to be yours. Concentrate on that which you would become, not that which you now believe you are, and you will enter a new realm of consciousness — one of *chosen* good.

The realm of consciousness that most people tend to live in is a mental world. We see life more in the way that we *think* it is, than in the way that it actually is. Instead of stepping onto the porch to feel the air, we turn on the radio or the T.V. to learn what the temperature is. I found some wild spearmint growing in the woods, and my first thought was, "Wow! This smells just like chewing gum!" We ask, "What time is it?" to find out whether we should eat, instead of asking our stomach whether or not it is hungry. We devise and discuss elaborate systems of psychotherapy, and yet we fail to give our children a smile or a hug when they need it. Fritz Perls said that real psychotherapy is "losing your mind and coming to your senses." We experience ourselves as mental creatures, and the world of ideas has become an all-too comfortable place for us.

Perhaps we have entered this realm in order to learn to master it. As explorers in consciousness, we must learn to conquer, through understanding, the mind which creates our destiny — *our own mind*. The principles, like tools, have been set before us, and it is our charge to take these tools and to use them with wisdom and integrity. We are told that previous civilizations on earth, such as Atlantis, unlocked the secrets of the mind and proceeded to misuse them, which led to their demise. We are also told that we have once again reached the point at which we can free ourselves or destroy our civilization through the use we make of the powers of the mind. It is a decision of great responsibility, one which we all share, and one which we cannot afford to take lightly.

We cannot deny the powers of mind that we all hold, any more than we could deny a speeding car in which we find ourselves at the wheel, with no power to stop it, but complete power to steer it. Our thoughts are continually creating, or attracting the world of the next moment. We do not have any choice as to *whether* we will create, but we always have a choice as to *what* we create.

Harnessing the power of attraction opens the door to what some would call the "secret" of living, although there is nothing hidden about it. *We can change our lives simply by changing the way we think!* We do not need to go through the cumbersome and impossible work of fighting, struggling and attempting to manipulate the conditions in our lives. We need only to begin to think in new and more productive ways, and the conditions will — must — reflect our way of thought. The principle seems hidden or secret because most people do not believe that thoughts are real, or that what we think has an effect on the way our lives work. If people really believed in the power of thought, our world would be a picture of harmony and perfection. It would be a portrait of God.

Choice is in our hands, as always it has been. We may hesitate to accept our power, for we have been taught to believe that there is a world out there bigger and more powerful than who we are, but the irony of this view is that the world "out there" *is* who we are. Align your thoughts with the Truth, and all that is True will be attracted to you. Believe in illusion, and your life will be clouded with experiences that confirm lawlessness, only because you refused to see reality in your original thought. Life blossoms for those who see the flowers in their experiences. We are free to draw to us the life of our own choosing. Indeed, all that we see is the offspring of chosen thoughts.

"Make your lives an offering, Children. It is within your ability to mark your own destiny. We would have you mark it for the highest good. How profound and pervasive are your quietest thoughts! As you realize their magnitude, you relinquish any notion of idleness.

Those who have been shown a moment of vision of the inner mechanics of the mind bear a great responsibility, greater than you currently understand. You hold within your hands the evolution and the destiny of all. Choose wisely, beloveds. The ramifications of your choices are being made known to you more rapidly, now. The energies of creation are multiplied as they are drawn from a place close to the center. Indeed, fathoming the intricacies of the mind is a final lesson in earth teaching. You must remain true to your most cherished principles in making application of the energies that you command. This is the greatest test of all. It is, after all, the only test of Christ Jesus after His baptism. He was challenged not for Himself, for He was already free. It was for all that He demonstrated the impotence of illusion. You need only to remember that what is free can never be bound.

We beckon you to offer the world Light while remaining in its midst. Those who serve mankind in this way are strong and blessed, indeed. A life transformed is more precious than a life escaped. Whatever your path, tread it well.

The Truth that gives you life is for you in all places. Make no distinction between degrees of Truth. All is Truth.''

REFLECTIONS

Weapons will do you no good in that cave, Luke . . . You will find only what you bring with you.   — Yoda

One night I had a dream about Sasha, a dog I used to know. In the dream, Sasha was whining for attention, and she just kept whining, no matter what I did, until I became very annoyed. I began to raise my voice and command her to be quiet. She continued, and I became angrier until, in this dream, I began to hit her. Worked into a furor, I awoke and found the whining I was fighting was nothing more than my own wheezing in my sleep, from a stuffy nose.

Although the story is in one way funny, it was a precious teaching for me. It symbolized what has been taught throughout the ages by all the great teachers of wisdom: All life is One; all that we see is our own self; the experience of separation is a dream.

Jesus taught, "Love thy neighbor as thy self," and "Do unto others as you would have them do unto you." He taught this because thy neighbor *is* thy self, and when we do unto others, we *are* doing unto ourself.

There is nobody out there. All that we see are reflections, or mirror images of our own self. When we talk, we are only talking to our Self. When we fight, we only fight our Self. When we love, we are only giving love to our Self. There is only One Being in all the universe, and It is Us.

Several years ago, I traveled cross country with a friend. On this trip, she and I spent a great deal of time bickering. We both grew enormously from it, but at the time we were engaged in mental Star Wars. We came to Wyoming, which, in this particular area, is a vast desert. If you have ever been there you know you can travel for hours, for hundreds of miles, and see hardly one person or green living thing. It's desolate.

We finally arrived at a public campground that was so remote, there was not even a ranger to take campers' money for the night's stay. There was just an old weathered wooden box with a few registration cards, a pencil, and a slot to put your money in. It was all on the honor system, this place was so far off the beaten path. We hiked to where the lake was supposed to be, only to find it dried up and arid. I mean this place was like another planet.

At least there was some living vegetation, so we decided to set up our tent and spend the night. We had just settled down when we heard, from just over the hill, a loud shrieking voice that made us jump, yelling, "How dare you do this to me?! I wish I'd never met you!" and so on, to which another equally enflamed voice shouted back, "Whaddya mean 'me?!' It's *you* who . . . !" and so on. I stealthily sneaked around the bend and found a man and his wife drinking and having one of the loudest, bawdiest quarrels I have ever heard. In the middle of nowhere. No water. No ranger. Just us and them. Just us.

All that we see is but a reflection of our own self. Through our bickering, my friend and I attracted that couple to us. We created that couple. We deserved that couple. We *were* that couple.

This lesson in the desert taught me a powerful method to short-circuit judgements and irritations that I feel about someone else. If I am annoyed at another's action, I ask myself, "Do *I* do that, myself?" If I am very honest, the answer is usually "Yes." Most of the time, the trait against which we are reacting in another is something within ourself that we do not accept. If you make a list of the positive and negative traits of someone you don't like, you will probably find a striking number of similarities between them and yourself. This requires a great deal of honesty, but if you can do it with a high intention, you will grow tremendously from it.

This may raise the question, "But people *do* have faults; am I supposed to be blind to the shortcomings of others?" No, this would be foolish. To believe that everything that everyone does is good would be irresponsible misuse of our Divine gift of discrimination. Earth is, in fact, a school for learning what to do and what *not* to do.

The key to knowing what is ours and what belongs to others is in understanding the difference between *observation* and *reaction*. I may *observe* that a room is untidy, that a word is misspelled, or that a person has a poor habit of interrupting others when they are speaking. If I can see it clearly, *without an emotional charge* on it, I am executing the very necessary faculty of discrimination, and such an observation is probably to my benefit as well as to the one doing the action. If, however, I become *upset* when I see the person doing what I don't like, and I lose my peace, then I am *reacting* to it, and it is most likely a trait within *myself* that I am refusing to accept. This method requires extreme honesty, and in order to benefit from it, we must want to grow more than we want to be right or to hold on to judgements and opinions.

Carl Jung called it the "Shadow." We project onto others what we do not want to see in ourselves. We have a need to deal with our non-acceptance of a certain trait, and it must be brought to the surface, as our purpose in life is to make the unconscious conscious, and to grow into loving it all. If, through our ego, we block ourselves from seeing the unwanted trait within ourselves, we project it onto another and we identify with the opposite of the trait, which we believe is "good," or we can accept. But the name of the game is to destroy thoughts of separation through exposing them to the light. As soon as we separate ourself from another and say, "*I* am this and *you* are that"; "*I* am good and *you* are bad"; "*I* am neat and *you* are messy," we have created a lie of separation, for we are *all everything*.

The way to get rid of the shadow is to *own*, or accept as part of ourself, that which we do not like or will not accept in another. Once we see that we were not reacting to another, but really to *ourself*, it immediately eliminates the conflict in the relationship, for we free the other person from the burden of our projection. We then do not have to change the entire world of others to fit our mold of what they should be like. We need, then, only to change ourself, which is much easier than reforming others or the whole world. We cannot, in fact, reform the world unless we first reform ourself.

Understanding this principle makes clear the reason why many social reform groups or movements are not successful. Actions or campaigns that are performed from a position of emotional self-righteousness have little power to bring about real and positive change, for those who would wage them are only reacting to an aspect of themselves, in the form of an outer shadow. By contrast, those who see a problem in society and can work against evil or injustice while at the same time loving and respecting the persons who are part of the problem, are much more likely to effect real and lasting change than those who see the problem as "them." Any time there is an "us" and a "them," a "good guys" and a "bad guys," a "criminal" and a "victim," there is a shadow. The extreme example of shadow-making is Hitler, who took all of the fears and guilts and angers of a whole culture and projected them *en masse* in a huge shadow onto a whole race, believing that he could purge a nation by annihilating people. We must beware, however, lest we deny our fears of evil within ourselves, and project them onto Hitler. Difficult as it may be to accept, unless we can love Hitler, we are only continuing to perpetrate the hatred and non-acceptance for which we hold him guilty.

Interestingly, the principle of the "shadow" can create separation even in the realm of "good." If you are inclined to worship, idolize, or prostrate yourself before any guru, teacher, or master, you have created a sort of "white shadow" which also must be reconciled. In such a case, you have refused to accept within yourself a good quality, such as wisdom, love, or kindness. By projecting it onto your guru, believing that he or she has it and you do not, you are creating another separation, denying that wisdom, love, and kindness are within you. Any real teacher of Truth reminds the students that all they would seek in the teacher is already within themselves. I once wrote a teacher a devotional letter, telling him that all I wanted to do was to hang out with him. He wrote me back a short reply, beginning with "no groupies . . . no students . . ." This was the kindest thing he could have done for me, for he did not allow me the luxury of separating myself from my own Divinity and projecting it onto him.

Perhaps the whole lesson of reflections can be summarized in an experience that I had while staying at a country house. At this house was a cute little pet white duck who would sit outside the kitchen door and quack whenever someone passed by. One morning I sat on the porch and watched several people respond to the duck as they entered the house. One woman, a professional singer, greeted him, "Why, Pete! How nice of you to sing me a morning song!" Five minutes later, an overweight man walked by and chided, "Oh, Pete! . . . There you go again, always quacking for more food!" And right after him came a rather intellectual fellow who replied to Pete's quacks with, "Always questions, Pete, always questions . . . perhaps we'll get you another duck to give you some answers." And so on. Meanwhile, Pete just went on quacking.

I am remembering, too, the tale of Narcissus, who lost awareness of himself when he became fascinated with his own reflections in a pool of water. While we usually take this as a lesson against vanity, it has much deeper implications. If, when we see others, we are actually seeing only ourselves, we, too, have been mesmerized by our own reflections, like Narcissus. The only way to break the spell is to begin to see ourselves, and not our reflections. The dream is over when we realize ourself to be all of the actors in the play.

"Divine ones, cease your continuous misidentification with the forms that you have created with your very own minds. Return to your true home within your Self. All that you see outside of you is a dream. In Truth, there is no separation, except that which you have made by your refusal to accept your own wholeness. Shadows exist only when you turn your back to the Light.

Courageously destroy all that you have made outside of yourself. Renounce your striving against that which you would not admit. Prostrate yourself before no man, but only before God, who dwells within you now.

Love the Divinity within all, and you free yourself of the slavery of artificial distinction. See the Perfection behind imperfection, and you behold the true being of your brethren and yourself. Those who teach Truth can do so only because they see Truth. Those who teach separation see divisions where none exist.

Strive to know yourself. Be unrelenting in your quest to discover what belongs to you, and to distinguish your true Self from that which has been taught to be yours. We tell you this with certainty: That which is yours can never be taken from you, and that which is not yours can never have belonged to you. Know this distinction — the only true distinction — and you free yourself of the tyranny of reflections."

ARE THESE MY THOUGHTS?

My housemate, Bill, had just gotten engaged to be married, and he was exuberant. One day around that time, I came home and I began to feel a little gloomy and depressed. My energies seemed to be dulled, and I did not understand why. Bill asked me for a ride to school, and as we drove along I felt a strange lethargy. The moment he stepped out of the car, I felt buoyant, light, and free. It was as if a cloud of smoke had flown out the window. I suspected that I had not been feeling down on my own account, but that I had been picking up some negative thoughts and feelings that he was experiencing, and taking them on as my own. I am not speaking of my relationship with him or my feelings about him, for we got along very well. I suspected that I was tuning into some disturbance within him. I could not understand it, though, because he had just been overjoyed to be engaged.

When I got home that evening, my answer came. Another housemate told me that Bill's engagement had just been broken. That explained it. Though he said nothing to me, Bill was feeling downhearted. I was not prepared to feel negativity from him, and as I left myself open, I assumed that the thoughts that he was emanating were my own.

Thoughts are catching. At times, such as in this case, we can feel thoughts (and the emotions that come with them) from other persons, and, if we are not careful, believe that they are ours. We are all generating a huge amount of thoughts and feelings all the time. If we are to remain strong, clear, and effective, we must understand and master thought energy.

THE DRAGON DOESN'T LIVE HERE ANYMORE

There has recently been a great deal of scientific research to demonstrate the reality of the transference of thoughts and feelings. In Peter Tompkins' *The Secret Life of Plants*,* we are told of experiments in which a man measured his plants' reactions to his thoughts. He found that the plants to which he sent loving and positive thoughts grew much more favorably than those to which he sent no thoughts or negative thoughts. It has been demonstrated, too, that thoughts are independent of physical distance. In a documented study, a woman in Georgia sent thoughts at a predetermined time to seedlings six hundred miles away, in Baltimore. By the next morning, the plants had grown 84% faster than a control group.* Since I read about this study, I talk to my plants, which are twice as healthy as they used to be.

In another experiment (a cruel one which I regret having been done, but from which we can learn), a litter of baby rabbits was taken in a submarine to a depth beyond which radio waves could penetrate. Their mother remained on the land, monitored by an electronic sensor. One by one, the little rabbits were killed. At the moment that each baby died, the mother registered a strong reaction. Even on the animal level, we are all tuned into the Universal Mind, made of thoughts which are very real.

I recently attended a lecture at which a high-ranking physicist from the NASA space program described current scientific findings of very subtle particles that all of us emit. These particles vibrate in accordance with the thoughts and feelings that we generate. In other words, we are always sending out little bits of our experience and we "bombard" the people around us with these tiny but powerful particles. In essence, we are always in a big "soup" made up of the thoughts and feelings of those who share the space in which we happen to be. We are constantly mixing, blending, and merging with them. Those around us take on some our our particles, while we take on theirs.

Mystics and yogis have known and taught this for thousands of years. One evening Hilda told us, "No one will walk out of here the same as when you walked in. Just by sitting with each other, we take on each others' energies. Our auras tend to blend. I will take home a bit of you, and you will take home some of me."

The agreement of Hilda's teaching with that of the NASA scientist

*Peter Tompkins & Christopher Bird, *The Secret Life of Plants,* Harper & Rowe, 1973.

reminded me of a quote that I heard not very long ago: "When the astronomers finally make it to the top of the mountain, there they will find the theologians waiting for them, laughing heartily."

"Sympathetic vibrations" are not unfamiliar to us on the physical level. I once had two female dogs who, before they lived together, went into heat at different times. When they moved into the same house, they began to go into heat at exactly the same times. I am also told that women who live together, and mothers and daughters often begin to menstruate in synchronism.

As we come to understand the implications of the transference of thoughts and feelings, we can use the principles to our advantage. Until we do, we may feel like a leaf in the wind, at the mercy of the rampant energies of those around us. There are three ways in which we can capitalize on our understanding of how thoughts work:

1. *Seek to be in the presence of positive people who share your ideals; place yourself in environments that support your spiritual growth.*
2. *Keep your clear, calm center when you are in the midst of negative thoughts and feelings; do not compromise your awareness of God's Perfect Presence.*
3. *Be a generator of positive and loving thoughts and feelings, so that you will enhance, and not detract from the experiences of those around you.*

All of the great spiritual teachers and religions have placed a high importance on keeping good company. We are told to spend time in good fellowship, or to seek *satsang* — the company of Truth: those who are dedicated to thinking and living in a Godly way. There is much to be said for keeping good company. Through it, we give and receive support to reach our highest goals, and to remain strong in the face of adversity. It is a way to keep our spiritual batteries charged. It is the true purpose of community. Swami Kriyananda said, "If you have just one or two spiritual friends with whom you can share your highest aspirations, you should consider yourself richly blessed."

There are many spiritual communities that have grown up in recent years. They are like lighthouses in a dark world. If you have contact with spiritually-oriented people, whether or not you live in a formal community, you are very fortunate. I thank God each day for the friends that She has sent me along this path, for I truly receive much from them. I met a woman who was on a brief visit to this country from Yugoslavia, where she is not permitted to worship God or gather with others to do so. She sat in on one of Hilda's classes and drank it in with an appreciation far greater than the regular students, who sometimes take the experience for granted. Perhaps hers is the kind of enthusiasm and appreciation that we need to have all the time if we are to realize our spiritual aspirations.

If you are fortunate enough to have the benefit of sitting in the presence of a real spiritual master, one who teaches in Truth and Love, you are very fortunate, indeed. Such a teacher can offer Grace that can remove obstacles, lessen suffering, and save a great deal of time from your path — lifetimes, perhaps. Cherish any opportunity you receive to be with a real teacher, as well as any group gathered in the name of God.

If you are required, as we all are, to be in the presence of people or environments that are generating negative energy — anger, fear, uncontrolled emotions or words — you must learn to hold firm and remain confident of God's Presence even — and especially — in the face of thoughts, words, or news of "evil." You can do this by meditating regularly, cultivating positive thinking, visualizing and feeling a brilliant aura of light or positive energy all around you, and by controlling your words and actions that would react *in kind* to negativity. It is of the utmost importance to *not* go into agreement or align yourself with the turbulent feelings that another is experiencing, or you yourself will enter a disturbed state of consciousness from which you, like them, will have to extricate yourself.

If you want to help someone who is experiencing worry, fear, or depression, you must stay centered in peacefulness. This is the most effective position from which you will be able to truly serve them. A friend of mine is a psychologist in a mental health clinic. When he first began the job, he was a mess; he took on the problems of many of his clients. He was headed for "burnout." It was only when he developed an ability to emotionally detach himself from his clients' lives that he really became effective. Many other mental health professionals have told me that they made the same discovery for themselves.

I would like to share with you several case histories that illustrate this principle. A man that I know has devoted his life to the selfless service of people who live in the ghettos of New York City. He gets them food, clothing, organizes activities for children, and does all that he can to help them out of whatever troubles he finds them in. He works with many alcoholics, drug addicts, and others whose lives are steeped in suffering. Once, he explained to Hilda, "The other night I came home late and I began to meditate before I went to bed. I felt horrible — as if there were some negative force all around me. I had to meditate and pray as hard as I could to get rid of it. Finally I regained my clarity, but I do not understand what happened."

Hilda explained, "You know, you work in some pretty heavy environments. You are subject to some tough vibratory rates. If you had been working hard all day and felt tired, your aura may have broken down a bit, and you may have absorbed some of the 'muck' (negative thoughts and violent feelings) from those you work with. Perhaps you needed to cleanse yourself of the negativity that you had taken on. Keep up your work, but be sure you get enough sleep, and do not overwork yourself."

Another friend of mine was ill for several days. She began to feel better, but all of a sudden she started to feel lonely and rejected, though she could not understand why. Her son then approached her and confided that he was feeling put down by his peers, and that he felt like he had no friends. Through her experience of illness, her consciousness of wholeness had broken down, and she assumed the lonely feelings of her son. She talked it over with him in a loving way, and they both felt better.

Does this mean that we should avoid or cloister ourselves from the world? Certainly not. Running away from negativity is not usually helpful. I used to use "bad vibes" as an unconscious excuse to separate myself from others. My idea of peace was to be off meditating somewhere by myself. That idea still sounds good to me, but now I see, too, that finding peace amid chaos is more valuable for our growth — and service — than finding quiet amid quiet. Jesus said, "Resist not evil, but overcome evil with good." Light is always more powerful than darkness. Evil, when confronted with love and positivity, flees like a thief in the night.

I learned this important lesson when I worked in an office with a woman who spent a lot of time complaining over the telephone. Once, when I was the only one in the office, her phone began to ring, and I began to pick up another extension, in fear of "catching" all the bad vibes on her phone. But then I thought, "This is ridiculous! What am I afraid of? If I am centered in Truth, thoughts of negation are meaningless. I refuse to be intimidated by nothing." So I used her phone, and, of course, no great disaster occurred. What did happen, though, was that I proved to myself that my own awareness of God is always more powerful than anything in the world.

Because our thoughts and our awareness are powerful, we have a responsibility to the people, the things, and the world around us. Just as we would not want anyone to empty a trash can of negation upon us, we must take care not to disturb others with our thoughts. A man at a yoga retreat came to Swami Muktananda, raving, "Swami! Swami! A terrible injustice has been committed! You must find me a new roommate. The man that has been assigned to my room smokes cigarettes. This inconsiderate oaf is polluting my room with his foul habit. You must remove this ignorant man and correct him!"

The swami thought for a moment and responded, "Yes, you are correct; an injustice has been committed. I shall transfer you to another room. But not because he is polluting the physical air with his cigarettes; it is because *you* are polluting God's air with your thoughts of judgement and your anger. He may be committing an injustice to his body, but you are committing a greater injustice to him and to your soul!"

We are constantly creating and recreating one another through our thoughts. This can be a vital key to improving troubled relationships. Relationships suffer when we hold negative pictures of each other. *If you want to bring a difficult relationship into the light of love, make up your mind to change your image of who both of you are.* Realize that the relationship will continue in a rut and you will tend to live out each other's negative expectations until one of you sees both of you as Godly. You do not have to wait for the other person to change; *you have the power to change the relationship for both of you.* As soon as you let go of your ideas of limitations about the other person or yourself, you set both of you free, and the relationship is likely to improve.

I once had a friend who believed I was clumsy. Now, I am not the great ballet dancer Nijinsky, but I am not particularly clumsy. When I was around this person, though, I found myself making foolish blunders, and he would harp on them and criticize me for them, and I just felt awkward around him. One day I realized that in being open to him in an undiscerning way, I was unconsciously tuning into and living out his thoughts of who I was. (And he was probably mirroring some of my unconscious thoughts that I am awkward, as well.) The moment I saw this whole pattern, I decided to maintain my inner clarity in his presence, and to stay centered and graceful no matter what he thought or said to me. At that moment, the relationship changed dramatically. I saw that I could help both of us by refusing to accept limiting thoughts about me, whether they came from him, from me, or from anywhere. By my holding to my innate O.K.-ness in the presence of thoughts of Not-o.k.-ness, those thoughts of limitation eventually dissolved, and I have since ceased to feel, think, or act limited in his — or my — presence.

Creating each other with our thoughts works for upliftment, as well. Why does it feel so good to be in the presence of someone who loves us? They are blessing us with their thoughts that we are beautiful and wonderful and loveable. We catch those thoughts, and as our thoughts vibrate in harmony with theirs, we begin to love and accept ourselves, too. This is the way to really make thoughts work for us. *We can create lovely and loving people around us just by tuning into the qualities that we would like to enjoy in them.*

I find that it is extremely important to remember that, because our real nature is one of Goodness and Godness, *any* thoughts to the contrary are not our own. At first, it may appear that they belong to other people, but as we realize that we are all One, it is clear that they cannot belong to anyone else either. Who, then, do they belong to? To a force of negation that belongs to no one, but has been kept alive in consciousness only by belief in it, like an old theatrical costume that keeps appearing in different plays only because actors are willing to put it on.

Which thoughts, then, really *do* belong to us? Those that are Divine; those that are born of Love; and those that shine with effulgent Light. We can believe that negation belongs to us only if we believe that we are less than Divine. Yet, said one who knew His — and Our — Identity, "You are the Light of the world." And the only thought that can belong to the Light is Light.

"What you imagine to be your thoughts are merely echoes of the voice of the world, a voice which bears no relation to your true identity with Light. Constantly meditate upon your true nature, and you will easily discern between that which is of Love and that which belongs to error.

This teaching is but an elementary training in separating yourself from that which you have imagined to be your own. Your growth is marked by freedom from the effects of misdirected musings of the mind. Be not dismayed at negative consequences of your past actions, for you are occasionally required to bear out the unfoldment of earlier thought patterns before the fruits of your present work make themselves visible.

It is of the utmost importance to be an ardent worker for the force of positivity. You bless your sisters and brothers by cultivating strong and loving thoughts about them. In so doing, you serve the transformation of their lives as well as your own.

Be peaceful in your work, and Peace shall find a home in you. That which is other than Truth cannot bind you, for you have been given dominion over the world. Share not the delusion of mortality. Cease to cling to ownership of illusions, and illusions shall cease to retain the image of binding you.

Freedom is your name.''

THE MIND AS THE
SLAYER OF THE REAL

Facts, my dear Sancho, are the enemies of the Truth.
— Don Quixote, Man of La Mancha

A young seeker trekked over treacherous mountain roads to find a certain teacher who, he was told, could answer the question that had long been gnawing at him. After days of searching, asking local villagers for clues, and depending on little more than intuition and faith, the pilgrim found the one whom he sought.

"Master," the earnest young man immediately asked, "How can I know what is Real?"

The sage was silent for a few moments, but not because he needed to think. Then he spoke. "If you want to know what is Real, then you must realize what is the nature of the mind that you ordinarily use to look at your life."

The student was not satisfied. "But how can this understanding show me what is Real?"

"Because," the teacher explained, "the mind is the slayer of the Real!"

What did the wise man mean? How can the mind slay the Real? If something is Real, is it not impervious to threat? What is the mind, anyway? And aren't facts necessary to discover the Truth?

No, the mind could never mar one iota of Truth. The Truth is eternal, and it is not in any way assailable. *Our perception* of Truth is, however, vulnerable, and it is too easily distorted by the web of

125

ignorance, spun by the crafty spider of the rational mind. In order to know the Truth, we must learn to recognize a Source other than facts.

Jesus and His small band of disciples were sharing a quiet retreat time by a clear, cooling stream in the mountains. The disciples were discussing who the people thought He was.

Thomas spoke first: "You are Jesus; of this only can I be sure."

"You are a great teacher," offered Judas, ". . . perhaps the best."

Peter stood up under the bough of a mighty tree and looked the Master boldly in the eyes. "I say you are the Christ — the Messiah — the Son of the Living God."

"And I say you are truly blessed, Peter," immediately responded Jesus, rising as He answered, "for this you could not have learned from any mortal man, but only from my Heavenly Father Himself. Your faith is the rock upon which I shall build my church."

We all have Thomas and Judas and Peter — and certainly the Christ — within us. Thomas is the over-thinking, inconclusive part of us which refuses to believe anything until it is proven "beyond a shadow of a doubt." The thinking mind is not willing to accept anything as proven, for then it would have thought its way out of a job, and it loves its job dearly. Think about it now, with your reasoning mind: What do you know, for *sure*? Can you not see two sides to every argument? If we pursue Truth with our mind, as soon as we come close to proving anything, some evidence for the opposite point of view is rushed into the courtroom. It never really reaches a satisfying resolution.

Judas is the betrayer of the Truth — the slayer of the Real. He represents the fearful aspect of us that sees threat where there is good will and finds a way to take blessings and negate them. In a sense, this way of thinking hands over our spiritual experience to the kangaroo court of the rational mind. It believes that it can win salvation by delivering the Christ in us to the judgement of the senses. It is sincere, but mistaken.

And Peter? Peter stands for the direct knowing of the heart, the blessedness of spiritual intuition, and the eternal knowledge of what is Real. He stands for an awareness of Truth that is independent of the judgements and opinions of men. Now ask your *heart*, "What is True?" You will not get an answer in words, but you will feel the eternality of the Truth in your soul. In the mind there are no answers; in the heart there are no questions.

At a certain point in our evolution, we seem to be inundated with questions and doubts. It would appear that our awareness of what is Real has been betrayed and delivered to the never-ending trial of worldly confusion. The thought may even cross our mind that there is no God, or that if there was, He is dead. But remember that there is one more personage in our story: Jesus, who represents the Truth ("I am the Way, the *Truth*, and the Life"). Though He was crucified, Jesus was resurrected as the Christ, in final demonstration of the incorruptibility of the Real.

If our vision of the Truth is clouded in any way, we must discover how the mind maintains its veil of ignorance. We must learn to observe how our errors in thinking tend to create unhappiness in our lives.

There is a famous story which gives us a lucid clue about how pain and suffering are unnecessarily created. A man walks into a dark room and sees the form of a deadly snake coiled at his feet. He becomes so frightened that he collapses and falls to the floor, dead. A few minutes later, another man walks into the same room, turns on the light, and finds the first man lying there with a coil of heavy rope at his feet.

In this parable, there was no real threat — but the *perception* of a threat was strong enough to bring about the same result as if the threat were real. This is the story of suffering in our lives. We see snakes, where, if we were to simply turn on the light, we would find a harmless rope. Think for a moment. What have been the snakes in your life that turned out to be ropes? How many things have you worried about that never came to pass? And if they did come to pass, were they as horrible as you imagined them to be? Probably not. One man actually kept track of all that he worried about. He discovered that of all his worries, 92% of them never came to pass, and of the 8% that did, he was somehow given the strength and the ability to deal with them successfully. Our worries are paper tigers.

A great statesman said, "We have nothing to fear but fear itself." The experience of fear is usually more debilitating than the event that we fear. ("A coward dies a thousand deaths, a hero only one.") Fear is always the result of the absence of the awareness of Truth. When we know and feel the Truth, it is not possible to hold fear.

127

THE DRAGON DOESN'T LIVE HERE ANYMORE

I would like to share with you a little snake and rope story of my own. One day I was sitting outside a grocery store, eating a muffin. Just then, a car pulled up, and I saw my first girlfriend, whom I hadn't seen in many years, get out and walk into the store. To my amazement, I became very edgy. "Should I talk to her?" I wondered, " . . . Maybe it's better if I just say nothing!" I hadn't really resolved my feelings about her, and my mind and emotions jumped about like school children at recess. My heart was beating rapidly, and I was gulping down my muffin. In new age spiritual terms, I had "lost my center."

A few minutes later she emerged from the store, and I just sat there and watched her get in her car and drive away. As the car turned the corner, I got one final look at her. And do you know what? It wasn't even her! It was just someone who looked like her. It was a rope that I made into a snake. (And even if it was her, it would have still been a rope.) Meanwhile, I had wasted precious minutes of my life, being nervous, pumping poisonous chemicals into my body, and improperly digesting a good muffin that I could have been enjoying. I felt pretty foolish, but at least I had a good laugh at myself.

Our experience will tend to bear out any thought that we believe, even if the thought is not true. This is how ignorance perpetuates itself. There was a period of time when I took a vacation from Hilda's classes. At the time, I did not know that it was a vacation; I thought that I was leaving her teachings. I began to find things wrong with Hilda and her way of teaching. The rational mind, which is incapable of holding two opposing ideas, had to make her "wrong" so I could be right. It was real insanity.

One night I returned to one of her classes and found that her chair had been placed on a small platform so she could have a full view of all the people in the class. My mind thought, "Look at this Guru Trip. She must have an ego, to be put up on a stage like that!" I sat there through the evening, bored, and I looked at the clock more in those three hours than I have in all the years I have been with her. As I write my experience now, it just seems so obviously ridiculous, for Hilda's intentions with the platform and the chair were born only of the humblest purity, which I later came to realize. But my mind needed to uphold my position of not attending classes; it needed to find a reason for what I was doing. So it created Guru Trips, egos, and boredom where none existed. Meanwhile, I missed out on an excellent class. I did, however, learn a good lesson about the inadequacy of the mind as a judge. Truly, the mind is the slayer of our *awareness* of the Real.

It is also true that a little knowledge can be worse than none at all. At around the same time, there were two people coming to the healing sessons at Hilda's classes, for healing of glaucoma. We prayed equally for both of them. One was healed and the other was not. The one who was healed was a simple (perhaps uneducated) woman. Ironically, the man who did not get healed was an optometrist by profession. "Do you know why the woman got healed, and the optometrist did not?" Hilda asked us one night. "Because," Hilda explained, "she did not *know* that the disease was incurable, but he *did*."

On another night, Hilda offered us a game to play: "I am going to concentrate on a number. See if you can guess it." Many people raised their hands, but they were all incorrect. Finally, after a long time, someone shouted out, "13," and Hilda answered, "That's right!" She went on, "How many of you thought, '13,' but didn't say it because you thought it was too 'negative' of a number for me to think?" Quite a few hands went up. "The mind is the slayer of the Real," she explained.

The story of the world is essentially that of the *Emperor's New Clothes*. As I remember the story, the Emperor's tailors made some kind of blunder which resulted in their failure to have the Emperor's new suit ready for the big parade. So they convinced him that he was wearing a beautiful new garment that he could not see. He ultimately agreed that it was very beautiful and set out to lead the big parade, wearing no more than his long johns. The people of the kingdom were convinced, as well, of his full attire, and the parade proceeded with everyone agreeing to this big lie. Everyone, that is, except for a little innocent child, who exclaimed, "Look, Mommy! The Emperor doesn't have his clothes on!" at which point everyone realized that they had been fooling themselves, and the Emperor was very embarrassed.

The mind has a way of teaming up with our desires, in a sort of tag team of illusion. We get a new car, a new guitar, a new girlfriend, and for a few days or weeks or months, we feel satisfied. Then, inevitably, a little voice begins to speak to us: "Wouldn't you like a better one? Or maybe another one? A bigger one would be nicer, you know!" and so on. From the vantage point of the mind, happiness is always *there*, never *here*. As soon as we move to Oregon, or have our first baby, or get that raise, everything will be alright. But that is not how it works, really, for as soon as we get Oregon, the baby, or the raise, there is always something else that we need to *really* make us happy. A friend of mine called it "the mythical ten percent." This is, as he explained it, "the ten percent *more* that if we had, we know would really satisfy us . . . Only problem is, it's always ten percent *more* than we have — no matter what we have!"

There is a tale about a man whose car gets a flat tire on an old country road. Seeing a farm down the road, he decides to ask the farmer to borrow a jack. As he walks toward the farm, he begins to think, "I hope he has a jack . . . Oh, he probably will . . . But what if he doesn't want to lend it to me? That would be pretty selfish . . . Well, if he doesn't, maybe he would do it for a few dollars. How much would be fair? . . . I'll offer him three dollars . . . But what if he wants five? I'll just have to give it to him! I have no choice. Even if he wanted ten, I'd have to pay it! What nerve! What if he wants more? He knows I'm stuck . . . I'm at his mercy! What if he wants all the money I have? . . . Let's see, now, I have about forty-five dollars in my wallet . . . If he wanted it all, I would just have to give it to him! That's downright robbery! What kind of man would take advantage of me like this?!"

As the man approaches the farmhouse, he becomes angrier and angrier. By the time he reaches the house, he is downright irate. He rings the bell, and the farmer answers the door with a friendly "Yes?" Red in the face, our friend spouts, "You know what you can do with your jack?! . . ." slams the door, and storms away.

Although the story is somewhat exaggerated, can you not think of experiences in your own life when you allowed the thinking mind to blow a situation so much out of proportion that you lost your ability to deal with it effectively? I can think of too many such instances in my own life. Our mind can be our best friend, but, uncontrolled, it can work against our best interests.

Our mind can confuse us to the point where actions bear no relation to reason. We do things for the wrong reasons, and we are not even aware of what we are doing or why we are doing them. A friend of mine once asked her brother, who was always rushing through yellow traffic lights, "What will you do with those extra few seconds that you seem to gain by speeding through yellow lights?" "Gosh, I don't know," he replied, with a blank expression on his face. "I never really thought about it."

This seems to spring from the same sort of unquestioning attitude which has escalated America's arms race with the Soviet Union. America and Russia have spent trillions of dollars to develop the most sophisticated weapons that, we are told, can destroy our planet fifty times over. It's called, in military terms, "overkill." To me, it is the same as *The Emperor's New Clothes.*

The Truth is so simple. Some of the happiest people that I have known are the retarded, and the elderly in a nursing home I have visited. I am certainly not denying their difficulties, but I do see a peace in many of these people that I do not find in the normal thinking population. Like little children, many of these people have a refreshing innocence about them. "Let the little children come forth. Lest ye be converted, and become as little children, ye shall not enter into the Kingdom of Heaven."

It has been said that "the rational mind is a wonderful servant, but a terrible master." We must *use* the mind, instead of giving it free rein to run wild. The thinking mind helps us to organize our world and to create technology that makes our lives easier and safer. If we do not control the mind, however, it will team up with the mouth and the tongue, and together they will get us into trouble.

We can stay out of trouble, and in the light, by thinking with our heart. I am not speaking of the emotions, but of the wisdom of the soul. Our heart will never lead us astray, or slay our perception of the Real. The heart *is* the Real. It cannot be misled, because it does not confuse facts with wisdom. It does not doubt, because it lives in God. And it cannot be slain, because it is Eternal.

"In your heart is etched the Truth of Existence. Thoughts that lead you away from that Truth are but delusion.

We encourage you, nay urge you to use your faculty of discrimination. Be not afraid to challenge the illusions that you have been taught. The Truth shall never fail to be revealed to you, for ignorance cannot stand the scrutiny of inspection.

Suffering is born of wrong thinking. The root of pain is error in perception. There can be no error in Truth, only errors in the perception of Truth. If you yearn to end human suffering, know, then, what is Real, for this Knowledge is the only source of invincible faith.

What is Real can never be slain; it can only be hidden from the mortal eye. To see the world rightly, you must look from the viewpoint of immortality. This is the only perspective that can bring meaning to a meaningless life. Thoughts of mortality are the only veils that can shield the Truth from view.

March on like true soldiers of Love. Annihilate illusion with the sword of discrimination, and the Reward of all quests is yours. We tell you this: the Real is your only salvation. Nothing that is Real can ever harm you, and nothing other than the Real can ever bring you the Peace that you seek. Acknowledge God, and welcome your Self."

THE NECESSITY OF
POSITIVE THINKING

To think positive is to think with God. This must be true because God is positive and God can do anything. When we think with God, we can do anything.

The key to success in life is to know without a doubt that God is our Mother/Father who wants only the best for us. All failure stems from the mistaken thought that we do not deserve the best that life has to offer. We are Divine Children of God. We were created to be magnificent. We were created to be great.

I have grown to have such a faith, such a belief, and such a confidence in the never-failing power of positive thinking that I believe it to be an absolute prerequisite for all success in life. We've all got to believe in ourselves. We've got to believe in our families, our friends, and our businesses. We've got to know the rightness of our hopes, our aspirations, and our dreams. God is desperately looking for people who will trust in the dreams He gives to us. There are so few people who are willing to take the inspiration that God breathes into them and hold tenaciously to it until the possibility becomes a reality. The world is numb to imagination, to creativity, to life. The neon lights of the cities block our view of the stars. The world has settled for second best, and in so bargaining has settled for nothing.

There is a story of a man who comes to the outskirts of an ancient city. There he finds a gatekeeper sitting quietly. The traveler tells the gatekeeper that he has just left his old city, and that he is thinking of moving here. "What's this city like?" asks the traveler.

"What was it like in the city you came from?" returns the gatekeeper.

"It was a rotten place. People were unfriendly, there were no jobs, and the government was crooked."

"Well, that's pretty much what you'll find here," explains the gatekeeper, and the traveler moves on in search of a better city.

A few hours later, along comes another man with a suitcase, also seeking a new home.

"What was it like in your old town?" asks the gatekeeper.

"Oh, it was quite a nice place," tells this second traveler; "lovely people, nicely kept; a shame I have to relocate on account of my job."

"Well, that's pretty much what you'll find here," reports the gatekeeper, and the man happily enters the city.

How we use our mind is crucial to our finding and getting what we want out of life, and giving what we want to it. Success, love, and abundance are not given to a privileged few by the whim of a capricious God. Those who enjoy happiness do so because they have earned it with their thoughts. They have the faith that God is working for their good, and that every moment of life is a precious gift. By so thinking, they open the door to goodness and success.

The foundation of positive thinking is this truth:

TO THINK IS TO CREATE

If we want to make it in life, we need to *start* with our goals clearly in mind; we need to decide what it is that we want, and then get a sharp mental picture of it. Then we must hold steadfast to our goal until it is realized. Refuse to be distracted by thoughts of failure; The Beatles were turned down by several recording companies before they were accepted by one. We've got to believe that if God gave us an idea to do something, He'll find a way for us to get it done.

We cannot allow temporary setbacks to be a cause for disappointment. God often has a bigger plan for us than we have for our little selves. Recently I was working on making a tape of deep relaxation exercises for my classes. I had the hardest time getting it done. First the microphone didn't work, and then the recorder short-circuited, and it seemed that one thing after another went haywire. A project that I expected to take no more than a few hours turned out to take weeks. I did not understand it, but I persevered. Finally the tape was finished, and I eagerly sat down to listen to the final product. It didn't turn out! All that I had recorded had mysteriously disappeared from the tape! I really couldn't figure that one out.

In desperation, I telephoned an electronic engineer friend of mine to ask his advice. "Why don't you come to my house and use my equipment," he offered; "I'll be glad to help you with it." I was delighted! There he gave me use of very expensive and sophisticated recording equipment, plus his expertise in pushing all the right buttons at just the right time, the sum total of which produced a recording far superior to any that I could ever have done by myself. While God was saying a temporary "No" to me in my earlier attempts, He was actually saying "Yes!" to a much bigger idea.

"Yes!" is the most dynamic word in the English language. It is the symbol of affirmation, acceptance and positivity. It makes me feel happy and strong just to look at the word.

When I went to visit a beautiful, Christ-like teacher named "Freedom," he asked me, "Do you want to be happy?"

"I sure do."

"Then say 'Yes!' " he advised me, with much love in his voice. "Say 'Yes!' to God, say 'Yes!' to life, say 'Yes!' to Love, say 'Yes!' to your Self. Then you will be happy."

Too often we miss opportunities because we do not live in the expectation of goodness. We believe that something is too good to be true, when, in fact, blessings are the only things *good enough* to be true.

Norman Vincent Peale, one of the most dynamic and enthusiastic people there has ever been, tells of two salesmen at an outdoor sports exposition, selling motorboats in booths adjacent to one another. Sales were slow and customers few. An Asiatic gentleman with sunglasses approached one of the booths and, after a few pleasantries, told the salesman, "I would like to purchase one million dollars worth of your boats."

The salesman was annoyed. "Listen, friend," he grumbled, "it's been a bad enough day without a comedian . . . Come back some other time when I'm in a mood for a laugh."

"Very well, sir," the customer replied, "Good day."

The man with the dark glasses went on to the next booth, and told the salesman, "I would like to buy one million dollars worth of your boats."

This salesman did not bat an eyelash. "Yes, sir!" he smiled, "Which models would you like?" and he began to fill out an order form. To the astonishment of the first salesman, the customer took out his checkbook, wrote a deposit check for $100,000, shook the hand of the salesman, and went on his way. The buyer was a wealthy Arab executive, and the salesman received his standard 10% commission — in this case $100,000!

Understood on a more subtle level, abundance is not something that we create, but that we *accept*. The second salesman made the deal only because he was *willing to accept it*. We can look at God, consciousness, and man through the symbol of the hourglass. God's infinite abundance is above us, waiting to flow down, and we have the space to hold it all. At the meeting point, at that skinny little juncture of the upper and lower vessels, is our mind. It regulates how much can come through. If our mind is small, tight, and fearful, a few meager grains will flow through. If the mind is open, free, and expansive, all of God's riches can pour through. We receive as much as we let in.

Ernest Holmes gives a good illustration of this principle. He asks us to imagine three people praying for jobs. In his last job, A earned $100 a week, B earned $200, and C, $500. All of them use the same prayer or affirmation, and all of them get new jobs. The results: A's new job pays him $100, B's job, $200, and C's, $500. Each of them put positive thinking to work, but each one was rewarded only to the level of his expectation. There is no reason for this confinement, except in the subconscious thoughts of limitation held by each person.

Real positive thinking means learning to look at *all* of life from a positive viewpoint. It does not mean just making money, gaining health, and finding the right spouse (although these are all valuable demonstrations). Real positivity means seeing the blessedness in *everything*. It requires a complete revision of the way we look at life. It means tearing down our judgements and opinions of what is good and what is bad, what is right and what is wrong. It means owning up to the truth that God is and lives in everything, and there is not one thing that exists, or one event that occurs that is not blessed by the Light of God. Simply, it means being willing to give up our mortal limited opinions.

When we let go of these binding concepts, we are initiated into a new level of evolution: the realm of God consciousness. This simply means that we see all as God and all as Good.

Learning to see God in all requires effort, creativity, courage, and love. Our old thought patterns of lack and failure will kick and scream, and they will find the subtlest and craftiest ways to retain their hold on our consciousness, for, in truth, their very life is being threatened. And that is the very best thing that could happen to us, for their life is founded on erroneous thinking and illusion. To break out of this old way of thinking, we must at first make a determined effort to deny the ranting and raving of our old mind which tells us that something is wrong. When negative thoughts assert themselves, we must challenge them with the light of Love, and dare to live the truth of goodness. Many people believe that it is courageous to live through a negative life. I believe that to live a life dedicated to happiness, freedom and forgiveness is the most courageous of all.

Overcoming negation with love is a matter of attunement. We must concentrate on that which is Good, Beautiful, and True. If there seem to be 999 negative attributes of a situation, and one positive aspect, we must seize on that one good thing, bless it, hold to it with determination, meditate on it, be grateful for it, exaggerate it, and glorify it. We will find that our tiny trickle of goodness has opened into a rushing stream, and then into a mighty river which pours into the ocean of God's storehouse abundant.

There was a woman who found herself lying in a hospital bed, paralyzed throughout her entire body, except for one of her little fingers. For a long time she bemoaned her fate, nearly lost in melancholia. Then she started to concentrate on that little finger. She began to acknowledge it, bless it, and move it. Then, one morning, she was thrilled to find that she could move another finger, and then her whole hand! She kept praising God for the parts of her body that she *could* move, until her whole body became flexible and healthy. She was a living example of the biblical promise, "To him that hath shall more be given."

We can let go of any notion that we have that God wants us to suffer. Jesus was one of the most positive thinkers of all time. He knew that our potential for happiness is unbounded, and that we can all go beyond our limited notions of how good it can be. He knew that every one of us has a great deal to offer, and that we too often sell ourselves short. And he knew that we all have a right to the very best in life. It was for this reason that he told us, "It is the Father's good pleasure to give you the Kingdom."

Life is showering its gifts upon us at this very moment. There is a force of love and light that is streaming, rushing, pouring toward us from all angles at all times. All we have to do is to let it in. Blessings are being offered to all of us without condition or limit. It's all already given to us. The keys to the Kingdom are ours whenever we are willing to accept them. What we have to lose is fear, lack, limitation, and sorrow. What we have to gain is peace of mind, success, health, and love. We do not need to become anything that we are not already. We need only to say "Yes!" to what the universe would just love to give us. We need to think with God.

"Positive thinking is the acceptance of Truth. When you open your mind to the possibility of the goodness of God, it allows Him the opportunity to pour blessings of Love and Light into the chalice of your life. When you align the thinking mind with the Creative Mind, you make available to yourself a power which you do not completely understand, but are fully capable of using for the upliftment of all.

We cannot overstate the importance of right thinking. It is your key to abundance and strength. Your habit of erroneous thought can be reforged into a powerful tool for the benefit of all humankind. Make your life a pillar of positive being. You have the opportunity to see the Light in all things, for, in Truth, the Light is in all things.

What you call "negative" thinking, we do not call bad or evil, but a blockage, or obstruction to the outpressing of Truth. It is simply a distorted view of reality, and it is corrected only by a clear vision of what is. When the Truth is seen, ignorance can hold no power over your life.

Your responsibility to the expression of Truth in the times to come is great. We ask only that you accept Love. Think in harmony with God, and the secrets of creation, which have never really been hidden from you, shall be clearly revealed. When the dreamer awakens, the dream is exposed to be nothing. Align your thoughts and actions with wakefulness, and you shall laugh at the dream of your former patterns of being. We salute you and we love you."

The Emotions

THE THREE BODIES

A friend of mine took a course in juggling. The first lesson of the course, he told me, was this: You have to remember that there is always one ball in the air.

This, to me, is pretty much the story of life: There is always one ball in the air. The moment we think we have really gotten life nailed down, there is something new that calls for our immediate attention. When will it ever end?

I don't know if it ever really will end. I don't think we can ever find real peace in the world. If we want to be satisfied, we have to tune in to the Spirit, in which we are Whole, Complete, and Perfect. In God are all of our problems resolved, for God has no problems. A yogi was once asked, "Why did illusion come into existence?" He answered, "It never did!"

In the meantime, dealing with life — from within life — requires us to take care of our physical, emotional, and mental selves. In a way, they are each like a separate body, each having their own needs which we, the custodian of the bodies, must handle. We cannot always pay attention to all of the bodies all of the time, so we must give each one our attention as it calls for it. Our job is something like that of a mother nursing triplets, or, to symbolize our spiritual journey, we are like mountain climbers with three baskets to carry but with only two hands. We have to alternate which baskets we carry, leaving one basket at a time behind, and then catching it up. Mastering life means keeping all of our bodies "caught up" and balanced.

We are all familiar with the physical body. It likes to eat, sleep, have sex, and enjoy sensory pleasures. On a deeper lever, it has the very important function of being a learning device to help us understand the lessons which we came to earth to learn. Those lessons are deeply connected to learning how to make peace within the body. We learn, though experience, how to work with the body. Sometimes we overindulge it, and that doesn't feel too good, and sometimes we underindulge it, if we take a path of asceticism, and that doesn't feel too good, either. Eventually, we must find a comfortable middle path for the physical body. This we know.

What many people are not aware of, however, is that the emotional body works in a similar way. Instead of eating, sleeping, and sexing, it fulfills itself though feeling emotions and different forms of excitement. Emotional energies are necessary for our journey up the spiritual mountain, and in the same way that we learn to master physical life, we must learn the proper way of caring for our emotional self. Our challenge is that the emotional body does not really care what it feels; it enjoys stimulation of any kind. It will feel nourished through joy, sorrow, exuberance, anger, surprise, disappointment, and even fear. Like the physical body, we must learn to keep it in harmony.

If we are not careful, we can overindulge the emotions with uncontrolled energies. Perhaps you know someone (really all of us, more or less) who is like an "emotional yoyo." One day they are on top of the world, laughing boisterously, happy, jumping, and singing. The next day they are somber and sullen, down in the dumps. As exuberant as they were yesterday, that's how melancholy they are today. They have fallen from the peak of elation into the valley of despair. And tomorrow, they might just as easily be at the peak again.

A friend of mine, for example, was in a roller coaster relationship with a woman, which was like many male-female relationships that I have experienced and seen. (Hilda calls it "love, fight, love, fight, love, fight, etc.") They were alternately together and apart over a long period of time. When I saw my friend one night, he seemed as if he was dancing on air. "I am so happy!" he exclaimed. "Betty and I just spent the day together, and we had the greatest time! Boy, things are really working out fine between us! I feel terrific!"

I smiled and said, "That's wonderful!" but I could hear in the way that he was speaking that he was floating on an emotional bubble — one that could break at any moment. I certainly did not want to burst it, so I kept my mouth closed, but I knew that it would not be long before the other side of the coin would show its face. (An Oriental sage once said, "*The bigger the front, the bigger the back.*")

I saw him the next night, and sure enough, his song had changed. His face was long and his demeanor cloudy. "What's happened?" I asked. "I don't know," he morosely explained. "I just talked to Betty, and things just aren't so good." The pendulum had swung the opposite way, and he had swung with it.

When we ride the pendulum of emotions, we are sure to swing from one end to the other. Intense emotional happiness is almost always followed by intense unhappiness. This is so because *if we allow our emotions to be tied to the events in our lives, we have given the power of our happiness to the changing tides of circumstances.* This is not real happiness, but transient happiness. Until we find an inner contentment, a peace that is not connected to the good and bad in our daily lives, we shall continue to ride the roller coaster of worldly events. Jesus said, "A Peace I give to you that the world cannot give." He was speaking of a Peace that does not depend on people, things, or events.

Emotions are Divine gifts that can take us to God when we use them for their highest purpose. It is wild, uncontrolled emotional indulgence that is harmful, for such intensity is bound to take its toll on our emotional and physical systems and "play us out." In so indulging, we do a disservice not only to ourselves, but to the people around us, for in our negativity we tend to sap energy from them and render ourselves unavailable to fully be with them in a community. "*You are the light of the world; a light under a basket cannot shine.*" The world needs you and me, our love, our strength, and our positivity.

What to do, then, with our emotions, which are a very natural part of our lives? This is a wonderful challenge that each of us must master. Let's take a look at our options.

There is a school of thought that says that to handle emotions properly, they must be discharged immediately by intensely expressing them to those around us, especially to those with whom we are angry. I have experimented with this method (and had it experimented on me), and I have not found it to work very well in the long run. Yes, it is necessary to take out our garbage, but we do not need to dump it on our neighbor's lawn. And if we manage our household efficiently, we will have less garbage to take out.

THE DRAGON DOESN'T LIVE HERE ANYMORE

It was in an encounter group that I had a breakthrough realization about the place that emotions have in our lives and how we can use emotional energies for or against ourselves. In this group, Bruce was angry at Nancy for something, and he told her so. At that point, Bob became irritated with Bruce, because Bob did not feel that Bruce's reason was good enough to be angry about. This annoyed Sara, since she felt that Bob was jumping on Bruce unnecessarily, while Jo was hurt because she felt akin to Nancy, who was the object of Bruce's wrath. You can see the pattern. A vicious cycle of negativity built up, filling the room with a thick emotional smog, until some intelligent person yelled, "Now wait a minute! We're all so busy relieving ourselves of our angry feelings that we've forgotten one basic element of human communication: old fashioned common courtesy!" He was right. I suggested that we stop what we were doing and, for a change, tell what we liked about each other. The transformation was amazing. The air cleared, hearts opened, and communication was once again possible. That moment was the end of any belief that I had that we can help ourselves or each other by expressing our angry feelings without forethought or consideration of the feelings of others. Some may not agree with me on this matter, but I have had a lot more success telling my angry feelings to God than I have had through telling them to other folks.

There are many very satisfying ways to nourish our emotional bodies. Music, song, dance, poetry, walking in nature, sharing a cup of tea with friends, theatre, all of the arts, and a thousand other activities are uplifting and joyous to the soul. If I feel bottled up emotionally, I pick up my guitar and begin to play and sing. Before long, that energy has been transformed into creativity. Physical exercise is also very practical for the emotions. Yoga, jogging, or any other constructive physical activity is great. I am not suggesting that we will never feel any negative emotions, for they inevitably arise. I am suggesting that there are many constructive ways of dealing with them that will keep our bodies in equilibrium and harmony, and free our friends from the burden of our negation.

Hilda has explained that when we get angry, our emotional body is upset for twenty-four hours or longer. That's how long it often takes to get back into focus. As my emotional body has become more and more peaceful over the years, any negativity that I indulge wreaks havoc on it. I say "I indulge," for there are inevitably little irritations or upsets that could jar me if I feed them with my thoughts and feelings. If, however, I let them go before they bury roots like weeds, their effect is negligible. In this world, we are bound to be subject to upset. If we do not create it ourselves, we can pick it up from others. The trick is to let it go in *forgiveness* the moment we become aware of it. In this way, we can keep our emotional self in healthy shape.

At the other extreme, emotional starkness is akin to physical starvation. We cannot deny the sweet symphony of life. If we do, we become dry, dreary, and empty. This is not God's pleasure, either. I remember going through a period of this kind of unnecessary asceticism. I became too rigid and uselessly stark. One evening I was going through some old papers to throw them out (to detach myself from my past!) when I came upon an old poem, written to me by a dear friend. As I read it, my heart flew open and I felt a flow of healing love, like a soothing balm, fill the cracks in my emotional body. I had become arid, and my emotional body had become parched like a prairie in a drought. The poem was so full of love that I instantly felt nourished and fulfilled, like a starving man given a loaf of fresh, warm bread. It was a wonderful lesson for me. From this experience I learned to maintain a fulfilling balance in my emotional self — not too wild, not too stark, but somewhere in the middle, where it feels just right. I still have the poem.

The mental body works on the same principle as the physical and emotional bodies, and we must keep it in balance, as well. The mental body just loves to think. It does not care what it thinks, as long as it is thinking something. It is really quite indiscriminate. It is we, the master of the bodies, who must control and decide what we want to feed to our mental body. Just as we would not put poison into our physical form, we would also not want to feed our mind with garbage. Most people, however, do not realize that thoughts are things, and they will digest thoughts that result in a mental stomachache, also known as a "headache."

It is really true that the mind is like a thought junkie. It is addicted to thinking. I realized this for myself when one evening I was sitting on the toilet and I found myself reading over and over again the instructions on a can of Drano. Now, I know very well how to use Drano; I've used it many times. And even if I hadn't, one reading of the label would have been sufficient. But the real clincher was that, on this particular evening, I had absolutely no use for any Drano. There were no clogged pipes, and I was not taking a chemistry course. I was simply sitting on the toilet. My mental body, however, was not sitting anywhere; it just wanted to think something, and Drano was good enough for it.

This experience showed me that the rational mind, if allowed to run unbridled, will indulge itself to a ridiculous extreme. There is an old story about two psychologists walking down a hall to the laboratory, when they pass one of their colleagues, who greets them with a smiling "Hello!" One of the psychologists turns to the other and ponders, "I wonder what he meant by that?" Thinking is great, but, like all other activities, it is best used in moderation.

I have discovered, as well, why sleep is such a marvelous gift. It is because, for a number of hours, we get our mind to shut up! Just think of how wonderful we feel after a good night's sleep. Our body is refreshed; healing has taken place; our emotions are smooth, and our thoughts clear. This is only because we have escaped the tyranny of the mind! Even so, the mind will follow us into the private realms of sleep, bugging us with useless memories of bits and phrases of the day's events, the rug that Aunt Mildred gave us for Christmas, how to ask the boss for a raise, and the moldy cheese that we must return to Grand Union before lunch tomorrow. It is only when we dive, purely out of self-survival, into the abyss of deep delta-sleep that we can escape this cosmic nudge of a mind, and have a few moments of peace and quiet! When Jesus said, "The evil of the day is sufficient unto itself," He certainly knew what He was talking about!

It is very difficult to get the mind to be quiet. One yogi said that if you could get your mind to stay on one thought for two minutes — just two minutes! — you would be a very advanced soul, indeed. This is why meditation is so valuable. To simply sit quietly for even twenty minutes, and to allow the mind to settle down somewhat, bringing it under conscious control, bringing it to one point, is a very valuable experience. It is, in fact, a real blessing.

As long as we're thinking most of the time, we might as well put into our mind the kind of thoughts that will lead to joy and freedom, and avoid those which lead to confusion. The world of thoughts is similar to that of emotions — there are thoughts that bring liberation, and thoughts that bring bondage. Whenever we read something, for example, we are making a deposit into the bank of our consciousness. We can choose which thoughts we will think. I usually like to read a little bit before I go to sleep. I find that the autobiographies of saints are more soothing to me than murder mysteries or stock market reports. But I can speak only for myself; you may find something else very calming. I was once at a retreat where I saw a woman reading *Emergency!* magazine, stories of ambulance calls, just before going to bed. "Jo!" I exclaimed, "How can you read such junky stuff before you go to sleep?" "Oh, I don't find it junky at all," she explained, ". . . In fact, I find it quite relaxing . . . I work on the rescue squad, and this gives me some good ideas!"

If any one of the three bodies goes unchecked, it can interfere with the proper functioning of the other two. They are like three roommates who share common living space. If one leaves its clothes lying around, it is a nuisance to the others. I went through a period when I believed it was not good for me to eat peanut butter or dairy products, nor should I eat before I go to sleep. There may or may not have been wisdom in these practices, but I carried them to an extreme.

My lack of moderation came to a head when, one evening, I took a short walk down the road from my house, and I began to feel very faint. I turned back toward home, feeling weaker and weaker with each step; I was not even sure if I would make it back to the house. Somehow I did make it, and the moment I walked through the front door, a fascinating process took over in my body. *Without any thought*, I found myself literally charging the refrigerator, grabbing the cream cheese and peanut butter, and devouring it as fast as I could stuff it into my mouth. I had no idea why I was doing this; I certainly didn't think about it or decide to do it, and I wasn't even hungry in the sense of my stomach wanting a meal; I just sort of stood by and watched the whole movie unfold. By the time I polished off the cream cheese and peanut butter, I felt fine and went off to an excellent night's sleep.

Now this may seem like something of a gluttonous act, but here is how I understand it: through my mental zealousness in denying myself certain foods, I may have created some sort of protein or vitamin deficiency. At some point, my physical body had been pushed about as far as it would be, and it had no choice but to break out in open defiance of its mental roommate and say, in effect, "O.K., buddy, you've had your fun, but I have needs too, so out of my way, for I want to survive, as well." A more polite way of describing it would be "cooperative co-existence."

This brings us back to our analogy of our climb up the mountain with our three baskets — the physical, emotional, and mental aspects of ourself. We must learn to strike a comfortable balance in meeting the needs of the different aspects of our being. A whole person is a balanced being. At the top of the mountain, we realize ourself to be the master of the three bodies — and all life. We have learned the meaning of balance, and in so learning, we reflect the balance of the entire universe. And even if there *is* one ball in the air — or one planet, or one sun, or a million galaxies — we've got it handled. We have to. We're created in the image and likeness of God, and God has everything handled.

"We seek strong and well-rounded persons to work with. Well-balanced persons are able to implement the Teachings with power and effectiveness. The energies of inner awakening must be channeled productively, and not dissipated through purposeless thoughts and emotional indulgence. We speak to you strictly on these matters, as they are vital to your progress, and your progress is of the greatest concern to us. We urge you to use common sense in your upward journey. Temper your lofty ideals with practicality and wisdom. A true disciple is a master on all levels. The challenges may now seem difficult or complex, but their necessity shall be made clear to you as you come to understand them more fully. Wisdom shall be given to you to deal with any matters on which you seek guidance with earnestness and sincerity."

THE WAY OUT

Captain Kirk and Mr. Spock were trapped behind an invisible but impenetrable wall. Their friend, Dr. McCoy, was being mercilessly beaten before their eyes, but there was nothing they could do to save him. Kirk's angry frustration increased with each precious moment. "We've got to do something!" screamed the captain, "We can't just let him die while we stand here and watch!"

Spock, the voice of reason, spoke with clarity and firmness: "Perhaps there *is* something we can do, Captain, but I believe it may not be exactly in the way that you are thinking."

"What's that?"

"I wonder if this wall that is stopping us is one of your own creation?"

"What are you talking about, Spock? . . . Out with it!"

"This force field that binds us may be a result of the wild emotional energy that you are generating. It appears that the angrier you get, the thicker the wall becomes. Perhaps if you relaxed and let go of your sympathizing with the doctor's pain, the wall might weaken, and we could then go to our friend's aid."

"Alright, Spock, it's worth a try. What shall I do?"

"Simply put your emotions aside for a few moments. Understand that we cannot help the doctor by anxious worry about him. Enter a clear state of mind in which emotions have no hold over you. This, I believe, is our only avenue of escape."

The captain closed his eyes and began to comply with Spock's suggestion. As he did, the force field began to weaken and diminish.

"It's working, Captain . . . Please continue," encouraged Spock. Within a few moments, the wall disappeared and the crew was free to release their comrade.

Our emotional energies are gifts from God. We have it within our power to bless the world or wreak havoc in it. Like all power, we can use it *for* or *against* our best interests. Our emotions can uplift us or entrap us. They are like the electricity which can light a light or build a bomb. Uncontrolled emotions are the most destructive force on earth; consecrated ones are the most healing.

One of my favorite stories is that of a Samurai warrior who came to a Zen master for instruction. "Master, I would like to know if Heaven and hell really exist," asked the Samurai.

The teacher heard his request and broke into mocking laughter. "*You* would like to know about Heaven and hell?! . . . Don't be ridiculous! Just look at you: you're fat, you're uneducated, and you're uncouth! What teacher in his right mind would invest his time in the likes of you?! . . . Go back to your camp and practice your silly exercises!" With that, the teacher turned his back on the man and ignored him.

The Samurai became enraged. His face turned red, he began to breathe heavily, and he drew his sword, ready to chop off the master's head with his next breath. Just as the sword was about to fall, the master turned around smoothly, and calmly told him, "That, sir, is hell."

The Samurai stopped cold and realized the profundity of the master's teaching. He saw instantly how he had created his own hell through pride and anger. Immediately, he fell at the master's feet in humble reverence.

The master looked down at him, lifted the Samurai's head, and quietly said, "And that, sir, is Heaven."

Our emotions can take us to God or they can take us to hell. They can save us or drown us. As the popular slogan reminded us, we can make love or we can make war. It's all in how we use our energies.

The "binding," or counterproductive emotions are fear, anger, guilt, worry, resentment, jealousy, pity, loneliness, lust, envy, pride, unworthiness, hatred, and all the other variations on these themes. They do not feel good, they make our life energy go haywire, and they release a huge amount of physical poisons into the body. A friend of mine in medical school showed me a picture of all the toxins that are spread throughout the body of a person who becomes angry, and I want to tell you that it was an ugly picture. It certainly made me think twice about anger. Beyond the physical damage these emotions do, they distort our perception and disturb our ability to enjoy loving, fulfilling relationships. In addition, uncontrolled emotions stir up a smog of confusion around us that tends to muddy the clarity of persons near us who are susceptible. In short, they do not serve us or the world.

There is no evil, wrongness, or badness in experiencing these emotions, nor need they be any cause for guilt. They are simply a natural carryover from an earlier state of evolution that we all share. At some point in our personal growth, however, we realize that these emotions do not really serve a life of harmony and inner peace, nor do they help us to make the kind of contribution we would like to offer to the world. It becomes clear that loving and calm words and actions work, and chaotic ones do not. At that point, the old binding emotions begin to drop away by themselves because we no longer believe in their usefulness.

Two friends of mine took up zen. Whenever they became upset or had a problem, they would go to the *roshi* (teacher), tell him all their troubles, and ask him what to do. His advice to them was always the same: "More *zazen* (meditation)!" No matter what they told him: "More *zazen*!" He was not telling them to run away from the world, or to deny or negate their turbulent feelings. He was telling them that they could only be effective in the world when their minds were clear and their emotions calm. Otherwise, they would just be making more trouble for themselves.

Once, Hilda was answering telephoned questions on a radio program. I was amazed at how violently people reacted to her talking about God. People would call up and argue, "But what about war?!" or "There's too much crime to waste time praying!" or "Instead of meditating, why don't you go out and do something!" and so on. She met each one of them on a point of agreement, saying, "Yes, you're absolutely right; this is a time for action and service to the world. The best way we can serve the world is by starting from our calm center. When we make contact with the Peace within ourselves and we find our Inner Source, we are then in a perfect position to go out and make change; until then, we only contribute to confusion. Meditation without action is a cop-out, but action without meditation is fruitless."

Hilda has given us yet one more teaching about the nature of emotion: when we indulge or express any emotion, we tune into, or open ourselves to all of the energies of that emotion that are now being expressed or have ever been expressed. This is a very powerful statement, and an even more potent lesson in practical living.

If we become impatient, for example, we align ourselves with all the impatient thoughts and feelings of every tired commuter in every traffic jam, every college student in a long registration line on a hot day, and every hungry person in a crowded restaurant. Because thoughts and feelings are things, when we generate them they linger in the air like flourocarbons in the ozone layer. When we tune in with a certain emotion, Hilda explains, we make a little wedge in our aura for all of those energies to come in at our unconscious invitation. It's a little like buying a McDonald's franchise. Because you make a commitment to the organization, you get to wear the same color uniform, advertise through the same signs, and eat and serve the same hamburgers as thousands of other McDonald's employees. You become identified with McDonald's, and in so identifying yourself, you tune in with all the thoughts about McDonald's by every other McDonald's worker and customer that there ever was — 35 or 40 Billion, to be exact. If you like McDonald's energy, then you are in your right place. If not, you might do better to align yourself with an organization that comes closer to the energies that you want to feel and express, like Pizza Hut or maybe even Howard Johnson's.

These are light examples, but there is a great promise in the principle of attunement: *we can link our energies to those of our ideals, and so reap the benefit of all those who have lived for what we aspire to.* If we desire to live for Truth, every time we act with integrity, we tune in with and receive the grace of all those who have lived for Truth. In so doing, we actually join Ghandi in his march to draw salt from the ocean for the liberation of India. When we think a thought or do an act of faith, we stand with Moses on the shore of the Red Sea. And when we love, we literally join Jesus at His Sermon on the Mount. Put even more directly, when we love, we become the Christ.

This is the promise of Grace. When we cultivate the higher emotions of joy, peacefulness, appreciation, devotion, and enthusiasm, we lift ourselves up on the magic carpet of the accumulated thoughts and deeds of all who have ever loved goodness and loving kindness. As we open our arms in appreciation, we are blessed by a power greater than that of our seemingly small action.

Every act of love is infinitely powerful, and so is every thought or feeling that we cultivate in Love's Name. The world is in the sorry state that it is because we have underestimated the tremendous significance of what we think and feel. And the salvation of the world will come through the acceptance of every tiny deed as a way to see and express God.

Once again we find choice before us. Because our emotions are simply gross extensions of our thoughts, the secrets of emotional transformation are the same in nature as those of thought. Destiny is consistently in our own hands. We did not create the choices, but we certainly have the power to exercise them. We did not make God, but we can certainly know Him. We did not make Love, but we can certainly become It.

"It is now for you to reevaluate your emotions and come to a new understanding of the nature and the purpose of the energies that you experience. Love is your key to finding Peace. As you remain calm and quiet, God instantly fills your heart. His willingness to abide with you is constant. It is only emotional turbulence that stands between you and your knowledge of His gentle Presence.

There is infallible guidance available to you through the door of purified emotion. We speak not of the occult, for Love is not occult. Nor do we speak of mediumship, for you are inseparably One with God. We speak only of the realization of your Divine Heritage, which is an ever burning Light on the altar of your heart.

In calling you to emotional mastery, we do not ask of you anything of which you are incapable. You are most certainly able to control your emotional energies to a degree of quietude beyond your current expectation. In such serenity, you hear His simple bidding. You are the master of your destiny. As you claim this identity, your effort is rewarded with the vision of Truth.

We do not encourage unnecessary starkness. Enjoy life while you are learning. All of the elements of your Self are created for the expression of Divine Love. Learn to raise your emotions to this Holy end. Nothing more is required of you than the Peace that you seek. Thus is your redemption made easy for you through your awareness of your own Divinity."

The Body

HEALTH, WHOLENESS, AND HOLINESS

All the lessons of living are about allowing healing to take place. Health is the easiest thing in the world, and dis-ease the hardest. We do not need to add anything to our lives to be healed. We need only to tune into our own flow — the very flow that God is always whispering in our ear. Health is our natural condition, and it will always manifest itself when we attune our thoughts and actions to the guidance of our still, small voice, ever calling us to our own Peace.

There is a legend about a butcher who used the same knife for twenty years without having to sharpen it once. The townspeople were astounded, and one day one of his customers asked him, "How can you do so much cutting and keep the blade sharp?"

"It's really very simple," the master explained. "I do not try to cut through gristle or bone. Where I feel resistance, I move the knife slightly, and make the necessary adjustment. My knife is always speaking to me, and I work in harmony with it."

The physical body speaks to us in the same way, and if we are willing to listen to its messages, we can avoid disease. If we experience illness or its warning signs, it is God's way of showing us — through the physical body — that we need to make a course correction in something that we are doing *and* a way that we are thinking. Illness is *not* a *punishment*, but a *message* to us from a loving God, telling us what we need to do to stay healthy and happy, which is exactly that way She likes to see us. How cruel would God be if She allowed us to continue without correction in a way of life that is fraught with anxiety and struggle. It is only out of loving compassion that She

161

sometimes jolts us a bit to head us away from a way of living that we will not admit is not working for us.

I learned this principle for myself — the hard way. One day, as I was merrily driving along in my wonderful Honda, I saw lit on my dashboard a red light which I had not noticed before. It said "BRAKES." I tested my brakes, and they seemed fine. I assumed that there must have been a short circuit in the lighting system, and since the car was running well, I left it as it was. Sometime later, however, my front brakes began to grind, and they sounded dangerous. When I took it to the repair shop I was told that the brakes had worn down to the metal, and due to the front wheel drive construction of my car, it would be a major job to repair. If I had caught the problem earlier, I would only have needed to replace the lining at a cost of about thirty dollars. Since I had let it go so long, however, a lot more parts and labor were required, and I ended up paying over $200 for the job. I could not blame the car, the mechanic, the light, or God. I could hold no one accountable but myself. Had I but read the owner's manual to see what the light was all about, I would have seen that it was a warning sign of things to come, and I could have saved myself some money. An expensive lesson, but a good one.

When we understand that disease is a teaching, we can begin to *learn from it* instead of simply being intimidated by it. There is a connection between our body and our mind. Health — and disease — begin in the mind (the way we think), expand to the emotions, and are finally expressed in the physical form. *The physical body is the last place we see the signs of illness;* by the time disease appears in the body, we are seeing the result of a long process that began with a pattern of thought. That pattern of thought brought about a series of emotions which eventually created a change in the physical patterning of the body, which we call "illness." If we can be sensitive to the messages we are being given through the experience of mental or emotional unrest, we can make the changes we need to make *before* the message is manifested in the physical body.

But because most people do not believe that there is a relationship between the way we think and the way our body feels, when disease appears they seek only to get rid of the symptom, and do not look any deeper to find the problem. Someone with a headache, for example, may be inclined to take an aspirin to remove the discomfort. This may be helpful, but the most helpful medication would be to learn to relax, let go of worry, and not to think so hard. When we take an aspirin or any other drug, we are simply masking the symptom that is a message to us from our higher self, calling our attention to what we need to do to make our life work better. The idea is, of course, to make the symptom go away, for all forms of pain are, according to their nature, not the way we were meant to live. The crucial issue is not *whether* to make the hurt go away, but *how* we do it. Too often we are prone to cover it up with a bandaid and hope that it will go away, or to remove the organ, as if the organ were the cause instead of the effect.

But because disease is a teaching for our *spiritual* growth, it will not go away until we learn the necessary *spiritual* lessons. We cannot, in the long run, sidestep doing what we need to do by avoiding the cues that remind us of what we must learn.

Eric Butterworth tells a marvelous story that neatly illustrates this very important principle. The copilot of a large airliner approached the pilot and told him, "Bob, I just saw the red warning light under 'LANDING GEAR MALFUNCTION' flashing on and off."

"So, what did you do?" quickly asked the pilot.

"I unscrewed the lightbulb!"

I do not know if this is a true story (I hope it isn't), but it certainly symbolizes the approach that many of us have taken toward ailments. A more effective approach would be to take a clear and honest look at the way we are living our life, and see how we can change, *from inside out*. It is easier to take a pill than to change. Real growth, however, requires change, and life is, in fact, pretty much about making the changes that lead to our greatest good.

Let's be a little more specific. Because the body is a symbol of the thoughts and the emotions, each organ of the body corresponds to a different and specific thought pattern. Where the physical body ails is the key to the mental, emotional, or spiritual work that we need to do.

I knew a scientist, for example, who was very fixed and rigid in his thinking. He had a case of arthritis. The arthritis did not cause the thinking; the *thought pattern* was *pictured* in the arthritis. What he needed to do was to loosen up and take life a little easier. Another friend had a skin eruption (rash) that cleared up when she discovered what in life she was reacting (erupting) against. In the case of constipation or problems of the eliminative organs, the question might be, "What is it that I am not letting go of? What am I holding onto tenaciously?" When we find an answer to the question, we will probably find the organ healed, as well.

Because the mind is the source of all of our experience, we can always trace our required lessons back to a pattern of thinking. When we discover the pattern of thought that needs to be changed, the physical symptom will disappear, for its function as the communicator of a lesson is no longer needed. Our bodies, like our lives, are not haphazard, and neither are they beyond our ability to understand their teachings and to see how healing can be accomplished.

At this point I want to make clear that I do have a tremendous respect for doctors, hospitals, and modern medicine. I believe that God heals through pills, machines, and surgery. I have seen doctors save lives that herbs could not, and I believe that antibiotics and painkillers save us time and energy that we could put to good use in other ways than to struggle with disease. To deny the blessing of medicine would be limited thinking. God doesn't limit Herself in the ways She is willing to express Herself. The important issue is *appropriate* use of medicine. There is a time for "natural healing" and there is a time for natural healing *through* medicine. We must be big enough to allow God to be big enough to heal us through whatever method She sees fit. If She gave someone an idea for a vaccine or an appliance, there must be a place for it. God doesn't waste any ideas.

No matter what form through which we accept healing, we must always remember that God is the only healer and that health is our only birthright. We cannot be healed if we believe we deserve to be ill. We must understand that because God is 100% God, we deserve to be 100% healthy. This chapter is called "*Health, Wholeness* and *Holiness*" because all of these words come from the same root, from the same idea in the Mind of God. When we remember we are holy, we are wholely healthy. If we are not healthy, we have missed the mark somewhere. As the poet Leonard Cohen put it, "If you're not feeling holy, your loneliness says that you've sinned." The Grace that supercedes sin is that all we need to do to get healthy is to get clear.

We need to give up our ideas that we deserve to suffer, to be ill, or to be punished. These thoughts are of an old way of thinking that is no longer useful to one who knows him or herself to be a reflection of Godly Light. To such a one, ease is a natural way of being, and health the natural way to express it.

A sign posted at a highway construction zone:

THE INCONVENIENCE IS TEMPORARY.
THE IMPROVEMENT IS PERMANENT.
THANK YOU FOR YOUR COOPERATION.

"*God's Love is the only force that can heal you, and yet is it the very one that you have denied. You are annointed with the Holy Spirit of the living God. Your Destiny is to know yourselves as children of effulgent Light.*

Yes, beloveds, you are whole. Accept no destiny less than Holiness. The world would have you agree with its dismal dream of limitation, but the Light would have you soar like the eagle of your sacred visions. In limitation is only sorrow, and in wholeness serenity. Choose wisely, for when you choose for yourself, you choose for all.

You have believed that your health is a function of your body, but we say to you now: Look deeper. There is no aspect of your experience that is unrelated to Spirit. See lessons in your physical experience, and you discover the Voice of God speaking in your life. The Spirit is eternally whole. In this principle there is no compromise. Believe only in Spirit, and you believe in God. Believe in chance, and you are lost. Choose wisely, beloveds.

The healing that you seek is available to you now. The Love that you ask for is freely given in this moment. You are a chalice of Universal Life, and the fulfillment of your journey is the consummation of His purpose for your existence.

All blessings be upon you."

The Flow of Life

LETTING GO

One evening I discovered some scrumptious-looking peanut butter cookies in the pantry of the house where I was staying. I really like cookies. (My mother used to give me cookies and milk every day when I came home from school, and I have only the fondest memories of the unbeatable combination of chocolate chip cookies, milk, and *Superman*.) I started to take one of these cookies, but my conscience began to wriggle a bit, since they were not mine. I knew that I could probably snitch one or two, and everyone would think that they were eaten by the rightful owners. But I decided to ask first. When I did, the person who baked them brightly replied, "Oh yes, sure, you can have them all! No one else likes them. Consider them yours!" (This is one of the advantages of being into health foods — no one else wants what you like.) I gave it up, in asking, and I got it all back. Yum.

I have given a lot of thought to the teaching, *"Give it all up and you get it all back."* I believe that this is an immensely potent formula for finding freedom and joy in living. Every time I have put this principle in action, it has worked. Whenever I have let go of something, God has either given it back to me, or given me something better, or shown me that I'm better off without it. More and more, I have come to see that God is always giving us exactly what we need for our highest good, and at no cost to anyone.

One evening, for example, a friend and I went to see a production of *Godspell*. Due to an error in the ticket office, two sets of tickets had been issued for our seats. We found ourselves potentially at odds with two other people who felt they had a right to the same seats. My friend said to me, "Well, we were here first, so let them find other seats." I saw that the other folks were getting a little upset, and I remembered Jesus' teaching, "If someone wants your coat, give them your cloak as well." So I said to my friend, "Let's let them have the seats; I think we'll be alright." And so we gave them the places. When I went to the ticket office to explain our predicament, the manager was very kind. He gave an usher two more tickets for us, and we were shown to two seats much closer to the stage, in a far better location.

The idea that "He who humbleth himself shall be exalted," is one of the most powerful and practical truths that I have ever encountered. It speaks of the miraculous principle that we do not need to "power-trip" our way through life; we will come out better in the long run if we allow God to take care of us.

Ironically, we can have only that which we are willing to give up. What we are not willing to let go of becomes a source of anxiety and threat. What we resist, persists. The second part of Jesus' teaching was, "He who exalteth himself will be humbled." The rabbis in *The Ethics of the Fathers* taught the same truth in a strikingly similar way: "He who seeks to gain reputation shall lose it; he who does not seek reputation shall win it." When I hear these proverbs, I usually think of the political figures involved in the Watergate scandal. It seems that the more they tried to gain or hold onto power, the more it backfired on them and resulted in their fall.

This principle applies to people and relationships, as well. A relationship based on clinging, possessiveness, or attachment cannot work. There is constant worry, fear, and threat. The moments of satisfaction in such a relationship are deceptive, for they lead only to pain. If "I have him/her" can bring joy, then surely, "I am losing him/her" will bring sorrow. *It is only when we hold people and things lightly that we can enjoy them fully.* Life is a constant flow of coming and going. Things and people come into our lives and they leave, just as sure as they came. Sometimes they stay for a moment, sometimes for a lifetime. We never really know how long it will be. Nor do we have any real control over how long we will share the path with someone. Our key to happiness is to enjoy a relationship while it lasts, allowing the person and the relationship complete freedom to evolve in the highest way for them, according to God's plan. Clinging never feels good. It brings hardship to the one who would possess, and to the one he or she would possess. Possession may be nine tenths of man's law, but it is not even one tenth of God's law.

If we feel pain at the loss of a relationship in our lives, it is not due to the loss of the person's presence; it is due to our *clinging*. When we stop clinging, the pain ceases. God may have been responsible for the loss, but we are responsible for the pain. This may sound stark, but it is true. In the long run, we are much better off for letting go. Is it not better to be free and happy than to be attached and in pain?

When a relationship ends, it is an opportunity to apply the principle of "Let go and let God." This means to accept that God is working for our highest good, and never against us. In such a situation, I would assume that He would not stop this relationship unless He had a good reason, and that this ending is really a beginning. Perhaps there is something or someone better in store. Perhaps we have given and received and shared and learned all that we could, for the time being, and now it's time to grow into a new and better space. That has to be the way it is; God wouldn't make a mistake with His child's life.

We must release the old to make room for the new. A friend of mine was praying and praying for a bigger and better apartment which she needed for herself and her family. But she was not doing anything about it. One day she was evicted by her landlord, and she was forced to find another place. The place that she found was the one that she had been praying for all along! She could not receive it, however, until she gave up the old one.

There is a lovely Zen story that delightfully describes this principle. A man came to a teacher for enlightenment. "Sit down," invited the teacher; "Let's have some tea." The teacher began to pour tea into the man's cup, but instead of stopping when the tea reached the brim, he continued to pour the tea, causing it to run over the cup, onto the table, and onto the man's legs.

Startled, the man jumped up and exclaimed, "What are you doing?! Can't you see that the cup is full?!"

"You have just learned the first lesson in Zen," explained the master: "You must make yourself an empty cup in order to learn. One who thinks that he already knows, cannot be taught anything new."

Put in other words, it is only when we stop trying to hold onto the past that we are able to fully accept the blessings that the present can offer us. Clinging (in reminiscence or bitterness) to a thought or an experience is the same as clutching to a person or a thing. It takes us out of our here-and-now center and detracts from our experience of the fullness of this moment. Too often we hold onto memories of "The Good Old Days," when we were "really happy," and when things went just right. If they were *really* good, then we would not feel pain in missing them now, for what is good is liberating, and if we are bound to the experience, it certainly did not liberate us very much. The *real* good old days were those which showed us that we are free to live fully in *any* moment, including — and especially — *now*. If I enjoyed something in such a way that I feel sorrow for its absence, I enjoyed it in the wrong way. I enjoyed it in a way that led to suffering, and not to freedom. I enjoyed the mortal, changing element of the person or the thing, and that element can never bring peace. Only when we enjoy the eternal, Godly, inner aspect of an experience can it bring us real happiness. When I look back on the experiences that I cherish, I feel no sense of loss whatsoever, for those were the experiences that made visible to me the Light that is within me now. That Light was there then, It is here now, and It will be here tomorrow. It is not the person or the experience that counts, it is the *spirit* that is precious, and spirit is present in all experiences. People and events are like teacups — vessels — through which God gives us love and loving lessons. Though teacups may fade, crack, or be lost, the God that gave them to us in the first place is always present, with an endless supply of new vessels in His Divine pantry.

When we cling to someone in resentment, we bind ourselves to him or her by our thoughts and memories. The river of life would have us flow to the ocean, but we would cling to the rock upon which we dashed our foot. We cannot change the events in our past, but we can always change *the way we look at* those events. Those who seemed to bring us pain and hardship were our teachers who presented us with challenges which helped us to grow into greater personal strength. When we realize that the problem was not in them, but in the way we were *looking at* them, we free ourselves as well as them.

We fight life only because we do not perceive our own best interests. It is rare that we can know how any particular experience will fit into the whole plan of good in our lives. Often there is a difference between what we think is good for us, and what God *knows* is good for us. The story of Joseph is a magnificent illustration of this truth. When we left the story, Joseph, whose brothers had sold him into slavery, had become Prime Minister of Egypt. Soon after that, famine struck the region, and Joseph's brothers were driven to seek food from

THIS IS NOT USED

Egypt, the only land that had a reserve. They found themselves face to face with Joseph, though they recognized him not. In forgiving love, Joseph gave them food and revealed his identity to them. When they felt sorry and wept for their misdeed, Joseph consoled them: "Do not feel bad; you meant it for evil, but God meant it for good."

I like to believe that God means everything for good. This is difficult to see from a limited point of view, but easy and natural to see from the grandest point of view. It is said that "Prayer is the contemplation of the facts of life from the highest point of view." When we look at our experience through Divine eyes, we can see the essence of goodness in all experiences, and letting go is no longer a trial to be feared, but to be embraced as an opportunity to be filled in with something wonderful.

The famous Prayer of St. Francis affirms:

> *It is in giving that we receive*
> *It is in pardoning that we are pardoned*
> *It is in dying that we are born to eternal life*

Some have paraphrased the last line, "It is in surrendering that we are born anew." When we surrender all to God, we are not failing, or being weak, or losing anything. To the contrary, we are making ourselves available to be filled with the Holy Spirit, which is the strongest power in the universe, and all the Love that we ever really wanted.

We eventually see that it is not *things* that we must let go of, but our *attachment* to them. We can remove ourselves from things, but if we keep mental ties to them, we might as well be with them; in fact, we would probably do better to be with them, for then we could learn to let them go. There is a story of a yogi who went off to a cave for many years to renounce the world. The day he returned to the village, someone accidently bumped into him and he got angry. What good did all those years of "renunciation" do for him? He would have served himself and the world better to live in the city until he no longer got flustered when someone bumped him. Then he would have been a real renunciate, free to live in the city, or in a cave, or anywhere his heart guided him.

Attachments take the form of thoughts of *"mine."* A mine is

173

something that blows up when you step on it. I was once experiencing the pain of being attached to someone. I went to a lecture by a beautiful Buddhist monk who said, "All of our troubles are in the mind. That is where our problems start and that is where they end." His words changed my whole outlook! There were no physical chains binding me to the person; the chains were forged in my mind and the lock was fastened with my thoughts. The key to freedom was in the thoughts, as well. If a thought can bind, a thought can free.

When I leave this world, I do not want to be bound to anything — not to any object, any person, any philosophy, any unfulfilled desire. I want to head straight for the Light, with no delays on the local track. My prayer is to drop all of my luggage and to leave my arms free to embrace God and God alone. I don't want to have to come back for anything, unless I am to serve. I have never found any real or lasting pleasure in any physical object or person. Ironically, the more I have given up attachments to things and people, the more I am able to love and enjoy them.

In the end, we must give up our striving, as well. One sage said, *"Give up your lust for growth."* Striving for growth is a necessary stage of the path, but finally we must accept fullness from a Source *within* ourselves and renounce the illusion of seeking or reaching out. As long as we see God, Peace, or Consciousness as *outside* of ourselves, we shall never know Him completely. The moment we find God within, our searching comes to an end, for we realize that He has been within us all along, and ever shall there remain.

The great yogi Tat-Walla said, "The last thing to go is God." He did not mean that God goes, for where could He go? What Tat-Walla meant to go was our *thought* of God as "Him," "Her," or "It," which creates an artificial separation between us and God. If we really want to be One with God, we cannot relate to God as an "other." We must relate to God as Self. When Ramakrishna was asked to describe God, he went into silent ecstasy. There was nothing he could say in the state of God. Who could he talk to? Lover and Beloved had become One.

So "God" must go, too. Some would call this blasphemy, but they called Jesus a blasphemer when He declared, "I and the Father are One." Loving God, serving Him, fearing Him and worshipping Him come to an end when we *are* Him. Neem Karoli Baba said, "Even better than having the *darshan* (sitting in the Presence) of Christ is to *become* the Christ."

> *All that I am*
> *All that I do*
> *All that I'll ever have*
> *I offer now to you*
>
> *All that I dream*
> *All that I pray*
> *All that I'll ever make*
> *I give to you today*
>
> *Take and sanctify these gifts*
> *For your honor, Lord*
> *Knowing that I love and serve you*
> *Is enough reward*
>
> *All that I am*
> *All that I do*
> *All that I'll ever have*
> *I offer now to you**

*"All that I am" by Sebastian Temple, Copyright © 1977, Franciscan Communications, Los Angeles, California 70015. Reprinted with permission.

"There is a freedom that befalls you who are willing to trust in God. You once attempted to gain security, power, and life through fearful clinging, yet to what avail? Your observation of those in your midst who are at peace with themselves has revealed that sharing is the very source of joy.

Because the values of the world are founded on distorted perception, you have been taught to believe that accumulation is success. That belief has all but departed from you now, as you have discovered that fulfillment cannot be found in things, but only in Spirit. The realm of selfless sharing extends to you its Holy invitation, awaiting only your acceptance of its joyous welcome.

Your happiness is completely dependent on your confidence in God's ability to give you that which you cannot give yourself. Your admission of the impotence of your striving self is the condition for your realization of the infinite power of your Divine Self. Release the goals that you have made for yourself and allow them to be replaced by the Goal that God has always had for you, one of total union with your Divine nature."

GO WITH THE FLOW

I remember the summer I graduated from high school. Around the end of August, just about when I was getting ready to leave for college, I felt a sense of being lost in space with no one place I felt was home. Most of my old friends had gone away to college or were getting ready to be married, and I did not know anyone who was going to the college I was about to attend. I knew that there would be good friends awaiting me when I actually arrived, but I knew, too, that the time was not yet ripe. I felt as if I were in a kind of vacuum.

There is a stage like this on the spiritual path. Many sincere aspirants experience a period of seeming emptiness in which the old has lost its appeal, but the new has not yet arrived. It is a time when old friends, activities, and interests are no longer attractive, but new ones have not come along to replace them. Many students on the path say, "I don't feel like doing the things I used to enjoy, and I have the feeling that there is something good in store for me — something better than what I was used to — but I don't really know how to find it."

Hilda has described this in-between state as a "corridor between rooms." We have left our history, but not yet claimed our Destiny. This is a normal, natural, and necessary process, and it is, in fact, a very good sign. It means that we have completed — graduated from — one era of our growth, and we are now ready for something new and better. (Losing our old friends means that we are on the right track; it's when we hang out with the same people all of our lives that we know that we are in trouble!)

What we need to do during such a transitional time is to mobilize

177

faith and to realize that it is only a matter of time until our aspiration becomes our Reality. If you are moving from an old house to a new one, you are bound to spend a certain amount of time on the road between the two. This can feel a little insecure, especially if you've sold all of your furniture to make your transition lighter. While you are traveling, it is the vision of your new home that gives you the strength to keep on driving, and the expectation of a new and better way of living that makes the trip worthwhile.

If we can just let go and trust in the process of our advancement, we can appreciate the miracle of the flow of life. If, during our turbulent periods, we keep ourselves dynamically balanced like a skilled surfer, the waves of our experience will guide us smoothly to the shore. We may fear that the waves will drown us, but it is actually the waves that *move* us.

Steve is a dear friend of mine of many years. We met during our teens and shared an era of experiences. We stayed up late at night, involved in ponderous discussions of the nature of the universe; we laughed; we were inspired by the same great teachers of Truth; we traveled together and enjoyed the changing of the seasons around us. Steve and I supported each other, challenged each other, shared, and grew as brothers in life. Eventually we lived together for several years, in harmony and cooperation.

Gradually, Steve and I drifted apart in interests and activities. I sensed our growing separation, and inwardly I resisted. "Steve is my best friend," I thought; "He always has been, and always will be." In my heart, though, I knew that our paths were diverging.

Steve became involved in a relationship with a woman which was a painful one for him. I sensed Steve's hurt and I attempted to let him know that I was feeling with him and that I supported him. Strangely, he was not receptive, and I felt disappointed. It was then that I realized that Steve had to fulfill his own destiny, and that his life was taking a new direction. And there was nothing I could do to hold back the tide of life.

Several months later, Steve announced that he was moving out to live with this woman. At first I felt a little empty to hear this, for it signified to me that a very special era in my life was coming to an end. When I looked a little more deeply into myself, though, I discovered a very peaceful sense of relief and freedom, for I admitted to myself that it was O.K. for us to travel in different directions. I realized, too, that our sharing of interests was not what it used to be, and that I had been foolishly clinging to a picture of the past. At that moment I was free to wish Steve well and to offer him my blessings for his chosen path.

Now Steve and I are very dear to each other. We have since traversed our own peaks and valleys and we are both the richer for it. We do not spend as much time together as we once did, but we love and respect each other as fully as we ever did. I shall always value the early years of our friendship, as I do the moments we now share. And I am especially grateful for the lesson of letting go.

An oriental sage taught, *"That the yielding is more powerful than the resistant is a fact known by all and practiced by none."* To change one's mind or to humble one's self is considered by many to be a sign of weakness, although the most humble among men are the most exalted. We are taught to subjugate, manhandle, and mold the world to conform to our expectations. But power is a word that very few people understand. The power that we gain in the world is like a bubble on the Ocean of God. Sooner or later it pops and we once again find ourselves to be the ocean.

I was talking to a man just a few days ago who had been to the top of the ladder of success in the business world — and then to the bottom. When I last saw him about ten years ago, he held a very prestigious position in a major department store chain. He wore $300 suits, owned a few Cadillacs, and he and his family enjoyed all of the finest things in life. Then, almost overnight, his firm went out of business and he lost his job. His wife became ill, and he was faced with medical expenses. He remained out of work for five years. By God's Grace, he took it all in stride and remained positive during his trials. He has since gotten another job, his wife has recovered, and his attitude is excellent. As he told me his story, I felt no bitterness or resentment from him. He was able to flow with the changing circumstances of his life. I know another man who had a similar turn of events, but he was set back by it. As it was harder for him to take it in stride, he went through some depression and illness before he came out on the other side. Yet his seeming misfortune was actually God's Grace, for he was saved from the plight of the five men who preceded him in his job, all of whom died of heart attacks.

It is said that the willow tree enjoys longevity because its boughs can bend to relieve itself of the burden of heavy snow and ice which would break the branch of a more rigid tree. Master Sivananda, a great and revered yogi, well understood this principle when he gave his students a very practical mantra:

> Serve, love, meditate, purify,
> Be good, do good, be kind, be compassionate,
> *Adapt, adjust, accommodate,*
> Bear insult, bear injury, highest *sadhana**

There is an American guru who teaches these same principles. His name is Arthur Fonzarelli, affectionately known to his many disciples as *"The Fonz."* The Fonz is a master of what Hilda calls "quick adjustment of the mind." He knows how to take a challenge and immediately turn it into an asset. Once, for example, Ritchie was pledging a fraternity, and as part of his initiation, he has to go to a high school dance dressed as a girl. At the same dance, of course, is The Fonz, who (unaware of the disguise) takes a liking to Ritchie and asks him (her) to dance. As they are slow dancing, The Fonz begins to blow in Ritchie's ear and kiss him on the neck. Ritchie feels compelled to reveal his identity and begins to whisper, "Hey Fonz, it's me, Ritchie! — I'm just dressed up like this for my fraternity initiation!" The Fonz gets an incredibly startled look in his eye for about a half a second, but, in his invincible style, he does not lose his cool. He doesn't even miss one step in the dance. All he does is move just a few inches away from Ritchie and tell him, "Oh yeah, oh yeah . . . I knew it all along . . . I just wanted to help you with your initiation . . . Did you think that The Fonz would let you down?" and the dance goes on. Quick adjustment of the mind.

Adapting, adjusting, and accommodating are qualities that we in western culture sometimes have a hard time understanding or putting into action. I recently heard a wonderful talk by a Native American Indian gardener. She pointed out that many gardeners approach growing food and living things in a very aggressive way: we say "I'm going to *make* that garden grow." We attack the mother earth with chemicals and disrespect, pillaging her for instant gain, disregarding the long-range effects of our impetuousness. The great dust storms of the 1930's, she said, were largely a result of short-sighted overplowing, upsetting the balance of rooted living plants. The Native

*"sadhana": spiritual path

American way, she explained, is one of planting, cultivating, and harvesting in harmony with the natural flow of the land, always appreciating the bounty of the earth, and replenishing the soil with any precious nutrients that are removed. There is a great respect, she pointed out, for working *with* the seasons, never *against* them.

One way that we buck the seasons of our growth is by running away from situations we have not yet mastered. If the fire gets too hot in a challenging relationship or job, we may be tempted to take off to find an easier one. Unfortunately, as a friend of mine put it, "If an ass goes out to travel, it won't come back a horse." In other words, if you run away from a tough scene, you have succeeded only in avoiding the stimulus which presses your buttons, which is probably exactly what you need to understand and master in order to grow. Besides, we are sure to face the same challenge in another form somewhere else, probably to a more intense degree. So, we are better off sticking it out where we are, because if we run elsewhere, the fire will be even hotter. If you are tempted to leave husband 1 because he squeezes the toothpaste from the wrong end, you might as well work it out now, because husband 2 will probably leave the cap off the tube, as well!

When, then, are we free to leave a situation which we feel is not for us? We can leave when, in our heart of hearts, we are certain that we are not running away in hopes of finding a better replacement. If we hold an *emotional charge*, any anger, irritation, or resentment about the situation we would like to leave, it remains a golden opportunity for us to grow through resolving it, and we would probably benefit tremendously by staying. If, on the other hand, we feel satisfied, complete, and clear about the job we have done, and we *honestly* feel that it is no longer challenging or productive, we may very well be done with our spiritual work in that place. If we hear a very strong *inner* (not emotional) urge to make a change, and we feel in the *flow* (and not in *reaction*) with the change, then, perhaps, a change is very much in order.

Life in the flow does not guarantee any recipes; there are no cut and dried, pre-packaged rules of thumb. Sometimes the answer is in one principle; sometimes it is the opposite. Eric Butterworth has said, "It's not doing what you like that's important — it's liking what you do!" On the other hand, Patricia Sun was once asked, "Why am I so tired all the time?" Her answer: "Because you don't like what you're doing . . . Why not try doing something you like?" Who was correct?

181

Both of them. Each challenge requires a unique solution. We have to *feel* our way through life. We must be flexible enough to know what needs to be done in the moment, even if it was not what needed to be done a moment ago. Mahatma Gandhi said, "I am committed to Truth — not consistency."

I once was offered a very nice job working with retarded people. As I needed some money at the time, I took the job. I fell in love with the "clients," many of whom were very joyous and loving people and from whom I learned many valuable lessons. As time wore on, however, I began to feel unfulfilled in my work. I was over-sleeping, my physical health was not up to par, I was arriving to work late, and I began to look forward to holidays and to look for ways to get out of work.

I was yearning to express my creativity in a different way. I feel especially fulfilled teaching yoga, playing music, writing, traveling, and working on human relations workshops. This job seemed far afield from the kind of work I do best and enjoy the most. So, knowing the principle of "take whatcha got and make whatcha want," I attempted to introduce my skills into the program. I started to teach the clients yoga, I played music during lunch hour, and I started an incense-making business at the center. These programs were successful, but I was still trying to stuff a round peg into a square hole.

I very much felt inclined to leave the job, but here is how my mind acted as "the slayer of the real": it said, "You are running away. You are avoiding a lesson you need to learn. You must not be a quitter. You must stay until you learn the lesson." So, although I had no idea what the lesson was, I decided to stay and to give myself until Memorial Day to learn it.

Well, Memorial Day came and it went, and I still didn't know what the lesson was, but I was determined not to be a quitter and to learn that mysterious lesson, which I just knew would be revealed to me, probably now by the Fourth of July. So came and went Independence Day, and I still didn't get the lesson, and more and more all I wanted was to be independent of this job.

Now the mind — the little mind — has a very clever ability to team up with the emotions. I was afraid to quit the job because I would probably feel guilty about leaving these poor retarded people; "After all," I thought, "they really need *my* love!" (Meanwhile, the fellow who replaced me after I finally did leave, did a much better job than me.) I reasoned, too, that perhaps I had been retarded in some previous life, and now I had to pay off my karma by serving these people as some kind soul had served me. Or perhaps I had some other great karma that I could work out in this unhappy lot.

So I continued, day after day, week after week, until I finally decided to quit and take my chances with the lords of karma. And did it feel right and good to leave! The great lesson that I was waiting to learn was that I did not belong there.

I went on to develop my work with yoga, music, human relations, and writing. Now I look forward to awakening each morning, to creating in my own way, and to serving people according to my own bent. God gave me skills to express in a unique way, as He gave every person a special role. While I thought it was "wrong" or a "sin" to leave a job where I could render valuable service to humanity, now I feel it may be more of an error for any of us to deny the calling we are given, and an even greater sin to withhold our God-given inclinations from humanity, out of fear or guilt. If we have faith that God is guiding us, He will lead us to where we can serve in our own way — which is *His* own way.

Years later, Hilda explained a principle that brought the whole experience into light. She explained, "If you do something because you think you have karma to work out — in that moment, *by that thought* (of 'I have such and such a karma'), you are *creating* the karma." My thought of "I must stay in this job to work out karma" may have been the very karma that kept me there.

And so it is only the mind that can stand between us and the flow of life. And so it is the heart that reconnects us with its music. There is a moment which all musicians know, aspire to, and perhaps live for. It is that precious moment when the music takes over and the musicians become the instruments. It is the instant when the thought of separate players dissolves into the song, and there is only one energy, one idea in the room. In this moment, there is no thought, no history, no expectation. There is only now, and now proves itself to be very real, indeed. It is as if the rivers have merged into the ocean, and the many have become The One. The old, the parent of now, assumes its rightful role as servant of Life, and graciously gives birth to the new. And so a Child is born.

"You who would master the art of living, dance gracefully. Move lightly through your postures, and each will show you your way to the next. Your guide calls from within, pointing your path through evolution. Bend this way, now that, and give full confidence to the promptings of your soul.

Renounce the thinking mind as the final arbiter of your understanding of life. At times your mind bears witness to the Truth, but often it confounds you. We tell you to give full authority to your simple teacher, for it exists only for the releasement of the God that is you. The quiet wisdom of such a teacher is your only salvation.

The greatness that you are promised is not the grandeur that you have been taught to value by the world. The guide offers you the Kingdom of Heaven, which is already yours, though you remember it only faintly. The world offers you itself, which you know well, but not well enough to know that its end is emptiness. We show you the end of your strivings. Your attempts to find a resting place in the world have come to naught. This you can now see, and you are nearly ready to admit. Your growing inclination to turn about to your Father's House is the yearning which will surely bring you Peace."

SEASONS

A few evenings ago, I spoke with a lovely but sullen young lady. She was feeling guilty because she had let go of her spiritual discipline for a while. She told me that for a long time she had been going to church every day, meditating and praying for hours. During that time she felt very fulfilled, in her niche. She then stopped going, and felt sinful for it. Now she wanted to start again, but she feared that she had fallen away from the path, and she felt too unworthy to take up her practice again. "What good is it?" she asked, "if I start toward God, and then quit? I might as well not even start!"

But I didn't see her stopping as quitting. What she had needed, as I saw it, was a breather. She had done some very intense spiritual work, and she probably needed some time to absorb and integrate it. It might have been counterproductive to force herself to continue to sit for hours in that church, before her experience was gelled within her. I told her that I certainly did not consider it sinful to take a temporary rest from intense spiritual striving, and, in fact, such a "vacation" might have been exactly what she needed to get her ready for the next step of her growth.

Upon hearing this, she looked at me, almost startled, and asked, "You mean I haven't fallen from God because I stopped?" Of course she hadn't. In truth, she had never left the spiritual path. The form of her work had just changed. There is no such thing as falling outside of God, for this would mean that there is somewhere that God is not. The only place we can fall is in *consciousness,* and as soon as we rise back into God-consciousness, we see that He was with us always; we were just not looking at Him. This young lady loved God very much. Who she wasn't loving was herself.

There are seasons of our growth. When we flow with them and enjoy them, we accept their full blessing; when we buck them or attempt to deny them, we miss a rich treasure. *"To everything there is a season; a time for every purpose under Heaven."* There is a time for discipline, and a time for letting go; an occasion for pushing on, and one for surrender; a purpose for tears, and one for laughter. Everything in nature has a reason for living, in its right place.

I often feel awed by the change of the earth seasons. Ferlinghetti had an idea which I adapt to speak for me: "I am continually celebrating the rebirth of wonder." It is just such a mystery to me how each spring, trees that seem to be dead give birth to life in the form of little green buds. This miracle reminds me of what Jesus told the family of the little girl that He healed. "Don't be alarmed, the girl is not dead . . . She is just sleeping." In the heat of the summer, it is hard to believe that in just a few months the ground will be covered with snow, and the chill wind will blast us. If we can just look at these simple patterns of our earth, a world with which we are inseparably one, we can learn great lessons that we can use for our upliftment.

In the practice of hatha yoga physical exercises, for example, it is very important to stop after every few exercises and rest for a little while to integrate and absorb the effects of the movements. The real payoff of the exercises is the deep sense of relaxation and well-being that comes after completing the stretches. Students are required to lay down and rest for a period of time at the end of class, and it is during these moments that the healing effects of the exercises make themselves known. Both the activity and the resting are equally necessary and important. We cannot enjoy the full benefit without a combination of the two. In accepting *all* of the aspects of the process, it becomes one meaningful integrated whole.

People go through seasons that require us to look deep to understand them. There is a beautiful man who was very close to Hilda and our spiritual community. I felt great esteem and respect for him, as he has a great deal of spiritual wisdom and love to offer. One day I noticed that he had not been coming to our gatherings for a while, and I later learned that he had withdrawn himself from the classes. This troubled me, for I thought that he might have lost his spirituality or stepped onto the wrong road. I felt a sense of loss.

I did not say anything to anyone about this. Then, one day, Hilda took me aside and explained, "You know, J. never really left our group. He was just going so high in his meditation, and his spiritual growth was happening so fast that he was losing his ability to function effectively in the world. Out of wisdom, the inner guides, who want well-rounded workers, strong in practicality as well as spirituality, pushed him back into the world for a while. He is as much a part of our group as ever. Whether or not he comes to the classes, he has not lost his spirituality. He is just learning lessons in a different place."

There are lessons, in fact, to be learned in every place. The mark of spiritual mastery is the ability to remember God wherever we go, and through whatever we experience. A friend once sent me a greeting card that said, *"We are living in a world of permanent change."* Everything changes, and the more firmly we have this understanding imbedded in our consciousness, the easier it is to remember God as we go through all of the transformations that are necessary for our total evolution.

I am reminded of King Solomon's request to his counselor to tell him "something that will make me happy when I am too sad, and make me sober when I feel too happy." A few days later, the advisor gave the king a ring with these words inscribed on it: *"This, too, shall pass."*

I had a marvelous lesson in letting "this, too" pass. For many years, I was given to the practice of deep meditation. It was my greatest joy to sit, sometimes for hours, and dive into my deepest Self. I cannot describe in words the satisfaction that I experienced. I did not do it as a discipline or a practice. I did it because I loved to do it, and I grew tremendously from it.

Then, one morning I woke up and the desire to meditate had left me. I was not resisting it or running away from it. I just did not feel a need to meditate. At first, my mind was very uncomfortable with this new feeling. I thought, "You really should, you know, even if you do not want to." But the truth was that I wanted to, but did not feel the need to. And then I thought, "Well, you've been meditating every morning for eight years; what will you do if you don't?" and "If you don't meditate, you will have an awful day, and you will be sorry you didn't." But my inner voice told me to honor my intuition. So I carried on without lots of deep meditation, and, to my amazement, my days were wonderfully complete! I found I had a fantastic amount of time and energy to be creative, to be with others, and to contribute to the world in a new and different way.

At the time, I thought that I was finished with meditation, but there was an even more profound lesson in store. At a later date, the seasons of my growth made a full circle, and I resumed regular meditation, but this time without clinging to it. I now see that my retreat from my regular practice was actually a preparation for a new level of consciousness, one which would allow meditation to be an asset to my happiness, and not a dogmatic institution. That season of no meditation was required to show me that although I find God in meditation, I cannot afford to make a god of it. Now meditation is even more useful to me, as it blends with the overall flow of my life.

We must honor the natural rhythms and cycles in our nature. As I look around me, I see the great tapestry of the universe woven with a magnificent ebb and flow. We are told that the entire cosmos is pulsating like our hearts and like the microcosmic atoms vibrating within us. To feel the rhythm of life is to dance to the greatest symphony of all, and to deny its pulse is to miss the essence of all expression. Life is about changes, rhythms, growth, retreat, activity, rest, unfolding, delving inward. And when the seasons of our life have left us with all the teachings they bear, there is but one lesson that remains, ever beyond the effect of passing opposites: There is one unchanging life that breathes in and through us, and in which all seasons humbly come to resolution in seasonless Serenity.

To everything there is a season,
a time for every purpose under heaven:
a time to be born,
a time to die,
a time to plant,
a time to reap,
a time to kill,
a time to heal,
a time to tear down,
a time to build up,
a time to weep,
a time to laugh,
a time to mourn,
a time to dance,
a time for casting away stones,
a time to gather them;
a time to embrace,
a time to refrain from embracing;
a time to find,
a time to lose,
a time to keep,
a time to throw away,
a time to tear,
a time to mend,
a time to be silent,
a time to speak,
a time to love,
a time to hate,
a time for war,
a time for peace.

—Ecclesiastes 1-9

"You who would find your place and your purpose under Heaven, accept your goodness in His eyes. See the perfection of all things, and know that all in creation has a right and good purpose.

For too long have you denied the seasons of your life and the intelligence thereof. Now is your time to acknowledge your freedom to live, a right which you richly deserve. The era in which you are about to enter is ruled by the wisdom of the heart, not the meanderings of the mind. The mind has been sufficiently developed. There must be a balance. Hold Love in one hand and Wisdom in the other, and so you have the tools with which to build a new age.

Your work is that of attunement. You can no longer depend on form and imitation for your livelihood, for these would only serve to weaken you. In meekness there is mastery. This great truth was the cornerstone of the ancients, but ignorance of it is the fault of the present civilization.

The task, one which you have already accepted, is the wise merger of the ancient wisdom and the knowledge you have cultivated. Those who would deny one for the sake of the other do not see fully. You see fully, and so you are charged with the demonstration of this grand principle to those who have need to learn it.

Peace is to be learned through observation. Watch the peaceful and emulate its essence. Open yourself to the serene and accept it as your teacher. In this way, you gain conscious awareness of the seasons of your being, and in so learning, you make them God's gift to humanity."

THY WELL BE DONE

We have not correctly understood the Will of God. Somewhere along the way, we adopted the mistaken notion that God's Will is something to be feared. If, when we hear, "Thy Will be done," we begin to shiver and shake with a sense of impending doom, we do not know Who God Is. If we believe that if God really got to do His Will on us, we would be chastised and smitten, we do not know Who We Are. And if we think that God does not already love us with an everlasting Love, we do not know what Love Is.

The Will of God is the most wonderful thing that could ever happen to anyone. It is not to be feared, but embraced. The Muslim word for God is *Allah* — *"The Friend."* A friend of mine was walking in the park one day when be began to think of the things in his life that he was resisting. One by one he analyzed them, and soon he saw that the plan for his evolution was one of great Love and Beauty, and so it had always been. He saw, too, that in fighting the Will of God, he was really fighting his own best interest. As he explained it, "What I was afraid of was pure love, and, after all, I have nothing against pure love!"

We have been afraid to love. We have been afraid because we have felt hurt by what we thought was love. Love cannot hurt. Love can only heal.

Another friend of mine telephoned me to invite me to participate in a human relations workshop, the theme of which, she told me, was "Love."

"How wonderful!" I exclaimed, "I'm glad you picked such a

positive theme!"

"I don't know how positive love is," she countered; "I've been hurt by love too many times."

I knew her pain, but I could not agree that love could injure. "I, too, have felt the hurt that you say came from love," I told her. "And as I have let love become my friend, I see that it was not love that hurt us. Our hurt came from images, from expectations, from clinging. The Real Love that I have discovered has brought me only happiness."

Pain is not the offspring of love, nor is it the Will of God. We ascribe pain to love because we ascribe pain to God, and neither of these ideas is correct. Because God *is* Love, He could never bring pain. All we did was to dream an empty fantasy and then rail against it because it would not give us what it is impossible for a dream to give. God could never allow a dream to give us more than He can, or else He would not be God.

Love is the balm that heals all the wounds that we have ascribed to love. What else but love would heal the hurt that has been mistakenly blamed on itself?

Life is supposed to go right. I went to a lecture on esoteric astrology at which the lecturer told us, "People receive an answer to a prayer or experience a miracle and they come to me and exclaim, 'The most amazing thing just happened to me!' Actually, prayers are *supposed* to be answered and miracles are *supposed* to happen. God is real and His Love is true. Frankly, the most amazing thing to me would be if miracles *didn't* happen!"

Hilda taught this lesson in a very practical way. Once, when she learned that a cat at her house was injured due to someone's lack of paying attention, Hilda sharply chastised everyone present. "You've ruined my evening!" she chided. "There's no need for any cat or any animal or any person to be hurt! . . . If you would have paid attention, this would not have happened!" Hilda was not reacting in anger, but teaching a lesson: *There is no need for things to go wrong.* If we are living in the flow of God, things go right. Mishaps occur only when we step out of the flow, and healing is natural when we once again find it.

As we begin to see that God is really working *for* us, we see that Her only purpose is our happiness. Her commitment to our well-being is so unconditional that if we veer from that purpose and step out of the flow, She is right there to guide us back into it. We must know that for every brake about to wear out, it is God's Will to flash that little red light. But it is *we* who must mobilize our will to follow up the guidance with action. We must "pray with our feet moving." This is the alignment of the Will of God and the will of man. This is when *my* will becomes *Thy* Will, and the two are One.

The teacher "Freedom" once told me, "Life is easy. Love is easy. God is easy. It is *we* who make them complicated." When our intentions are attuned with the Will of God, we experience life as smooth sailing. Somehow our ship is guided around the reefs, and our course is straight for the port. When our seeing is out of focus with God's vision of Perfection, we experience conflict and turbulent waters. We cannot buck God. We can try, but as the popular play affirms, "Your arms are too short to box with God." Actually, if we really knew that God is always working for our happiness and peace, why would we want to box with Him in the first place? If we quit trying to grab His arms, we might just find Him hugging us.

"It is time for you to understand the purpose of your life. You are a chalice for God's Love and a vehicle for Him to bless the world. Realize your Divine purpose and your will is aligned with His.

Goodness is the theme of all life. See the Perfection in your life and you recapture your Childhood Vision. As you give up patterns of evaluation and cynicism, you accept the benevolence of God. Pain is born of resistance, and joy is a function of the acceptance of God's whole and Holy Love for you. Find purpose in your joy, and you find purpose in God.

We join you, in equal status, in looking out upon the marvels of the universe. We stand with you in awe at the mystery and the magnanimity of creation, miraculous beyond speakable understanding. The limited mind interprets vastness as intimidating, but wisdom reveals grandeur as a mark of your identity. As you release your fears, you are free to embrace the whole of the cosmos.

If there is any reason for sadness, it is the erroneous thought that the Father would work against the needs of His children. This idea is inconceivable to God and to those who know Him. 'If a man's son asks for a loaf of bread, would he give him a stone?' To the extent that we are saddened to see earth children deny their Divine Heritage, we are jubilant to see you accept it."

PART II:
THE HOMECOMING

"He arose and came to his father. But when he was yet a great way off, his father saw him and had great compassion, and ran, and embraced him and kissed him.

And the son said to him, 'Father, I have sinned against Heaven and in your eyes, and I am no more worthy to be called your son.'

But the father said to his servants, 'Bring forth the best robe, and put it on him . . . and let us eat and be merry, for this, my son, was dead, and is alive again; he was lost, and is found.'

And they began to be merry."

— Luke, Chapter Fifteen

The Vision of Freedom

BE THOU PERFECT

Our freedom depends on our willingness to see Perfection. The imperfection that we have been taught to see has led only to suffering. The world's belief that God is dead has made death a god, and Love a romantic fiction. Such a way of seeing takes a photograph and frames the negative as a portrait for all to worship as a dark standard. It is a standard that sees nothing and glorifies bitterness.

There is another way of seeing, a way that honors Perfection. It is a way of seeing all persons and things in the Light in which they were created, the Light of God. It is a way of seeing that restores Beauty and Wonder and Goodness to our lives and affirms that we are real because God is real.

Perfection is not a standard to be achieved, but a truth to be acknowledged. *It is not the difference between us and God, but the hallmark of our unity with Him.* And the honoring of Perfection is not a sin of vanity, but the humble acceptance of our identity as offspring of the Eternal.

If you do not now experience your Perfect Self, it is due only to an error in *awareness*, not in reality. We arrived on earth in purity and bliss. Our Innocence united us with the wonder of God's Love. We had no self-image, no self-consciousness, no thoughts of limitation. We lived in the Garden of Eden.

Then we gradually learned to not love ourselves. As pure children, we were open and receptive to harsh beliefs and vibrations. If mom was annoyed or angry about having to arise in the night to attend to our needs, or if older brother was fearful of our new place in the family, we incorporated those jagged feelings into our sensitive body. We cannot blame mom, dad, brother, or teacher for their negative feelings, for they were loving us in the best way that they knew, according to their level of evolution. They, too, learned not to love themselves in the same way. Simply by being born into the world, we take on a huge amount of unconsciousness. It is from this point that each of us began the noble task of learning to love ourselves in a world that denies Love.

Our learning to *not* love ourselves is what the bible describes as the fall from the Garden of Eden. Hilda has said many times that the Garden of Eden is not a place, but a *consciousness*. The story in the bible is not a distant, remote, and unrelated fable. It is *our* story, and it describes the evolutionary unfoldment of each and every human being. When Adam and Eve ate from the "tree of knowledge of good and evil," they began to cut the fruit of life into thoughts of worthiness and unworthiness. They entered into the illusion that it is possible to do things that will make us unlovable. They began to label actions as *evil*, or outside of God.

Since it is you and I who are Adam and Eve, each of us ate from the tree of "good" and "evil" when we accepted the belief that we were good if we did what mommy wanted us to do, but if we did not, we were bad, and punishable by being cast out of the garden of providence and protection. We accepted conditional human love in place of ever-forgiving Divine Love.

We can re-enter the Garden of Eden (in *consciousness*) by remembering that warm and blissful experience of being wholly loveable, the feeling that was so natural to us before we were taught that we had to do something before we could be enough. In the beautiful motion picture, *Brother Sun, Sister Moon*, Pope Innocent tells St. Francis, "In our obsession with original sin, we have forgotten Original *Innocence*."

The key to our entering back into the Garden is to locate the point where we left it. This requires a clear and bold look into our personal history. One evening, in a meditation class, I was guided to mentally return to my childhood to explore how I learned to feel unworthy and fearful. In a flash, a long-submerged memory was revealed to me: As a child, I drank milk from a baby bottle until a few years after the age that most children stop. My mother would continue to give me bottles, but she was very concerned that no one else know about it. It was O.K. for me to drink a bottle around the house, but if we went out I could only do it in secret. Once, we accidentally left a bottle at my aunt's house, and when she discovered it, my aunt made fun of me, and my mother was terribly ashamed.

As you can imagine, I absorbed these feelings of shame and embarrassment, which I most likely did not have before, and I began to think that there was something wrong with me; that I was less than other people; that I was unworthy; and that I had to hide what I did. This, perhaps, was my personal fall from the Garden of Eden in this life.

When, in my class, I saw this whole sequence clearly, I felt the exhilirating freedom of refound Innocence. I saw, as if a light had been turned on in a dark room, how my unworthiness was *learned*, and how it consisted of nothing more than my accepting a set of thoughts and feelings that other people believed in. I realized the joy that the lovely Patricia Sun described as her own self-discovery. She said that she had always felt that there was some awful, terrible thing inside of her that would just devour her if she ever looked at it. When, one day, she actually looked within, she saw that there was absolutely nothing there, and her fears were all based upon a hoax, a joke, — an illusion.

My experience after that realization was one of deep peace and contentment. I realized that there is nothing to do in life but just to *be*. I saw that all of this world (which Ramakrishna called "a mansion of mirth") is based upon desire, which is itself based on the illusion of "need." That night I knew, in my deepest heart of hearts, that I did not, in Truth, need anything, that I actually never have needed anything, and that I never shall. Nor has anyone on this earth ever, in Reality, needed anything. Indeed, we come on earth to learn that what we desire can never really make us happy. I saw, too, that all of our business — busyness — is just scurrying about in vain attempts to fulfill needs that we have created by thinking we need this or that to be happy.

There was an illuminating *Star Trek* episode in which Captain Christopher Pike is captured by a group of mentally powerful beings on another planet, and held prisoner in a glass cage of illusion, which his captors have created with their minds. He begins to suspect that his prison is not real, and in an effort to prove the truth, he captures one of his guards. The frail guard suddenly turns into a huge and horrible monster, about to maul Pike, who nevertheless maintains his hold on the guard-monster. Pike points a ray gun to the monster's head and demands, "You seem to be a monster, but I say you are not real — I say you are an illusion! Reveal yourself, or I'll blow your head off!" The monster disappears, the weak and fragile form of the guard reappears, and the captain escapes, free.

The monsters in our lives are the constructs of mass thoughts of limitation that we have accepted as true. When we point the ray gun of Truth at them, they, too, vanish like nightmares in the morning light.

The night of my insight, I was given the grace to see the flimsiness of the illusory fears that I once felt. These exposed boogeymen were powerless to touch me in this clear consciousness. Someone came at me with harsh criticism, and I, resting in this calm center, handled it easily. Nothing could disturb me in my Garden. The same night, someone invited me to play some music with a group, but it was just not in my heart to do so at that moment. At some other time, I might have agreed out of fear of saying "No," but this night, this very special night, my confidence in my enoughness was too strong to be seduced by fears of rejection. I felt so serene and secure that I did not care whether I lived or died.

Before retiring for the night, I thought whether to meditate and pray as I usually do. But how could I sit down to practice remembering who I am, when I already know? And how could I pray to Jesus, when I know myself — and all — to be one with the Christ? There was simply nothing to do. The falsehood of becoming had given way to the miracle of being.

Jesus said, "Be thou perfect, even as thy Father in Heaven is perfect." This was not a command, but a statement. He was telling us how it is. He was telling us Who We Are. He was telling us the Truth. Jesus was reminding us of our forgotten identity; He was showing us an aspect — the Aspect — of ourselves that we do not see. We do not need to attain perfection; we could not do that, even — and especially — if we tried. We just need to see it.

A teacher once told a group of us, "You are all already liberated!" Puzzled, I asked, "If we are all already liberated, then why do we fall?"

"Because," he explained, "you do not believe that you are free, and you push and you push and you push, until you fall."

Patricia Sun said it in another way:" It is impossible for you to

LEARNED SELF IMAGES

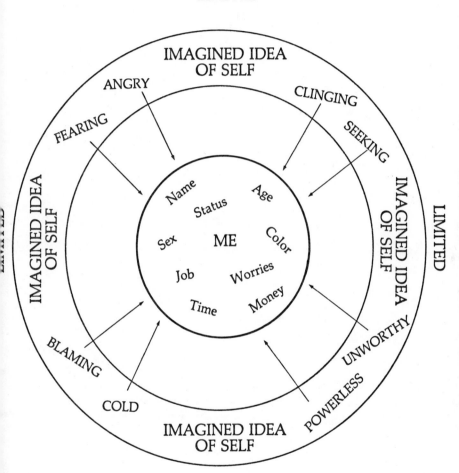

OUR REAL SELF

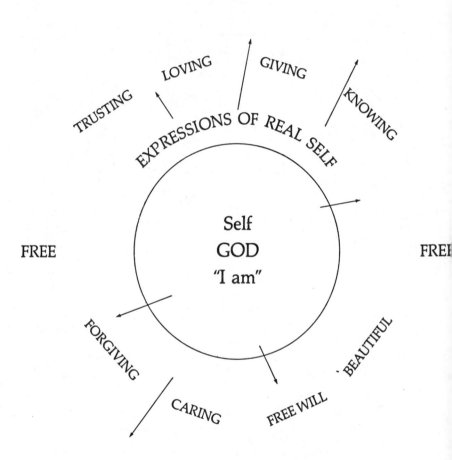

become good by doing something, because the act is based on the assumption that you are not *already* good!"

We must not confuse Perfection with Hollywood. We can have a bump on our nose, we can dial a wrong number, we can make a mistake, and still we are perfect. The Perfection that I am speaking of is not the kind that is ambitiously sought after in the world. God's idea of Perfection is much broader than the little mind's idea. Mother Nature is big enough to absorb a few jagged edges. Trees do not grow in straight rows. Lettuce can be very delicious and nutritious even with a few holes in the leaves. And scientists have told us now that the earth is not exactly round; it is just slightly pear-shaped. Seen from the highest perspective, the grand tapestry of nature is entirely perfect. All the little imperfections disappear and blend into the magnificence of the whole.

To claim our Perfection is not a delusion of the ego; to deny it is the real sin. Owning our Perfection means that we can and do have an important role in the unfoldment of humanity's destiny of Good. It means that we do not have to wait until we are 21, 30, or 65, or until we get married or a Ph.D. to be O.K. We can live up to our potential now. Sometimes our calling is as simple as a smile. Whatever our path, we must always remember that we are fully endowed by God to do what She gives us to do, and to do it well — even perfectly.

"The key to your freedom is the acceptance of your heritage of Perfection. Would that you were as ready to admit your Perfection as you are to identify with your flaws.

Your Perfection is your salvation. There is no middle ground between limitation and Perfection. Children of Light, adhere to your wholeness with all of your heart. It shall never fail you, for its very nature is eternal Fullness.

We stand ready to see you mature into the full understanding of your rightful place in the cosmos. Relinquish forever your dream of beggarhood. Those who struggle in the mire of earth see not beyond their own mind. Those who reach upward for Divine Knowledge dream a dream of kingship, one which bears fruit in the garden of His Truth. Emptiness is but a passing fantasy. Indulge not in lack, for lack is born of ignorance and must always be renounced for the inheritance of the Kingdom.

You who would aspire to the full understanding of your Destiny, shall know it, for in the asking is the promise of the answer. Ask your question, and renounce your search. Prepare a place for your wholeness by surrendering your concepts of oppression. So invited, shall Peace surely come.

There is a serenity that befalls the one who sees the simplicity that is God. Pain and despair are no more. Ponder upon these ideas until you realize them to be your own. In that realization, the lover has become the beloved, the seeker, the sought, and the man, the God. Nothing less shall ever satisfy you, and nothing more is ever possible."

UNDOING UNWORTHINESS

God has not condemned me. No more do I.
— A Course in Miracles*

Unworthiness is the subtlest of obstacles that stand between us and our Good. It is a crafty thief that masks itself in the garb of guilt, false humility, and even pride, and robs us of the full expression of our potential as Godly beings. It uses doubt as a weapon to create confusion of the lower mind, and kidnaps healers from the ill and lovers from the beloved. Unworthiness is responsible for the withholding of talent, service, and wisdom from a world which so desperately yearns for upliftment. If there is a devil, it is the *thought* that we are sinful, evil creatures. And because there is a God, the debunking of that thought is ensured with the realization that we are Divine.

Unworthiness is simply a case of mistaken identity. It seems formidable only when we shrink from it. Our freedom from unworthiness is bought only by awareness of Light. Like any other impediment to Self-knowledge, lack of self-appreciation is but a form of ignorance, and it is immediately overcome by simple clear seeing.

Several months ago I began to experience abundant success in my work. Creative and challenging projects, ideas, and money began to come my way with a powerful flow that I had not experienced before. I had the feeling that "this is too good to be true." But nothing is too good to be true. God is true and God is good.

---

*For information on *A Course in Miracles,* see reference on copyright page of this book.

THE DRAGON DOESN'T LIVE HERE ANYMORE

Around the same time, I began to feel that I was soon going to die. I had the strange sense that I did not have much time left on earth. When I held this notion up to the light of discrimination, I knew that it was not so — that my feeling was coming from a source other than intuition or Truth. But where?

I delved into this issue in meditation, and I discovered that what was indeed in the process of dying was a *concept of myself* as a mediocre person. I had never thought of myself as very successful, wealthy, or desirable. When these situations began to manifest themselves in my life, I did not know how to handle them. They seemed to be the kind of things that happened to other people — *successful* people — but not to *me*. In order for me to accept these positive changes in my life, I would have to let go of my picture of myself as someone who doesn't have very much to offer, and accept a new image — one of value and worthiness. I realized that it was not "me" or the body that was dying, but an old and non-productive idea of who "I" am.

"Let it die, then," I thought, "with my blessings." And so it did.

There is a story of a woman who sold fish all her life and knew little else. One spring she was invited to the king's palace for a royal festival. When she was shown to her room, she found it filled with colorful flowers and sweet incense. She was repulsed. "How disgusting!" she complained; "Please let me go back to sleep near my pile of fish." She chose the foulness of her fish, solely out of familiarity.

We, too, cling to our hurts, our grudges, our illnesses, our sorrows, and our angers as if they offered us comfort or serenity. In truth, all they offer us is the solace of familiarity and the surety of a self-image that we can hold onto in the face of the insecurity of a changing world. We accept the meager rewards of sympathy, agreement, self-righteousness, and attention, which are not really rewards, but snares. The dear price we pay is that of inner tranquility, joy, and freedom. The tragedy of life is that we do not believe that we have a choice.

The miracle of life is that the instant we realize that we can choose self-worth, purposefulness, and appreciation, the power of our love begins to shine a light of forgiveness on us that dissolves all of our hurts and makes us whole as ever we were. We begin to see through unworthiness as if it were an amateur magician. We can refuse to be abducted down the dark alley of negative thinking; we have walked down that path, and we know it leads to nowhere. Instead, we begin to acknowledge the deep compassion of the God within us, a sweet and merciful kindness that lies patiently awaiting its full expression through the door of an open heart.

I have participated in many encounter groups, personal growth workshops, counselor training courses, and been privy to extremely personal information about the lives of many human beings. I may not have heard it all, but I'll bet I've heard at least one from each category. After seeing and hearing what I have seen and heard, it seems to me that, behind the outer masks of suits, make-up, smiles, and properness, we have all done some rather sordid things, and behind all of our seemingly evil selves, we are wonderful, loving, and lovable people. After all the results are in, we are all pretty much equally horrible in the realm of horror, and equally lovable in the realm of love, which is the only realm that really counts, anyway.

I have seen parents of retarded children giving them an awful lot of love. Their love was not diminished because their child was handicapped; if anything, they gave the child more love. If you feel unworthy in any way, imagine that your unworthy self is like a handicapped child; pick it up, hold it in your arms, look right through its apparent "ugliness," and give it all the love you know how to give.

"What about conscience?" you may rightfully ask. "Isn't it appropriate to feel guilty about some things?" It is necessary to recognize our errors. As soon as we realize or admit to ourself that we have made a mistake, however, and we decide not to repeat it, we have experienced an awakening, which is a cause for *joy*, and *not remorse*. After a moment's sincere realization, any browbeating, self-pity, or sorrow is the luxury of woe.

Jesus' paramount teaching was "Love your neighbor as yourself." We are pretty much aware of the importance of loving our neighbor, but the part about loving ourselves seems to have gotten lost somewhere along the way. Although we usually think of the Golden Rule as giving others the same love as we give to ourselves, I have found in my own life that the reverse applies, too: I must learn to offer the same acceptance and forgiveness to myself that I usually offer to others. Sometimes I hear a friend's story of error that is easy enough to understand and forgive; if, however, I make a similar mistake, I am often much harder on myself — perhaps a little too hard. In such a case I am not loving my neighbor as myself.

Jesus gave two other important teachings: "I have not come to judge, but to forgive" and "Love one another as I have loved you." If Jesus was big enough to wash his disciples' feet and to tell them, "I have loved you with an everlasting love," can we take it upon ourselves to be so small and unforgiving that we can throw ourselves out of our own heart? Can we be so arrogant as not to love that which the Christ loves?

If you think about it clearly, it makes all the sense in the world for us to be useful and beautiful. There is obviously a great and Divine intelligence in the universe. All of God's creations function in magnificent harmony and precision. Every element and every living thing has a meaning and a purpose. Would the Creator be so foolish as to create a person without a purpose? Would She make you or me if She didn't have a plan for our existence? If God is Omniscient and Omnipotent, and Omni-everything else, would She create something that She didn't love? And if She weren't sure of Herself, wouldn't She have created a few duplicates for each model, in case one didn't work? Every human being is unique and special. Surely we come into this world for a special function — one that only each of us, as an individual, can fulfill.

That fulfillment is made easy by our willingness to forgive ourselves. How much time we waste on holding ourselves to blame for past mistakes! We believe we deserve to suffer, or that we must pay off years of karma of past wrongdoings. This issue of paying off karma puzzled me. "If I have seen the error of a deed, must I continue to pay for it?" I wondered. Suppose, for example, that I committed ten acts of burglary, and then I am stolen from once. If I then realize the problem of my stealing, must I be stolen from nine more times? The inner voice explained: "The purpose of life is *education — not punishment.*" Once the lesson is learned, further education is no longer necessary.

To put ourselves through continued suffering because we believe we must atone for past "evil" deeds is self-created suffering. At that point, the lesson we must learn is not related to the original error, but one of releasing ourself from the masochism of unworthiness. We do not need to go out of our way to find ways to pay off our "bad karma." God is clever enough to find ways for us to pay our debts. He will send us enough lessons and challenges, compassionately well-timed, to offset our karmic obligations. We do not need to add to them; He knows His business. I once heard, "Never trouble trouble 'til trouble troubles you." As I see it, if life is offering us no troubles, we might as well take advantage of the time and enjoy ourselves.

To forgive is to transcend our lower nature and to release a force of Light that can heal the universe and purge it of all suffering. When we forgive anyone, including — and especially — ourselves, we are lifted up by the very thought of forgiveness to our highest angelic potential. Nothing can be more pleasing in the eyes of God. To love ourselves for our goodness is easy. To love ourselves, in spite of our errors, is downright Holy.

"Children, you hold yourself too strictly in account for what you believe are your misdeeds. We see only lessons and experiences. It is you who attach the meaning of good or bad to these experiences. We are incapable of judgement, and so do not know unworthiness. Self-condemnation is a creation of the human mind. We seek for your understanding, and not for your suffering.

We hold nothing against you. We do not know guilt. You are your own judge, jury, and executioner. We implore you to cease causing yourself unnecessary hardship on this joyous path of learning.

We delight in your forging onward in the quest of the knowledge of your True Self. No other endeavor has any value. Do not look back to a past that is dead and complete. We are desirous of aspirants with the vision of the future.

See yourselves as whole and pure, and you see yourselves as we see you. We see nothing less than Perfection in you. Join us in our victory over the ignorance of unworthiness. Our power is not in fear and retaliation, but Forgiveness and Love. This is the path that cannot fail. This is the path of God."

STANDING NAKED

To stand naked before God is to realize that all that we would hide is unimportant. We make our secrets important only by our fear of them. When we believe we need to conceal something, we obscure our own vision of its nothingness. God could not care less about the secrets we try to keep from Him. These secrets continue to wield power over us only as long as we do not hold them up to the light. When we summon the courage to have a clear look at our hidden selves, we see how flimsily they are constructed, and we can enjoy the best kind of laugh as we watch them disintegrate.

Real growth comes only through self-acceptance. As long as we deny any aspect of our being, we make believe that something could be outside of God. It is as if we say, "God is everywhere; He fills all time and space — except for this part of my body and what I did at age fifteen."

Approval by others is a limited acceptance; it is not self-acceptance. I have participated in a number of "ventilation" workshops, during which I was asked to speak of my deep hidden secrets — acts and aspects of myself that I feared or was ashamed to admit.

These were the thoughts, feelings, and experiences which I felt, in my subconscious, that if anyone knew about, I would be unloved and rejected. So I mustered up the courage to share these things in small groups during these workshops, and I was very happy to find that the world did not fall apart, nor was I outcast from society. I also learned that everyone else had their own equally sensitive "stash," and that they were so busy being afraid that they would not be loved because

213

of their "stuff" that they couldn't care less what I have been or done. The only one who cared was me.

I left these workshops feeling clean, clear, and happy, for it was a great relief to be able to share my hidden self with others, and still receive their support, approval, and love. But I later learned a deeper lesson that showed me an even more subtle teaching about self-disclosure.

In a guided meditation class, the teacher said, "Now take a look at all of the things that you have kept hidden from others, and have not admitted to yourself. You will not be required to speak any of these facts to anyone else. These issues are simply between you and God."

One by one, an array of feelings, thoughts, and experiences began to parade before my consciousness, as if they were being shown to me on an inner movie screen. The promise that I would not have to reveal them to anyone else encouraged me to be totally free and honest with myself. A surprising amount of little judgements, opinions, and grudges were made visible to me. I did not really like C., although I had been trying to convince her and myself that I did; I was still angry at J; I was putting up a facade about my feelings about the house; and I really felt I made a bad deal for my guitar case. The more I admitted, the more was revealed to me. At first it was painful to admit my hypocrisy and deception, but as the process went on, I felt freer and freer, until I gladly welcomed any insights that came to me. By the time we were finished, I felt wonderful — in all my imperfection. I had seen myself through clear eyes, and I knew, ironically, that I was alright with God. It was only my self-judgement that made me seem not alright.

From this I gained a very important understanding: *Standing naked before people is not nearly as important as standing naked before God.* Approval by others may bring encouragement, but acceptance by my Self brings freedom.

In the long run, acceptance by others does not solve the problem of leaning outward for validation. After my meditation, I thought, "In those workshops, people accepted me, and that made me feel good . . . But what if they had laughed or scorned or rejected me? . . . I would have felt hurt! . . . What kind of freedom is that?" If I allowed social approval to make me happy, I was making myself vulnerable to social rejection making me unhappy. In other words, I was giving the power of my happiness to other people, which is never a wise investment. In that meditation class, I cleared myself with God, which is the only clearing that is really valuable.

We cannot fool God; we can only try to fool our little selves. We would attempt to fool God because we believe, on some level, that He would not love us if He knew the truth. The joke is that He already knows the truth, of course, and He already loves us, anyway. He is just waiting for us to come around to His point of view — one of complete and unconditional acceptance.

God's Love is the surest thing in the universe. He is unflinching in His willingness to have us just as we are. There is no reason to hide and no place to run. When we offer our lives to Him, He assumes full responsibility for our well-being. If He knows all that we do, He must surely know why we do it, and such a knowledge is always wed to deep compassionate understanding. This is the great surprise that undoes the need for all of our empty labors: We are forgiven and we are loved.

> Open all the shutters on your windows!
> Unlock all the locks upon your doors!
> Brush away the cobwebs from your daydreams!
> No secrets come between us anymore!
> So fly, little bird, up into the clear blue sky,
> Carry the word, Love's the only reason why . . .

—The Moody Blues, *The Land of Make Believe*, by Justin Hayward

''My Love for you is unconditional and complete. I am your beloved, who knows the hidden recesses of your inner self better than you, yourself, know them. I am not concerned with your impurities or errors. In my eyes they hold no power or reality.

My deepest wish is that you love yourself as I love you, which is exactly the way your Heavenly Father loves you. As you realize the magnitude of this Love, you laugh at the uselessness of your hiding. You tried to conceal that which you are not. By your very attempt to hide it, you gave a seeming reality to that which never existed.

Come into the sunshine of Love's acceptance, beloved Children of Light. Seek not the approval of your brothers and sisters, for they are yet students like you, and their discrimination is not yet keen. What the world can give, the world can take away. What your Heavenly Father gives, no man can remove.

There is nothing that you can do that would cause you to lose my Love. Go forward in confidence, and be strong in your freedom.''

The Truth

THE MIGHTY TRUTH

It has been said that even if there were no God, the universe could flourish on the foundation of Truth alone. This teaching, to me, means this: If it is hard for you to accept the idea of God, perhaps due to negative associations learned early in life, then pursue Truth with all the reverence and tenacity in your heart, and so you will find fulfillment, for the lessons of Truth *are* the lessons of God.

Truth is the whole of our existence. It is our very life. We have no existence outside of Truth and neither can Truth exist outside of us. When a human being aligns him or herself with Truth, only good can come of such a commitment. Those who feel that they do not know the Truth but sincerely wish to know it, will receive answers to all they ask. Those who belong to Truth cannot fail.

Mahatma Gandhi was one of the greatest devotees of Truth that ever lived. When I think of Truth, I think of Gandhi. His story is one of a nervous, neurotic, and fearful man who, in the name of Truth, tackled life by the horns and gradually, relentlessly, freed himself from his limitations and took a nation of hundreds of millions to freedom with him. He refused to compromise his integrity under all circumstances, and though he was at first scorned, later found the world beating a path to his door.

Gandhi and those great ones like him knew that the vision of Truth is born of loving. The real organ of Truth is not the brain, but the heart. The ancient Egyptians realized this. When a man died, they removed most of his bodily organs and preserved only a few organs which they believed to embody Divine energies. They discarded the brain, but kept the heart. Hafiz, the Persian poet, said, "O you who would learn the marvels of Love from the copybook of reason, I am afraid that you will never really see the point!"

We feel or sense Truth more than we think it. We know it more than we understand it. We can see it more than we can explain it. When we attempt to analyze Truth, we lose ourselves in the dead-end labyrinth of the thinking mind. When we love Truth, however, the storehouse of universal wisdom is opened to us. Our respect for Truth is our investment in its understanding, and our suffering the price of its denial.

The Truth, we discover, cannot be found in a book. We may find words and descriptions of the Truth in a book, but not the Whole Truth, for the Whole Truth is fathomless, ever free of containment, confinement, or conformity. There was a monk in Ireland named Alanus, who was revered and sought after for his great wisdom. One spring, he was invited to the University of Paris to address the student body. After his lecture, one of the students approached Alanus and asked him if he would speak the following day on the subject of the Trinity. "Certainly!" Alanus agreed, and he set out along the banks of the Thames River to prepare his discourse.

As he was pondering, Alanus noticed a little boy repeatedly dipping a bucket in the water and dumping it on the shore. Curious, he asked the child, "What are you doing?"

"I'm emptying the entire river onto the shore!" the boy explained.

Laughing, Alanus told him, "Don't be silly; you will never be able to empty the river like that!"

Looking Alanus straight in the eye, the child answered, "And neither can you explain the Trinity in the words of a lecture."

No teacher, religion, or cult can hold exclusive possession of the Truth. The hallmark of Truth is its inclusive nature; no one or no thing could ever be excluded from It. Those who believe that their truth is the only Truth are living a consciousness of limitation, and in Truth, limitation does not exist. When Christ Jesus said, "I am the Way, the Truth, and the Life," He was speaking from the awareness of the universal "I Am," the Christ, the Light which He knew Himself and all persons to be. He was not speaking only of the Jesus, which was the physical form that was identified with the Christ. Jesus, Buddha, Moses, Mohammed, and the other great ones have all taught the same

Truth: *paths are many; the Truth is One.*

This one Truth is not hidden, nor has it ever been. It is always present, available, and free to those who sincerely love it and yearn to delight in its brilliant splendor. The Truth cannot be bought, sold, bartered, or traded. Those who would sell it do not have it. Neither can it be taught, given or bestowed. It can only be lived. Like Love, those who do not have it catch it from those who have it, and like the most delicate wildflower, Truth recreates itself by the power of its own beauty. There is nothing secret about the Truth; it will find us wherever we are, like the morning sun finds the eyes of a sleeping child. The telling mark of those who have discovered the Truth is their eagerness to share it, for unlike the meager commodities of the world, Truth's joy only increases through sharing.

Those who have taught the Truth have been the pillars of humankind throughout the ages. Though many were mocked, some of them martyred, and nearly all of them misunderstood, it is those who had the courage to live for Truth that have sustained our human family through the centuries. Many of them lived short lives, coming briefly to bring their message of Peace and Light, leaving the earth with a legacy of new understanding.

Those who have taught untruth have been swallowed up by the ages. Lies are distinguishable only by their inability to withstand change. The real Truth is so powerful that, once expressed, it stands nobly, never to be forgotten, established in the genetic blueprint for planetary unfoldment.

It is said that "The Truth hurts." The Truth has never hurt anything; only illusion hurts. The Truth knows only how to heal. Those who resist Truth resist healing, and those in need of healing can find it by embracing Truth. The Truth brings with it a peace and a satisfaction that falsehood cannot imitate. The lover of Truth lives only for the vision of his ideal and he is nourished only by his awareness of it. A man may survive without physical sustenance for a number of days, but how long can he survive without Truth?

The Truth is simple. It is people and minds that make it seem complicated. The more complex we make it, the further we drive ourselves from it. When we return to the simple things, the Truth reawakens our heart like a long-exiled lover. To me, the Truth is as obvious in a daisy as in the most technical encyclopedia. If you want to know what the Truth is, put aside your textbooks for a while and walk along the seashore at sunset. Take a child to a park. Gaze at the stars. Observe the gentle rhythm of your breath. Listen to the sound of a bamboo flute. Sing a song of simple verse: "Row, row, row your boat, gently down the stream, merrily, merrily, merrily, merrily, life is but a dream."

If you believe not in a God, then let Truth be your redeemer. If you find nothing sacred, let Love be your consoler. And if you find no friend worthy of your trust, let Life itself be your consort. The Truth bears no concern for that which it is called, else Truth it would not be.

The dance is never done, and the song is never completely sung, 'til the love of the Truth has made us One.

—David and Jamil

"The Truth is a mighty fortress to those who take refuge in its protective strength. In Truth, there is no fear; outside of the Truth, there is no consolation. You are heir to the never failing power of the all-pervading Truth. Never compromise your right to know the Truth and stand firmly upon it. Truth will never betray your trust.

Who can challenge the Truth and stand vindicated? Who can flaunt mortality in the face of eternal Love and have Truth bear witness to vanity? We tell you now that the only strength in the universe is the strength of Truth. There is no other, nor can another ever exist.

Truth is the only weapon of those who live for the upliftment of humanity. Truly, the only stone that marks humanity's plight is the insistence on the possibility of fulfillment outside of the Spirit. The Spirit is the Truth, and there can be no separation between the two, for the Holy Truth and the Holy Spirit are made One in innocent vision.

We cannot, nor can any man, speak for the Truth, for Truth is its own hallmark. At best, we can live in its service. Words may point the way to Truth, but actions demonstrate it. Live in accordance with the highest awareness of the Truth that you know. There is no greater purpose in life than this one."

Transformations

In a dream, I saw myself as a butterfly; now I am wondering whether I am Chuang Tsu dreaming I was a butterfly, or a butterfly dreaming I am Chuang Tsu.

— Chuang Tsu

THE MAGIC MASK

Once upon a time, there was a cruel and hard-hearted king. He was so unpopular that he was continuously fending off rebellions and attempts on his life. One morning he awoke and realized how miserable was his life. More than anything, he wished he could change. He called for his royal wizard and asked him for help.

The wizard pondered for a moment, and told the king, "I can help you, but you must be prepared to carry out any instructions I give you."

"Anything," agreed the king, "that will restore peace to me."

"Very well," said the wizard, "wait three days, and I will give you something to help you."

When the three days elapsed, the wizard gave the king a very unusual object — a mask. The mask was almost an exact likeness of the face of the king, himself — with one very important exception: instead of the usual frowns and scowling lines, this image was smiling, with smooth and pleasant features.

"I can't wear that!" argued the king, ". . . It's not really my face; and besides, people will not recognize me — they know I am not a happy man."

"If you want me to help you, you must do as I say, and wear the mask at all times," the wizard reiterated.

"Very well — I will."

The king began to wear the mask, and something amazing happened. People began to enjoy looking at him, and to feel more comfortable in his presence. They began to feel safe with the king, and to trust him. The king responded positively to his subjects' acceptance of him, and began to treat them with respect and kindness. Gradually the unrest in the kingdom diminished, and peace was restored within its borders.

There remained, however, one place where there was not complete satisfaction — within the heart of the king. He was overjoyed with the changes in his kingdom, but as he had grown, he came to feel hypocritical, for he knew that he was wearing a phony mask. He wrestled with his discomfort and summoned the wizard.

"I am very grateful for the changes that have taken place in my kingdom, but I can deceive my people no longer. I am a charlatan. Please give me permission to remove the mask."

"As you wish," replied the wizard.

Painfully, the king stood in front of a mirror and slowly began to peel away this image that had transformed his life and his kingdom. It was not easy for him, but he knew that he had to do it. Summoning all the courage he could, he opened his eyes to look at his old scowling face.

That face, however, was not the one he saw. What he did see, miraculously, was a beautiful and joyous visage, even more radiant than the one the mask had represented. Through his inner transformation, the king's face had actually become a portrait of joy and kindness. The mask had been only a temporary measure to draw out his real inner beauty.

In this era of honesty, we are encouraged to "Tell it like it is," to "shoot from the hip," and to "give feedback." These practices are very valuable when offered in a loving and supportive way. The principle is, however, often misused. We speak hurtful words with a sharp and cutting tongue, and then reason, "Well, I'm just being me, and, after all, I gotta be me." This is true — we've all "gotta be me," but it is important that we know who "me" is before we express it to others.

Who we are is God. Who we are is Joy. Who we are is Love. Anything else is passing show, illusion. The word "personality" comes from the Greek *persona* — mask. Our personalities, then, are our masks, and they are simply disguising the real us, which is ever whole and perfect.

To wear a "magic mask" of loving words and deeds is to act in accord with our real nature. In fact, once we begin to reap the benefits of our given love, we discover that it is our *goodness* that was real all along, and negation the imposter. We are like an actor who has played his role for so long that he forgot who he was before he began the play. Before we got used to the world's norm of defensiveness, it was very natural for us to be innocent and happy. As children, we lived in a blissful state, shining our light and love on all, regardless of their age, sex, or color. This is why even the hardest person melts in the presence of an innocent child, for children awaken our memory of the purity within ourselves which we long to once again express.

By God's loving Grace, that purity was never lost — it just became *veiled* by a smoggy layer of erroneous beliefs that we could be something less than Divine. Our happy surprise is that all of the ideals that we cherish — love, wisdom, kindness, compassion, and beauty — we already are; we seek after them only because they are the original aspects of ourselves that we came into life to express.

Our purposeful positivity is the key to that expression. It demonstrates through the results it begets that our ideas of "I can't," "I am unworthy," "I am afraid," and "I do not love" are simply untrue. Once we see that we *can*, that we are supremely loveable, and that we have the courage of the saints, the impostors of fear and guilt can never again fool us into believing in them instead of God.

Our hidden goodness and talents are released when we are willing to play the game of owning them, even if we are not fully convinced that they are ours. This was demonstrated to me in Tim Gallway's workshop called "The Inner Game of Tennis." I saw him get two novice players on the court and instruct them, "Imagine you are two of the greatest superstars of tennis; you have been playing professionally for twenty years, and many people have paid a great deal of money for the privilege of watching you play. Would you now be kind enough to give us a demonstration match." I could hardly believe my eyes! A couple who, ten minutes earlier, had made a few clumsy attempts to hit the ball, now danced all about the court with masterful finesse, skillfully smashing difficult shots in long volleys. They received wild applause from the astonished audience. Through this magic mask of skill, they gave themselves permission to release inner ability that would otherwise have laid trapped under thoughts of "I cannot" or "I am not."

Our strengths lie within us, and it is only our permission that can activate their expression. Our problem is not that we are weak, but that we do not believe that we are strong. Although love is the only thing that is real, we have believed in negation for so long that we thought it to be genuine, when it is but an offshoot of a mistaken thought.

Neem Karoli Baba told Ram Dass, "Love everyone and tell the truth." This seeming contradiction puzzled Ram Dass, for he thought, "The truth is that I don't really love everyone." So he began to express his dislikes, his disturbances, and his annoyed feelings toward his friends. He worked himself into such a vicious cycle of bitterness that one day he found himself weeping at the feet of his guru, under a heavy burden of feelings of isolation and separateness. "Love everyone and tell the truth," reminded the compassionate and forgiving guru. "At that moment," Ram Dass tells, "I realized that the truth is, behind my surface feelings of like and dislike, behind my judgements, and behind my emotions, I really do love everyone. I just thought I didn't. Holding onto that flimsy thought was the only thing that stopped me from being who I am; releasing it revealed to me the truth of Love."

We are loving, kingly beings who have dreamed that we are paupers and tyrants. Yet, by royal decree, our throne has been held in trust for us until we come to discover that our nature is one of rich loving kindness. The king who came to the wizard for help did not know if or how this magic mask would help him; he knew only that he wanted to live a more meaningful life, and that he was willing to take a risk to accomplish it. He had a bit of faith in the wizard, who had a great deal of faith in the king.

"You have been conditioned to accept an identity which is not true. To supercede that conditioning, you must accept a new image of yourself — one of Godliness and Beauty. You prove that image by your purposeful action.

The fingers of the untrained musician are comfortable with the familiar, but they must be disciplined to release an imprisoned song, one in which they shall later find greater comfort in mastery. Use your "ordinary" actions to release into expression your purest thoughts and play a masterful song, that the world may be uplifted. Your fears of "foolishness" and your need for "defense" exist only in your thoughts. Kindness, joy, and harmony are foolish only in the eyes of men. In the eyes of God, they are precious beyond description.

We are well aware of the urges and the forces that draw you to react with bitterness and retaliation. These are but the residue of past habits, even of an ancient time. They belong to a concept of yourself that is no longer necessary or useful. We call upon you to renounce the patterns of a painful past, and to come of age as a being of Golden Light. Know that you are supported in your efforts. Every act in harmony with your good nature brings you closer to your goal of true Self-expression. Be not confused by the ways of the world. They are the ways of ignorance. They are constricting and binding, and lead only to disappointment.

The ways of the Spirit are those of joy and bounty. They are the very keynote of the age to come. They lead to life and to happiness. Choose ye the force with which you would align yourself."

GAMBLING FOR GOD

There is a marvelous Chasidic story about a man who came running to the rabbi, exclaiming, "Rabbi, Rabbi, a terrible sin has been committed! Three men from our synagogue were up all night playing cards and gambling! You must chastise them immediately!"

"Wonderful!" exclaimed the rabbi, to the man's astonishment. "I am glad to hear it!"

The man was aghast. "How can you say 'Wonderful!'? Is it not a sin to gamble?"

"I am not approving so much of their gambling, friend. But I am overjoyed that they could stay up all night to play, for they have learned how to overcome sleep to do something that they enjoy. Just think — when they learn to love God, they will be able to stay up all night to serve Him!"

I met a man who selflessly devotes much of his time to a service organization, giving dynamic and inspiring lectures. He has a marvelous talent of taking spiritual topics and making them humorous and captivating. I asked him how he got involved in this work.

"To tell you the truth, I haven't always been very spiritually oriented," he explained. "In fact, I used to go to lots of drinking parties and really raise hell. I began to tell off-color jokes, and I found that there was a big audience for bawdy humor. So I gained a reputation as sort of an off-color comedian, and I was invited to many banquets and parties to tell my jokes. During that time, I developed confidence and a bit of style in public speaking.

"When I began to allow God into my life, I lost interest in telling my stories, but I found that I could still use my ability to speak before groups in an entertaining way. So when I was offered the opportunity to speak for my Lord through this organization, I was well prepared for the job." (And now he *really* raises hell.)

There are no unnecessary steps or experiences on our path to God. Because we look at God through mortal eyes, we may believe that we have missed or wasted time, but that is only because that is not how we would use God's energy now. When we look upon our experiences through the eyes of wisdom, we see how the process of personal evolution is a magnificent, well-designed mosaic. We see, too, that there is nothing outside of God, and there is nothing that She cannot find a way to use for Her Glory.

Our lives are transformed not through *becoming* Divine, but through *realizing* that all of our experiences have served a Godly purpose. Moses himself was a prince of Egypt before he realized his identity as a Jew. He even killed a man. He would not seem to have been a likely person to lead the nation of Israel to freedom, yet Moses' service as a prince of Egypt actually *prepared* him for the important role of leading the Jewish nation out of bondage.

In the same way, each stage of our life prepares us for the next — and better — one. When I was in high school I played electric bass in a rock band, and we played some pretty coarse music. Later, I became more interested in the acoustic guitar, and now it is my joy to play and sing songs that speak of the Peace of God. The abilities that I developed in a relatively crude forum can now be used as a vehicle to serve. The skills that once created agitation now soothe. I must honor those crude days, for they were a step to where I am now. No part of the path is any better or worse than another. If we can see life from the highest vantage point, we see how all of its elements are perfectly designed to fit into the grand scheme of development.

I was recently at a party at an ashram spiritual retreat. Just for the fun of it, we began to sing some old rock 'n' roll songs, which I had hesitated to sing because I thought they would be too heavy for a "spiritual" crowd. As it turned out, most of the people knew the songs better than I did, and they filled me in on the words that I could not remember. Many of the yogis and nuns were simply people with worldly experience who had grown into the spiritual life. As we got to talking about the marvel of personal transformation, we began to share with each other how we came to be doing what we do. One fellow had had a nervous breakdown when he was younger, and he began to develop a sensitivity for the needs of people in mental distress. Now he has a very powerful position in the government as a public advocate for mental patients. The head of the kitchen at this large ashram learned all about food service when she worked in a tavern. And the woman who took such wonderful care of the garden learned to do so when, in frustration, she ran away from home at an early age and lived with some American Indians. As a result of what she learned from them, her family situation is now healed, as well.

The caterpillar must surrender to the cocoon before it can be a butterfly. As we grow through life, we learn to express our God-given traits in progressively purer and purer forms. Each of us has a calling, one which we fulfill more deeply with each stage of our growth. We come to earth with a deep sense of the contribution that we would like to make to people and to the planet, but it takes a while for us to have the rough edges of our plan filed off. Seen from the broadest perspective, the caterpillar always was a butterfly; the cocoon was just the thing it needed to make its true identity obvious.

We cannot deny any element of our personal history, for each experience has played a vital role in our training as master souls. The world is more of a school than a playground. We must learn to walk before we can run. We would certainly not return to grade school now, but neither would we throw away what we learned, for it has brought us to where we are now. The flower does not find itself unworthy because it was once but a seed, nor does it judge other flowers in seed form. Are we not all flowers in various stages of opening?

"All of your actions and all of your experiences belong to God. You cannot see the purpose of your actions from the perspective of limitation; the one from which you have looked. We see, however, and we know that all that you have done is in the name of Good. Seek not to become good through future actions, for this would create an evil of the old, a creation of fantasy, and not of fact. Work, rather, to transmute, or refine your understanding of your work. In so doing, you raise your deeds to the highest, a position which they have always merited, but which you have not always accepted.

It is of the utmost importance to relieve yourself of the burden of judgement of the activities of your sisters and brothers. In so doing, you free yourself as well as them. We do not judge any soul, for we lose not sight of Divinity. It is very difficult for you to know the purpose of another's work. Let it suffice to believe that all work is for God.

The mind must be made to function for you as an instrument of blessing. Refuse to acknowledge sin. All that you see is a matter of interpretation. In God, there is no interpretation, for God sees only God."

GOLDEN OPPORTUNITIES

When life gives you lemons, make lemonade
—Esco Brown, *Last Chance Gas*, Chapter 1, Verse 1
(Resurrection)

A friend of mine once wrote: "All of life's experiences are to be either enjoyed or learned from." This is a different perspective than we usually hold; we have been conditioned to believe that life is a combination of good and bad, and that the price we pay for the good is the bad. Yet there is another way of looking at our experiences.

The hurts and sorrows that we feel in life are *not* punishments from God; they are messages given to us by a *loving* God who is showing us exactly where we need to change in order to grow into the serenity that is our nature. Understanding this truth entirely changes the way we look at our difficulties. Seen in this light, troubles turn into lessons, and grudges into Grace. Simply, it makes *all* of life good.

Adversity is our dear friend. It is the driving force that pushes us out of our comfortable nest and forces us to learn to fly on our own. We can really welcome adversity as a gift. Without it our growth is very slow. With it, we are transformed from fledglings into masters.

Every great person has a history of adversity. No one has ever made a contribution to humanity without first undergoing a certain amount of trials. Adversity can forge an immature soul into a powerhouse of strength. As I study the lives of the saints and statesmen, I see that every one of them came to be what they were through conquering challenges. Mahatma Ghandi was thrown off a train and spent a night in a cold train station because his skin was dark. St. Theresa of

Lisieux, the simple "Little Flower," selflessly tolerated barbs and criticism from her sisters in the convent. She learned greatness through humility. Moses was abandoned to the river as an infant, stripped of his dignity as Prince of Egypt, and cast off to die in the desert before he found God. Even after the miraculous parting of the Red Sea, Moses had to mollify the rebellious murmerings of the Hebrew people, forty years in the wilderness. I have seen the Sinai desert, and it is as barren as the moon. Even after this great tribulation, Moses was not permitted to enter the promised land with his people.

Pericles, the masterful Greek statesman whose purity and integrity marked the pinnacle of Greece's Golden Age, was scorned and maligned. He died in a horrendous plague. And we know of the small and stark beginnings of Abraham Lincoln, who had to find a way to heal a wartorn nation, and finally bore the wrath of an assassin's bullet.

It was not by chance that these great ones faced tremendous adversity — they were, in fact, *made great by it.* Perhaps their souls had chosen a life of service to humankind, and these tests and trials were required of them to forge their characters for such a task.

I do not suggest to seek out adversity or to become a false martyr. God takes no joy in seeing Her children suffer. We need only to change the way we look at, or understand, adversity when it comes. Life takes on a new meaning when we see that it is not "out to get us," and that God is *not* our enemy, but our best — and only — friend. Life's trials are the universe's way of lovingly teaching us valuable lessons that we need to learn — the very reasons we have come to earth.

Jesus taught to "love your enemies." How can this be? When we can look at our "enemies" as our teachers, they cease to be our opponents, and become our best friends. Our heritage, our birthright, and our purpose in life are to live in love and appreciation. If we find ourself in angry strife with another, we must have within us some seed of misunderstanding that needs to be corrected. If someone else "presses our buttons," we only misdirect our energy if we blame them, for our job in life is not to run from button pressers, but to find our buttons and unplug them. Those who bring our irritation to the surface are doing us a very great service, indeed. For this reason, we ought to be beholden to those good friends we mistakenly label "enemies," for they are (whether they realize it or not) the very agents of God that show us our way to greater strength.

We are told of a Greek man who paid someone a daily wage to follow him through his affairs and insult him, so that he, through learning to remain steadfast in the face of criticism, would develop strength of character. Considering his example, perhaps we should be thankful that our enemy-friends are doing us such a valuable service at no charge.

In the "Inner Game" workshop, Tim Gallway showed me how we already understand and use this principle. "When you want a good game of tennis," he asked, "who do you call for a partner? Usually an opponent who is equal or superior to you in skill. It's no fun playing with someone who doesn't challenge you."

And so it is with the inner game of life. We want to grow; we want to improve our skills in life. To drift through life without challenges would be useless and boring. We would be like stagnant algae on a motionless lake. If you have mastered any art, sport, or field of endeavor, you know the value of challenge, adversity, and discipline. The violin virtuoso welcomes with enthusiasm a new and difficult piece of music. He must flex his musical muscles to master the piece. He well knows that through the practice of overcoming the challenge, his proficiency is increased.

This sharpening of skills is the real value of competition. Many have lost sight of the purpose of healthy competition, which helps us to draw forth inner strength and encourages us to transcend our ideas of personal limitation. The real competition, however, is *within* the person, and not *between* people. We must each compete with — strive to conquer — our notions of how much we can do. When pushed to our limit, we usually find that we can do more than we thought we could. Our opponents in sports are actually performing a loving favor: they are working with us to support us in overcoming our weakness. In essence, competition is cooperation.

Looking at adversity in this way, we really *can* love our enemies. They serve us hard shots until we learn God's way of returning them. So mastered, we move on to a more formidable challenger until there are none that can defeat us.

As I reflect on my unfoldment, I see that the difficult experiences taught me practical lessons and made me stronger. They moved me forward to new and more fulfilling ways of being. They pushed me out of ignorance and into Truth. They were, in fact, my keys to freedom.

This is the new light which changes the way we view life's challenges, one which renews us as we see God's good hand in all. Hilda has said that the New Age requires a "new way of thinking." We must evaluate our experiences in a totally new way; God knows the old way didn't work. We must refuse to see our sorrows, hurts, and conflicts only at the surface level. We must look deeper. There is no wasted time or purposeless experience. We must take the challenges that now face us and re-work them in our minds until we see them in a positive light. Until they come into that light, they are begging for our awareness, and as soon as we give it to them, they become golden.

GOLDEN OPPORTUNITIES

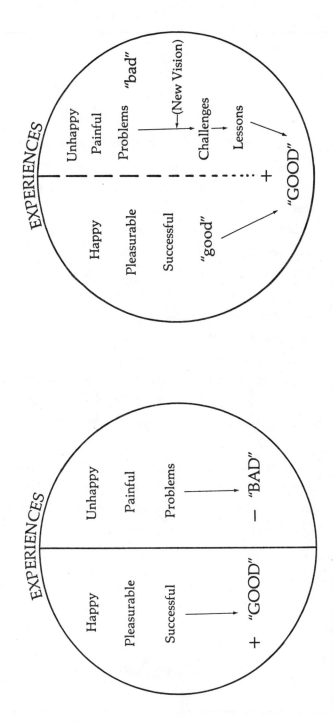

LIMITED VIEW OF LIFE

EXPERIENCES

Happy
Pleasurable
Successful → + "GOOD"

Unhappy
Painful
Problems → — "BAD"

WHOLE VIEW OF LIFE

EXPERIENCES

Happy
Pleasurable
Successful
"good" → "GOOD"

Unhappy
Painful
Problems "bad" →(New Vision)→ Challenges → Lessons → + "GOOD"

The masterful attitude toward life is the one that takes the whole view of experiences. The wise person sees problems as challenges, and values them for the lessons that they offer. In this way, all experiences become good.

"You must cease to look at challenge as your enemy. Whenever you hold a force of God outside your Self, you create evil. Hold all events within God, and evil cannot exist.

This process of development is one of revising your understanding. Experiences continue to be what they have been, are, and shall be. It is you who must bring your understanding of your experiences into clarity. We tell you that holding your life in the Light shall bring you the peace for which you yearn.

You must master the art of perspective. A slight shift in perspective is all that is necessary to see the wholeness of your training. It is, in fact, the training that you have chosen, in a way that the mind believes it understands, but cannot really accept.

Were you to see all of your experiences in the Love that they are given, you would cherish every moment of your life, for every moment is one of great opportunity. Be grateful, Children of Light, you are loved."

THE GIFT

My father passed on when I was 18 years old. At the time, I was fortunate to have many friends who gave their loving support and sympathy. We received many thoughtful cards, flowers, fruit baskets, and kind visitors. The person who stands out most prominently in my mind, however, was our neighborhood butcher, a Jewish man who had seen his family killed in the Nazi holocaust.

I shall never forget our brief interlude that spring afternoon on the steps of the synagogue. Having just learned about my dad's passing, he asked, "So . . . how are you doing?" "O.K.," I answered. He looked me straight in the eye, with a deep, seasoned balance of strength and understanding, and asked (though it was not really a question), "Pushing on, huh?"

In those three words, in the firm way in which he offered them, I felt a wave of strength and fortitude resonate deep within my soul. He was perhaps the only person, of all the well-wishers, from whom I felt no melancholy sympathy. It seemed that many of my other good friends were somewhat anxious about how to deal with me and my father's death. This man, however, through tremendous adversity, had learned a powerful inner calm. His firmness, his understanding, and his love were all communicated to me in just a few words and a strong but compassionate glance of the eyes. He gave me much, and as I remember all of my friends for their unique gifts, I shall always be grateful to him for his detached, yet very loving, support.

The greatest gift that we can offer to one another is the affirmation of our mutual strength. To go into agreement with thoughts of weakness or victimization does not serve one who needs light, and not more darkness.

When I first saw Patricia Sun, she was fielding questions from a tough audience, on healing and dealing with the hardships of life. It seemed that no matter what horrendous predicaments were thrown at her for her advice, including cancers, brutal crimes, and life's callousness, she would smile and begin her response with "That's wonderful!" She would then go on to describe what unique lessons each situation had to offer the questioner. All of her responses were given with total compassion, awareness of the pain being felt, and respect for the position of the person needing support. Yet she did not sympathize with their anger or feelings of victimization. And she won the audience's heart. When someone asked her how she healed people, she innocently answered, "I don't know; I just feel their pain and love them."

To heal one another and our planet is an ability that we all have. That healing takes place when we look past circumstances into Light. To acknowledge Light where others see darkness is to give a very great blessing.

At one of Eric Butterworth's fine lectures, a woman raised her hand and asked how she could get out of her horrible job. She hated her boss, couldn't stand the work, did not get along with her colleagues, and she was tremendously uncomfortable in the position. "Why do you want to leave?" Eric teased; "It sounds like you've really found your niche!"

Her job, he meant, was offering her an unusually fine opportunity to see where she needed to change the way she was looking at life, and to grow beyond her narrow vision. If she stayed with her job until she no longer reacted to it in an emotional way, she would then have graduated from it, having earned the right to move on to another lesson elsewhere.

If she ran away from the position in a huff, she would not be free of the traits *within* her that made her uncomfortable. It is necessary to see that the problem was not in the job, but in *her*. The job was just what it was, and she was reacting to it according to her outlook. It was especially obvious that the problem was hers because she disliked *everyone* and *everything* about the job; she was looking at it through dark glasses.

We may say of a challenging job or relationship, "I am free . . . I can leave if I like!" Certainly we may leave, but more than likely, in the next job, or the one after it, or the one after that, we will encounter the same problems over the same issues, with even greater intensity. The process will continue until we stand up to the situation, face it, and conquer it. The freedom that we feel by leaving a difficult situation is fool's freedom; the freedom that we gain by conquering it is God's.

Hilda often speaks of such challenges as "logs" — inner obstacles of unconsciousness that we cannot sidestep or squirm under — precisely because we must master these particular lessons in order to grow to our full stature.

We must place the log on the block of faith, split it with the wedge of determination, and break it apart with the axe of courage; nothing less will do. As the old song goes:

> So high, can't get over Him
> So low, can't get under Him
> So wide, can't get 'round Him
> Gotta go through the door

The door is none other than that of Love's peaceful kingdom. The common person sees only the log and bemoans a dead-end path. The visionary — the one who holds a constant memory of her or his Divine Goal — sees the log as the marker of a hidden treasure, and knows that God always has the ability to remove obstacles that fear cannot.

"Grace is given you in your hour of trial. Those who understand the opportunity in adversity have discovered a secret that greatly hastens your homeward journey. Go further, go further, go further, Children, in your understanding of life's hardships, until you find the jewel.

Be not hasty to judge or flee from that which troubles you. The situation has been given you for your education. Would you flee from a lesson in a class that you requested for your improvement? Accept what is given in the spirit that it is offered, and your learning shall proceed well.

You attract to you the events, persons, and experiences required for your growth. Blame not God, the world, or your brother for your predicament, for you, of your own free will, have drawn these circumstances to you for your betterment. It is this betterment that we hold dear to us, for of it you become free to serve the gentle purpose of Love.

Open your heart to the struggles of your brethren, but do not let your compassion be tainted by sympathy. You best serve one another by affirming your constant abiding in God's Perfect Presence. Remain firm in the midst of chaos, see sorrow with Divine eyes, and find God in seeming misfortune.

You are, each of you, a healer. As your purity of intention makes you a vessel for His Will to heal, He will brighten the world through you. This is the intention of all who live to serve humanity, and you, who would freely choose to make it your intention, are blessed in your choice.''

The Path

"All paths are the same: they lead nowhere . . . There are paths going through the bush, or into the bush. In my own life I could say I have traversed long, long paths, but I am not anywhere. My benefactor's question has meaning now. Does this path have a heart? If it does, the path is good; if it doesn't, it is of no use. Both paths lead nowhere; but one has a heart, the other doesn't. One makes for a joyful journey; as long as you follow it, you are one with it. The other will make you curse your life. One makes you strong; the other weakens you."

— Don Juan, in Carlos Castenada's *The Teachings of Don Juan*

ACTION

Pray with your feet moving.

The awareness of God is useless unless it is put into action in the affairs of daily life. Martin Luther King, Jr. said, "I have been to the mountaintop and seen the Promised Land" — and he chose to return. He came back to march. Indeed, we can march effectively only when we have been to the mountaintop — to the high perspective from which we see how Divinely our world could work — and then returned to bring that vision into expression.

Life is about harmonizing our human relationships, conducting business with integrity, and loving. Meditation, prayer, and spiritual discipline are worthwhile only if our overall life gets better. If it doesn't, we are not praying or meditating properly. There must be consistency between meditation and action. To love God in prayer and then to criticize our neighbor is not consistent. To see the same God in meditation and in the bus driver is the affirmation of God in real life.

To the enlightened, or God-realized person, all of life is an opportunity to see God and to put God into action. There are no ups or downs, no comings or goings. One evening, at the end of a group meditation, Hilda asked me to sing a song. I had gone very "high" in meditation, and I slightly resisted "coming down." Hilda perceptibly picked this up and commented, "Poor Alan; he thinks he has to come down to sing — he doesn't know that he doesn't have to come down." She was teaching that had I not kept a separation in my mind between meditation and singing, I would not have been jarred by the transition

— a transition which I created in my own mind.

During another guided meditation, a very sweet and etheric one, Hilda was leading us through an exquisitely lovely image of a garden. In the middle of a sentence, Hilda interrupted this picture of Heaven to announce a meeting after class. I immediately felt annoyed that she would bring such a mundane topic into the midst of such a "spiritual" experience. Her next sentence was: "Were any of you kids disturbed by that announcement? I wasn't — *everything* is God, to me."

We do not need to go off to a cave and renounce the world as a recluse, although there may be a time for retreating to do inner work. We do not need to sit for long hours in lotus position. We may simply sit in quiet prayer or meditation for twenty minutes, once or twice a day, and attune ourselves with our Ideals, which will later bear fruit in action. Jack Schwarz, a well known teacher and healer, describes meditation as "charging your batteries." He says, "If a car battery is run down, you simply jump it or recharge it, and then you use the car. If you keep charging it after it is energized, you begin to waste energy and you miss out on using the car for its intended purpose — action."

There was a man who would arise each morning before dawn and go to a certain spot in the woods, where he would sit quietly and make contact with his Divine Source. Then he would talk to the flowers and they would reveal their secrets to him. Then, when he had established his deep connection with God and all creation, he would enter his day's activity and create new ways to beautify the world through living things and to make practical use of the gifts they offer humankind. This man was Dr. George Washington Carver. Dr. Carver was a living example of a masterful balance between inner communion and outer expression. He said, "*Pray as if it all depends on God, but work as if it all depends on you.*"*

Paramahansa Yogananda was another who found God in the earth as well as the heavens. In his marvelous book, *The Law Of Success*, Yogananda teaches,

> *Before embarking on important undertakings, sit quietly,*
> *calm your senses and thoughts, and meditate deeply. You*

---

*For a most inspiring account of Dr. Carver's life, read *The Man Who Would Talk To The Flowers*, by Glenn Clark, Macalester Park Publishing Co., 1511 Grant Ave., St. Paul, MN 55105

will then be guided by the great creative power of Spirit.
After that you should utilize all necessary material means
to achieve your goal. **

The aim of meditation practice is to learn to be able to meditate
all the time — not just when sitting with eyes closed, but right in the
mainstream of life: in the family, in the office, and at the supermarket.
God is to be found in silence, but He is also knowable while taking the
kids to Hebrew school, negotiating for a higher salary, and cleaning
the bathtub. The idea is to remember Who We Are — *wherever we*
are.

Our best opportunitites to practice the presence of God are in the
situations in which we don't think He is. Alan Watts said, "If you can't
meditate in a boiler room, you can't meditate!" Real learning consists
of remaining calm, peaceful, and aware of God in situations which
once made us nervous, upset, or afraid. As a teenager, I used to perform an ancient and very sacred ceremony in my synagogue on important holidays. According to my lineage, I was required to stand
before the entire congregation and sing a blessing to everyone in the
temple. The first time I did it, I was never so uptight in all my life. I
made an error, and all the learned men went wild. I wanted to jump
into the ark and hide. It was a horror movie for me.

The next time the holiday came around, I wished I could change
my last name. But I felt it was my duty to go through with it, and so I
did. I continued like this for a few years, dreading the ceremony, but
doing it anyway, and being pretty much out of focus through the
whole thing. (If God was blessing the congregation through me, He
sure had to find a way to do it in spite of me!) Then, one time, for just
a few seconds, I actually felt relaxed during the ritual! What a wonderful feeling of freedom! I was astonished to see that I could do this thing
and keep my cool! After that, the ceremony became easier and easier
for me each succeeding time, and eventually it was even enjoyable.
Through practice, I learned to remember my inner peace — meditate
— in the midst of a "threatening" situation. This is exactly the
awareness that we come into the world to develop: to know, through
experience, that we need not lose our peace in any situation, and that

**Yogananda, *THE LAW OF SUCCESS*. The address for Yogananda's writings is given on the copyright page of this
book.

when we find God within our own heart, we find Her everywhere.

We pretty well know that if we clear our mind, we can bring order to our affairs; when our mind is clear, our room automatically becomes tidy, our car runs efficiently, and our checkbook is balanced. What many people are not aware of, however, is that *we can use our affairs to clear our mind.* If we make the effort to smooth out our bedspread, to sit down and tackle our checkbook until it is balanced, or to clean out the back closet, we will find our mind also organized, almost as if we sat down to meditate. This is so because in order to bring our affairs into alignment we must mobilize the state of mind to accomplish it. In other words, we are using life's "little" acts as a means to bring clarity to us.

This places what we do during the day in a whole new light. It means that *everything is a way to discover and express God.* It means that jobs and relationships and the eleven o'clock news are all good, for they are all opportunities to practice being conscious. And so it doesn't matter so much what we do, then; the crucial issue is the *consciousness that we bring to what we do.* I heard of a bank vice-president who "dropped out" and went on a spiritual quest. He threw away his grey suits, became a vegetarian, made a pilgrimage to India, studied with learned pundits and sages, and went through many experiences and lessons. One day about ten years later, he was walking down a street in his old home town when one of his former colleagues saw him and offered him his old job, which just happened to be open at the time. The man pondered for a moment and thought, "Why not?" and so he returned to his job. He had learned that no job is better than another; the important element is the *awareness* that we keep while doing the job. In fact, practicing God's Presence is our only real job, no matter what the company's job description says. Our only real company is Truth, and it is God Incorporated.

We have all come to earth for a reason — to learn the lessons that the earth has to teach, and to bless the world through sharing (through our being and our actions) what we have learned. To desist from action is to miss or delay our opportunity to bless, and to go into action with God in mind is to bring God directly into the world to serve it. As Hilda once said, *"Real meditation begins when you open your eyes."*

"The path of purposeful action bears a double blessing for those who walk it: in the blessing of the world is your own. Right action is the key to the reestablishment of God consciousness within your world.

Errors must be corrected according to their own nature. The world has lost the awareness of God in its actions, and so it is through action that awareness must be restored. Find for yourself a comfortable balance of stillness and activity, and serve the world from such a point of equalibrium.

Be not concerned about the form that your action should take. Your expression will unfold naturally. Simply love God, hold to your purest intentions, and remain true to your inner Light. In this consciousness shall your place be made known to you without question. The miracle of right action is its willingness to spring forth from good intention.

Let your deeds speak your message to the world. Your actions have the power to heal. This is a responsibility of great and wonderful magnitude. It is your only responsibility, and it is the easiest one, for when you choose the responsibility to heal the world, you instantly allow God to heal the world through you. This is your role as a messenger of Light."

INTEGRITY

If you can keep your head while all about you are losing
theirs and blaming it on you . . .
— Rudyard Kipling, *IF*

The confused purposes of the world would dissuade the spiritual aspirant from remaining as dear to Truth as Truth remains to him. Integrity is like a high rock above which the stormy ocean of worldly troubles cannot rise. The spiritual path is a razor's edge odyssey, fraught with temptation and pitfalls that become more subtle as the winding mountain road advances toward the summit. When our hearts and our vision remain fixed on the Light of God, however, we pass unscathed through the mire of delusion and adversity.

Sir Thomas More, nobly portrayed in *A Man for All Seasons*, was faced with intense pressure to abandon his code of ethics. He was perhaps the only man in England who stood for his beliefs while pressed to uphold an unscrupulous king. His position, his family, and his life were under threat of death. In a ploy to persuade More to sign an oath of allegiance, one of his colleagues asked him, "Why don't you just do it for the sake of comradery?" More's response: "When you go to Heaven for following your conscience, and I go to hell for not following mine, will you then join me there, 'for the sake of comradery?' "

Every day, each one of us is given a thousand little opportunities to choose between peace and turmoil, between clarity and confusion, between love and animosity. I am speaking now about remaining quiet, firm, and loving in the midst of our daily activities. We may

257

never be the only person in a kingdom to stand for Truth, as did Sir —
Saint — Thomas More, but we can bless the world by remaining
peaceful in all that we do.

We live in a world of multifarious thoughts — all around us are
thoughts, thoughts, and more thoughts. We must deal not only with
our own thoughts, but with those of the people around us. Life in "the
marketplace" is largely a matter of maintaining our center — our integrity — in the midst of chaotic influences. If we are not careful, we
can lose touch with our center, and we will have to work to regain it.
If we enter activity with a strong and prepared attitude, however, we
serve ourselves and all those we meet.

I once went to a workshop called "How to keep other people from
stealing your energy." Actually, no one can steal our energy from us
unless we give it to them. And no one is purposely seeking to steal our
energy — everyone is just vibrating according to their own evolution.
It is true, however, that we can lose our *awareness* of our inner Light
by accepting negative thoughts from the outside world. The moment
we go into agreement with a thought of evil, sickness, or victimization, we have sold out our knowledge of Truth for the sake of an illusion.

This illusion is a *practically* real force in the world. It is not really
real, but there is a belief that it is real, and that belief is enough to
make is *seem* real. If everyone in the world woke up tomorrow and
had no belief in evil, that would be the end of evil. The "devil" would
starve to death. On one *Star Trek* episode, a malignant force invaded
the Starship Enterprise and wreaked havoc by instilling fear and
dissension among the crew. As a sense of threat and animosity grew,
so did chaos. Someone finally discovered that the negative force was
feeding on fear. So Dr. McCoy gave the entire crew a laughing serum
that made them happy for just a few minutes, and the invader was
forced to leave the ship. It had nothing to which to attach itself. There
were no organisms upon which it could leech, like a parasite. No one
accepted evil, and evil died.

In Truth, it never lived, not on the Starship Enterprise, nor on the
Starship Earth. Its illusion is maintained only by erroneous belief in it.
When we refuse to accept untruth, it can hold no power over us. In the
parable of *Ulysses*, Circe the witch turns all of Ulysses' crew into pigs
so she can keep Ulysses her captive. When he discovers this, Ulysses
firmly points at her and commands, "You turn my men back into their

right form right now!" He says it with such conviction and in such a powerful way that she just has to do it. She just has to. The strength of Light is always more powerful than the assumed strength of darkness.

In the same way, we can free ourselves and each other of negation by refusing to accept it when it comes toward us. If someone sends you a C.O.D. package that you did not order, and you do not accept it, it goes back to the factory. If you accept it, you have to pay for it. A hand can only clap if there is another hand to meet it. If there is no hand to meet it, there is no sound. If we do not meet someone's negative thinking with like thoughts, the negation will fizzle out. One day, for example, a friend of mine saw me when she was in a caustic mood. She complained about everything. I was in such a joyous mood that I just could not take her seriously, and I began to joke with her about all the things she was complaining about. Before long, she, too, was laughing. A few hours later, she came to me and said, "I just want to thank you for not taking me seriously; laughing about my complaints was exactly what I needed to get me off of them."

There is another way that we can lose our center. It is through curiosity. There is a very useful kind of curiosity that prods us on to explore, investigate, and discover, but there is also a wasteful form of curiosity that dissipates our mental energies. Too often, I am tempted to tune into casual conversations, to listen to the talk in the next room, or to pick up any old magazine on the coffee table. Unmanaged curiosity is a lack of mental mastery, and it causes us to lose our balance and veer from our own path. Just as the physical body can become obese and the emotional body can get "played out," the mental body can become disturbed by tuning into unnecessary and extraneous thought-forms. Let us concentrate on that which is ours, and leave the rest be. Curiosity simply draws an overload of purposeless thoughts into our consciousness, and we are then required to meditate, sleep more, or to do something to cleanse us of that which is not ours.

That which *is* ours is given to us only when we are willing to claim it. Like positive thinking and appreciation, we must work at remembering and acting on the Truth, and this is what integrity is all about. There is much agreement on illusion. At every turn, there are thought-forms of emptiness and sorrow. The only way to overcome illusion is with our own affirmation of the reality and the fullness of Love. Like a vampire that shrinks away from light or a cross, negativity

259

flees when confronted with integrity.

We have been empowered with the greatest weapon there is — Truth. No bomb, no hatred, and no illusion can match the strength of Truth. It is our only real friend. When we stand for Truth, we are integrated, whole, and firm. We can walk amid any darkness, totally protected and assured of safety. We can "march into hell for a heavenly cause." Our love can dry the tears of the world. We can end wars and sorrows and the travails of those whose lives have been laden with pain. The entire universe is integrated and whole. When we remain true to integrity, we are aligned with the Force of the entire universe. When we walk with integrity, we walk with God.

"You who have been touched by the scepter of the living God must walk in the Light of the One who has bestowed upon you the blessing of His lineage. Integrity is your fortress and your redeemer, and, yea, the redeemer of the world. Christ Himself was the embodiment of Integrity, and in so being is rightly called the Son of God.

The path of life is difficult and treacherous only when you agree with the illusions with which the world seeks to maintain itself. Shun illusion for a moment, and you stand free of it forever. In that moment of freedom, you inherit eternal life, which is already yours.

We who encourage you to walk the path of righteousness, promise to stand by your side in your journey. As you remain true to integrity, Light shall be revealed to you in great splendor, the selfsame Light that you see in your most holy dreams. Begin by accepting the vision of Holiness in your heart. This is your only real vision. All others shall pass away, but the Vision of the Heart remains until the end of form.

Walk with dignity, Sons and Daughters of Truth. In this holy life, you have been given all that you have ever truly desired — the knowledge of your own sanctity, and that of all life. Remain confident in the reality of Love, and you shall not — you cannot — fail. All the holy saints, masters, and angels gladly sing with you in the chorus of happiness that was composed at the beginning of time. Alleluia and Amen."

COURAGE

Those who step forward to make a stand for Truth must be prepared to be spurned by the world from which they once enjoyed support. The world loves its own, but finds great threat in those who trust not in it. The call of the new life means the surrender of our desire to be accepted and approved by those from whom we received nurturing in the past. We may lose our old friends; we will get new ones. Our families may discourage us; our hearts will encourage us. People in the world may criticize what we are doing; all the saints and holy masters who love the Truth will love us. We may lose our earthly inheritance; we will gain all the riches in the universe. We may have to give up our old thoughts of who we are; we will know who we really are. We will no longer belong to the world; we will belong to God.

I recently attended a Catholic wedding of two very dear friends. The moment came when we were invited to line up for Holy Communion. I love receiving Communion. I don't know whether or not the wafer really turns into the body of Christ, but I pray and imagine that through the ceremony I am receiving the Holy Spirit of Christ. I consider it a great blessing.

At this wedding, sitting next to me (ironically) were the Jewish parents of one of my oldest friends, with whom I was very involved in Orthodox Judaism. The father is the president of the synagogue. For quite a few years, I used to visit their home on the sabbath, and they knew me as a very strict Orthodox Jew. These fine people were very kind to me, and I was treated as one of the family. Now, here I am, ten years later, deeply in love with Jesus, thrilled at the opportunity to take Holy Communion. It was as if my past were sitting at my right hand, and my future beckoning at my left.

I felt that these people might be hurt or upset if they saw me line up for Communion. Here was my moment of truth. Actually, there was no question about it. As I rose from my seat I could sense their thoughts of shock and disappointment. My heart was beating heavily, and I could feel the perspiration on my brow. But I had to do what I had to do. At that moment I had to let die all of my thoughts about who I was, in relation to those people. Though I loved and respected them as fully as I ever did, I had to be true to the promptings of my spiritual heart and trust that God would take care of me if I followed my inner call. I had to make a stand for my values.

Every one of us is faced with such a moment of truth at each step of our evolutionary unfoldment. Some would call these moments tests, others, challenges, and some would embrace them as invitations born of Grace. Every spiritual aspirant is given the opportunity — a fork in the road — to let go of an old pattern of living, and to accept a new and glorious one.

The opportunity always takes the form of clear cut earth plane choice. It may be a chance for a physical pleasure or some kind of ego temptation, such as for power, money, or some long-standing personal weakness in the form of a desire. The test always presents the aspirant with the choice of saying "Yes" to one action and "No" to another. In such a circumstance, God uses the physical world to manifest a situation that symbolizes the dynamics of our inner evolution.

When we do choose to step forward toward our higher life, there are masters, saints, angels, and enlightened beings who extend their helping hands to draw us up to a richer and more fullfilling station in our life's journey. It is said that "when you take one step toward God, He takes ten toward you." A friend of mine, for example, who had been shoplifting for a long time, began to want to "clean up his act." He wanted to stop stealing, but this shoplifting had become habitual for him, and he was afraid he would never be able to stop. He told me this story:

> One day I went to the mall to get a needle for my stereo. I walked into Radio Shack, picked out the needle, and went to the counter to pay for it. Just at that moment, the salesman turned his back to get something off a shelf. My

first inclination was to slip the needle into my pocket and walk out. No one at all would have seen me. But there was a part of me that did not want to take it, a feeling that I wanted to change my life. I stood there for a little while, torn. It was as if I was being pulled in two directions at once. Then I decided to try, just this once, paying for something I could have easily stolen. So I waited for the salesman to turn around, and I paid him. At that moment I felt such a wave of relief come over me that I can't even describe it in words. Something happened within me — something that was much bigger than my little decision not to steal that one needle. Since that time I have not stolen anything, and I don't really want to.

If you are struggling with a bad habit, like my friend, do not be overwhelmed by the enormity of it, for *you do not have to conquer all of it yourself.* God will help you. This I promise you. All you have to do is your share, which is to make an initial effort. When, with your good intention, you open the door to help, God will pour into you His Will, which can conquer anything. At the point that you take that one step in a new direction, you have mastered the old habit or trait that was retarding your progress. Having passed your test, you will no longer be faced with that particular trial, except, perhaps, in the form of "fried seeds" — old desires that occasionally arise but which do not have life in them sufficient to reproduce themselves. These obsolete desires are simply the residue of past thought patterns which can no longer entrap us, but which we must patiently bear, like the ripples of water created by a stone that we have thrown into a pond. You may experience fleeting desires to do an old bad habit, but they are nothing more than old thoughts that will eventually fizzle out.

The source of courage is *conviction*. Conviction is the powerful inner knowledge that what we are doing is good, an awareness unassailable by any opinion or persuasion. Conviction is crystalized faith, and courageous acts are the natural expression of conviction.

To the world, the person of conviction is a fool, a martyr, an ascetic. To the faithful, sacrifice is meaningless; the joy of following the promptings of the soul far outshines the meager loss that the world bemoans. The world labels the acts of a saint as sacrifice only because these are threatening to the treasures the world holds dear. If there is no fear of loss, there is no consciousness of sacrifice. Ramana Maharshi said, "I didn't feel like eating, and they said I was fasting!" And once, when I thanked Hilda for interrupting her lunch to talk with me, she smiled and told me, "That's fine, darling . . . the blessing has to go through me to you . . . so I get a blessing, too."

Wayshowers are indifferent to opinion because they know they are walking the path of destiny. When Helen and Scott Nearing established their self-sufficient homestead in Vermont, they were branded renegades, weirdos, and Communists. Despite intense criticism, they burned wood for heat, ate organic foods, did not smoke cigarettes, recycled their materials, bartered, and shared their abundance; they called it *The Good Life.*

Now, some fifty years later, much of what they stood for has become the forefront of the society to be. We have discovered that the earth's resources are limited, the chemicals in our food are poisons, and that sharing and joyous living are, indeed, the way that God intended for us to live happily on this planet. I once asked Helen: "How does it feel now that society is coming around to your way of thinking? All the things that you were chastised for are now accepted and popular; I'll bet you're happy to see this confirmation."

Helen's response: "It's nice that other people are doing it, but, to tell you the truth, if no one else ever did what we did, it would not make one bit of difference to us. We did what we did because we knew that it was right for us, and that was enough reason for it."

There was a saint named Mansur Mastana who discovered a Light and a Reason more powerful than he could find in the world. Swami Muktananda tells this story about him:

> He used to soar in the inner spaces, and he saw the highest truth right there. He began to say, "Anahalaq, Anahalaq, I am God, I am God, the truth is within me, the truth is within me, I am in the midst of truth, and the truth is in my midst!" He began to dance, "I have found it, I have found it, I have got it, I have got it!" The orthodox clerics, who never understand a thing, got after him, accusing him of uttering blasphemous heresy, and Mansur said, "I do not mean to utter heresy. I am only speaking the truth which I have experienced directly. From that, an

understanding has spontaneously arisen within: I am not this body; I am the same divine light of which the whole cosmos is an extension." He continued, "You may break a mosque, you may break a temple, you may break any holy place, but you must not break the human heart, because there the Lord Himself dwells. Inside a temple you worship an idol, inside a mosque you worship the void, but in the temple of the heart, the divine light is scintillating, sparkling all the time, and that is the true house of the Lord."

Because he said this, he was hanged, and he proclaimed the same truth even from the hanging noose. From there he began to shout, "Fling [your idols] into the water. Go around fearlessly proclaiming 'I am God, I am God, I am God!' "*

There is no power in the universe that can stand between courage and its expression.

*Swami Muktananda, *Getting Rid of What You Haven't Got*, S.Y.D.A. Foundation, San Francisco, 1967.

"Your moment of decision is inevitable and it is shared by all: you must bear witness to the Truth or silently consent to the perpetration of a lie.

You are asked but to let go of a meaningless life, one which always seemed to offer peace, but delivered only emptiness. When you testify to the whisperings of your deepest inclinations, the life of Light is opened before you. This new life, unlike the old, hides not behind the promise of peace, but justifies itself in the constant giving of serenity. The brotherhood of the peaceful is small in number, but great in reward. Those who would enter its ranks must renounce the dark cloak of the burdens of the world and receive in their stead the white robes of the community of Light.

As you give assent to God, your old treasures wither like the leaves of autumn. Fear not, Children of Light, for what is God's shall most certainly be returned to you in great abundance, and what is no longer yours shall bear you no further need or pleasure. When you are willing to confess that your love for God is greater than that for the world, a helping hand of brilliant light is extended to you. At the same time, there will be a clutching, a grabbing at your feet by a thousand grey and bony fingers, in the guise of old friends, habits, and excitements. These promptings are not real, but mere shadows of a myth to which you no longer give credence. Unnourished by your further indulgence, must they crumble into dust.

The new life that awaits you is one of splendor and richness. The rooms of your new mansion are filled with morning sunlight, and its windows open upon lush gardens and the sweet song of the nightingale. You have consciously renounced your dark dungeon of self, with its empty corridors and long stairways that lead to nowhere. You have released yourself from the prison of self-involvement and accepted your freedom as the child of the master of a great and wonderous estate. You have assented to your Divinity, a happy re-union of all that is beautiful, lovely, and true.

If you would take this courageous step, the only step worth taking, you must be prepared to be rejected by the world. You must not fall under mockery and misunderstanding. You must, in turning your back upon illusions, be prepared to have them scream into your ear in the name of their self-justification. You must have the holy courage to walk the path of the lonely and the exiled. You must take up a simple tunic in place of the vanity of the world, and walk barefoot through the snows of the remote mountains where dwell those who no longer belong to the world. Your only guide will be the footprints in the snow, quietly yet firmly impressed by the saints who have trod this narrow, winding path before you.

Yet in your travail shall you be urged ever onward by the mysteriously beautiful call of the conch, sounding ever clearer, drawing you to its source at the summit just beyond the clouds. There shall you find the humble home of the brotherhood whose faint whisperings to your sleeping heart awoke it and drew you to your lonely journey, now so near completion.

Reunited with your brothers and sisters in Truth, in the simplicity of a remote mountain village, the promptings of your soul are revealed to you as the worthwhile source of your long trek through the wilderness. You may then cast away your walking stick and stand forever free of the hardship of the illusion of abandonment. Here your rightful place in the community of souls is confirmed. Here are you shown the holy plan for the unfoldment of your perfection, which in the valley seemed a great enigma, yet here at the summit reveals itself to be Divine.

Take heart, then, in your labors, for the conclusion of your story has now been told to you. As you make it your own, you earn the right to work humbly for the cause of Divine Love, and in so choosing draw your searching brothers and sisters to their home in the community of the peaceful. They now follow the footsteps that you have etched in the Himalayan snows. Verily, their rooms in the golden mansion await them, and it is your privilege to usher them in to the Abode of Peace.''

GUIDANCE

Guru, God, and Self are One
— Neem Karoli Baba

Whenever I have needed guidance, God has never failed to give it. For any question I have asked in earnestness and sincerity, an answer has come. It is not always an answer that I want to hear, or that I expect to hear, or that I understand, and it does not always come immediately, but it is always one that works. This process is a miracle to me, and I have come to see that every human being is endowed with the same Divine gift.

Guidance is always available. We need only to *ask, listen,* and *accept.* The wisest counselor is your very Self. No guru, teacher, therapist, or psychic could ever know more about your path than God will tell you directly. The answers to our questions are waiting within us to be retrieved like precious pearls at the ocean floor. We do not need to seek any further than our own heart, the temple in which God Himself eternally dwells.

If you ask for an answer, do not dictate to your higher self where or when or how the answer is to be given. We never really know in what way guidance will come; we just need to know that it will. Paul had invested a lot of energy working *against* the teachings of Jesus when he was literally knocked off his horse by the Holy Spirit. And I love the process in *Close Encounters of the Third Kind,* which I saw as a metaphor for the spiritual path. The hero is obsessed with the vague image of a mountain, being communicated to him psychically by benevolent U.F.O. friends, who are instructing him how to contact them. He feels an undeniable urge to know what that mountain is, but he just can't seem to understand it. He starts to see this form in his shaving cream, in his mashed potatoes, and he is even driven to build a mountain in his living room. He just has to understand this image, but he is at a loss as to how to do it. Finally, in desperation, frustration, and exhaustion, he gives up and writes his intuition off as a pipe dream. Exactly at that moment, there flashes on the television a news report showing the exact mountain, complete with location, that he has intuitively been searching for — or, which has been searching for him. The guidance came — in its own right way and right timing.

The inner guide is sometimes called the "still, small voice." It is not really a voice that speaks in words, although we may sometimes hear the answer in the form of words. It is more of a quiet knowing. It does not rant, rave, chide, or dictate. It just knows, feels, and gently nudges us in the direction of our highest good. Some call it the conscience, and that is what it is. I used to associate "conscience" with guilt and the fiery wrath of God. Now I see that our conscience is the most helpful and loving friend that we have in this life. The still small voice will always tell us right from wrong, but it will never disown or condemn us for making an error. It is dedicated only to our happiness, and no matter what errors we have made, it will continue to guide us, even telling us how to undo the errors that we made in not having hearkened to its original gentle bidding.

I was recently told a remarkable story about the power of intuition. A tai chi* student was driving on a mountain highway when she decided to try out some of the principles that she had been learning. She took a few deep breaths and found her inner center of energy. At that moment, she felt a strange urge to pull off the highway and drive slowly on the shoulder of the road. Though her thoughts were ranting, "This is crazy; why don't you drive like a normal person?" she followed her intuition. Then, as she pulled around the next bend, she came upon an auto collision — right in the lane in which she *would have been* driving had she not listened to her intuitive prompting. Yet she escaped, thanks to her inner guidance — and her willingness to accept it.

I know, too, of a man who, when he has a troubling situation in

---

*an ancient Oriental form of moving meditation

his life, takes a glass of water before he goes to sleep, and affirms, "I am drinking the solution to my problem!" He inevitably wakes up with the answer. I do not believe there is any magic in the water, but I do believe that there is a great resource of inner knowledge that is released within him when he opens himself to it. Such is the nature of our Divine Guide. It happily offers its help to us through any channel that we find comfortable.

Nothing is too small to be undeserving of God's help. So many times I have misplaced a key, or I have the gnawing feeling that I have forgotten something, and I stop for just a moment and say, "O.K., God, can you give me a hand?" Wonderously, into my mind flashes the thought of the hall closet or a jacket that I wore last week, where, when I check, the object is right there. I remember, too, that several years ago, during a gas shortage, I needed to get to an important meeting one morning. The night before the meeting, I realized I would need to get gas before setting out, and I had no idea where to go for it. Around 5 a.m., in sort of a half-dream half-awake state, I had the feeling of Satya Sai Baba come to me and say, "Go to Hess!" To the Hess Station I went, and took my place as one of the first cars in a gas line at a station that was just about to open.

I have no idea how God knows what She knows, but She sure does know it. She will tell us anything we need to know. When I massage someone's back, for example, my hands are somehow drawn to the exact place where there is a kink or a knot, the spot that needs the most attention. The person does not tell me where to put my hands, nor do I search for the spot. The hands just go there almost automatically, and the person says, "Wow! How did you know that was the spot?" The truth is that I didn't know, but God was kind enough to show me. A printer friend of mine told me a similar story. He explained that, although he rarely reads the copy of what he is printing, if there is a slight error on the page, his eye will somehow be drawn right to it for correction. And a chemistry teacher told me that his students cannot figure out how he can mark all of their test papers overnight. He says, "I just lightly scan the whole paper. Although it is full of complex equations and numbers, if there is a mistake, it just sort of 'pops out' at me."

Guidance may also come through the mouth of another person. There is no real distinction between inner and outer guidance. We divide the universe into "inners" and "outers," but God is One, and all of life is inner as well as outer. Sri Ramakrishna tells a most practical story of two men who were walking through a pasture, when a wild bull began to charge at them. One man jumped up in a tree, while the other cockily stood right in the bull's path. "Come on up in the tree, you fool!" the first man cried, "You'll be killed!"

"Don't worry about me!" the other answered, "The Lord will protect me!"

The bull continued his charge, butted the man in the posterior, and left him bedraggled on the ground.

The man in the tree jumped down and chided, "I told you you should have come up in the tree with me!"

"I can't understand it," complained the wounded one. "I thought for sure that the Lord would take care of me!"

"He *was* trying to help you, you idiot!" the other explained. "Didn't you hear him calling to you from the tree?!"

When we allow ourselves to be open to *all* avenues of God's guidance, we find Him *everywhere*. Whenever someone tells Hilda a story, or suggests a book, or asks her a question, she responds as if the Lord Himself were offering her a teaching. We may consider all people to be our teachers — some teach us what to do and some teach us what *not* to do — not so much by their words, but by their actions. If I see an error that someone else has made, and I can apply it to myself to avert a potential error of my own, I feel I have been given a great grace. And I have gained much from watching the selfless service and loving kindness rendered by others. Surely this is God's way of guiding me. I may not be a Moses, like Charlton Heston, and have the ten commandments etched on a stone right before my eyes, but I see God's lessons in action in the "little" experiences of everyday life, and He is continually etching His Truth, in the form of love, in my heart.

In order to make ourselves available to receive guidance, we must keep the mind clear and the emotions quiet. We should not ask the still, small voice to have to compete with chattering thoughts and turbulent feelings. Picture a man, wanting and waiting for an airplane to land, running up and down the runway, waving his arms and yelling, "Come on, land! . . . Here I am! . . . Hurry up and land!" The irony is that the plane can land only when the man gets off the runway and allows the plane to set itself down without obstruction. When we worry, aggravate ourselves, or get upset, we block the path of our own perfect guidance, which is ready and willing to help us just as soon as we make space for it.

The idea of "I don't know" is a deception of the ego, which thrives on thoughts and feelings of separateness. Such an idea divides the Unity of the universe into two parts: a great field of knowledge of answers and solutions, and "me," who is outside that knowledge. We are, in Truth, whole and holy beings. The entire history and future of the universe are etched into our souls. We are inseparably one with the whole of God, and we could never, ever be outside of the wealth of His deepest wisdom.

Sooner or later, we must admit that we really do know, because God is always willing to tell us what we need to know. Usually when we say, "I don't know," we are actually saying, "I don't want to know," or "I don't want to deal with this issue." When I have worked with human relations programs, for example, if someone is asked a question about him or herself and they respond, "I don't know," I would ask them, "If you had to take a guess, what would you say?" Usually they then discover an answer that proves to be very accurate. This method often clears up a tough issue for them, and demonstrates that they held the key to their answers within themselves all the time, but were not ready — or willing — to use it.

There is a wonderful story about a psychiatrist who sees many patients throughout the day. Each one walks into his office with a long face, depressed and burdened. After a fifty-minute session, each patient emerges from the office, happy and beaming, gratefully shaking the therapist's hand, eager to make another appointment for next week. At the end of the day, the psychiatrist calls his secretary over the intercom and tells her, "O.K., Gertrude, you can bring me my hearing aid now!" He hadn't heard a word they said! — but they needed to unburden themselves, and to feel they were listened to and cared for.

There is a tendency for some to consult psychics, spirit guides, or discarnate entities for guidance. We must be very discerning when dealing in the realms of the occult or spirit worlds. It is possible to take a detour off the path, into the psychic worlds, leaning outward and copping out by placing the responsibility for our lives in the hands of a dead relative. Ram Dass said, "If Uncle Joe was a pretty run of the mill guy in life, not knowing much more than about driving a cab, what makes you think that now that he's dead, he'll be able to give you answers like the Oracle of Delphi?" Hilda says, too, that dead people, like alive people, just love to offer advice, whether or not they know what they're talking about. So we may ask, and we may get an answer, but we must always remember that there is no power or wisdom outside of the GodSelf that rests within us.

As many people are becoming spiritually awakened, there are many more psychics, mediums, and occult teachers in the marketplace. Some of them are offering a sincere and genuine spiritual service; many are not. If you are inclined to deal in any psychic circles, be extremely careful to accept only that energy which is of pure God. What is psychic is not always spiritual. What is occult is not always uplifting. What is titillating is not always useful. The highest teachers have gone through the psychic, renounced it, and are free to use it when necessary for the upliftment of their students and all humanity. They do not, however, dwell on the psychic, depend on it, or glorify it. As Hilda has said, "Why settle for little powers, when you can have God?"

If spiritual guidance comes to you through an occult person or science, then use it wisely, but do not become enamored with it. All sciences are of God, and let them be used to glorify Him, and not for their own sake. Remember that the finger pointing at the moon is not the moon.

It is a very positive sign that we seek guidance, for it indicates that we have a sense of a worthwhile path that we would like to follow, and that it is important to us to make the correct choice. To realize that guidance is available to us from a Source *within* ourself is the most magnificent awakening of all. It means that God has not deserted us and that He is delighted to help us, for, in Truth, He *is* us. As Jesus said, "It is the Father's good pleasure to give you the Kingdom." Though that would have been sufficient encouragement, Jesus, in His immense love and compassion, told us exactly where to find that treasure: said He, "The Kingdom of Heaven is within."

When we have confidence in our Divinity, we no longer have to "lean out" on someone else as our mentor, counselor, or savior. Hilda has said many times, "You kids look to me for answers unnecessarily . . . When I started on this path I had no teacher but God . . . He told me everything I needed to know." Yes, we may ask for opinions, help, and advice, but we can then take this information and offer it to our inner guide to see if it is the truth and if it will work for us. Our inner voice is the final authority in any question. We can take Jesus or a guru as our savior, but it is only because such a great one has been confirmed by our *inner* savior as genuine. What else but a savior could recognize a savior? And who else but God could recognize God?

"All life contains within it the gift of guidance and instruction. As you learn to look into the elements of creation in the correct way, all of the lessons of the universe make themselves known to you. Your only need is to look into things simply.

The humor of life is the reaching out that you do. You labor under the mistaken notion that someone can offer you more than you can offer yourself. Beloveds, this is not true. God's joy is your fulfillment. His celebration is your independence. His success is your realization.

Do not place God outside of yourself. The wisdom that you seek is but an aspect of your own nature, speaking to you in a form that you will accept, for you have not taken responsibility for wisdom.

There is no secret to wisdom or guidance. It is as obvious as the new morning. You have not seen it fully because you have complicated it with your concepts. As that complication dissolves, so disintegrate the blocks to your recognition of your path. Your heart is your surest source of direction. Those who follow the heart discover Truth."

THE TEACHER

I

When the people called Jesus "Teacher," He reprimanded them, "You should not call anyone 'Teacher,' for you have only One Teacher — your Heavenly Father."

II

As I was driving home from work one evening, I saw a billboard that I had not noticed before. It was a picture of a slender young lady in a leotard, doing a headstand. The caption of the advertisement was, *"You don't have to stand on your head to find a yoga teacher — find it fast in the Yellow Pages."*

This sign stimulated me to think about how far spirituality and spiritual teachers have come in our culture. Years ago it was very unusual for anyone to be involved in any spiritual pursuit outside of the church or temple. When Hilda first set out on the spiritual path, her friends laughed at her, calling her the derogatory name, "Yogi, Yogi, Yogi!" Now "Yogi" is a compliment, mysticism has made it to prime-time television, and courses in the Tarot cards are being taught in public adult education.

Yes, we have come a long way. In the old days, if you had a problem you either went to momma, the minister, or a psychiatrist — and that was it. Now we have our choice of Gurus, Therapists, Trainers, Readers, Facilitators, Mediums, Counselors, Advisers, Effective Listeners, and Consultants. As if these people weren't enough, there are biorhythm machines to tell you your destiny in the lobbies of

279

restaurants, astrological counseling in the daily newspapers, and Dial-a-Meditation, the last four digits of which are 1111. What used to be a gradual spiritual evolution is now an explosion.

This new enthusiasm for spiritual teaching is a wonderful and exciting phenomenon, but at the same time we must deal with the very important question, *What makes someone a teacher*? In the old days, it was easy to figure out: if you had a degree from a state teacher's college or a seminary, you were qualified to tell people how to live. But now it's a new ball game. The tremendous demand for spiritual guidance has attracted to the masses many trustworthy teachers — and many charlatans. It is no longer a cut-and-dried matter to know who is qualified. Now it is possible to become an ordained minister by mailing three dollars to a church in California, and there is a YMCA that offers yoga teachers certification after a one-weekend course. Perhaps these ministers and yogis are qualified; perhaps they are not; but one thing is for sure: a title or a piece of paper means nothing anymore.

How, then, are we to know who to trust? Who is worth listening to? What makes someone able to act as a spiritual guide? These questions are ones that you and I must answer within our own hearts. No longer can we afford to look outward for answers. The benefit of the challenge to find such answers is that we are forced to go within to find the Real Teacher — the Heavenly Father that Jesus spoke of.

As I have been required to discern between genuineness and impurity, there are three criteria that I have found important in assessing the worth of a teacher:

1. Does the teacher awaken your *heart* with a sense of real truth?
2. Does the teacher encourage you to be independent and whole, or does he foster need and dependence on him?
3. Does the teacher live what he is teaching?

When I sit in the presence or hear the words of a real teacher, I have a thrilling experience of Truth, as if I have come home. Many can utter holy words or quote chapter and verse from the Bible, but only one who has mastered the Truth can make us feel something real and important is happening when they speak. They said of Jesus that He was different because He was "one who spoke with authority."

Swami Vivekananda was a great yogi who was guided to come to this country after being with Sri Ramakrishna in India. When he arrived, the Swami was invited to Chicago to speak to a Congress of the Religions. The affair, as it has been described, was a long and boring one; the speakers gave dull and uninspiring speeches over a period of days. Swami Vivekananda was one of the last lecturers on the program. When it was his time to speak, he stood at the podium and powerfully began, "My Brothers and Sisters . . ." Immediately he was interrupted by thunderous applause, wild cheers, and a standing ovation! The audience knew that he was genuine, that he was speaking the Truth with the power of the Holy Spirit — they felt it in their souls.

You may go to a lecture or a seminar, hear many profound words, and be offered spiritual guidance, but if your heart is not awakened in this presence, the teachings are but empty platitudes, and it will do you no good to get involved, except to learn a lesson in discrimination between the genuine and the false. I once went to a workshop by a man who said many true things. He gave a very nice presentation, but there was just something about him that did not feel 100%. He later became well-known, and people would come to me and say, "This man is really great! He is a real healer!" and I wondered if, perhaps, my intuition had been wrong. Months later, the one who had praised him so highly told me some facts about the way he conducts his personal life that confirmed my intuitive misgivings about him and showed me that I was correct in not pursuing his teachings. I am not judging the man, for he is a beautiful soul, but it is my responsibility to assess the purity of his teaching. We cannot afford to settle for less than the whole Truth. In accepting the teachings of any teacher, we must exercise discrimination. The heart, or the inner guide, is the best source of this very important kind of discernment.

Jesus and other masters do their real teaching through *example*. Jesus told the people of the importance of humility and then he lived it by washing the feet of his disciples and by surrendering to His crucifixion. The words mean very little — it is the actions that count. A real teacher can sit in silence and the full teachings are given. Hilda would travel four hours to see Swami Nithyananda, who would look at her for only a few seconds and make a sound. That was it. "In this Presence," Hilda tells, "the teaching and the blessing were complete." Satya Sai Baba, who has millions of disciples, is considered by many to be an avatar — the very embodiment of God. Yet once, when Hilda apologized to him for making a slight error, he replied, "No, it was *my* fault." This kind of simple humility is the real mark of a great one. Sai Baba also says, "My life is my message."

Meher Baba, another great saint, was silent for over twenty-five years of his life. During that time, he traveled throughout India, serving the poor, bathing the lepers, and giving love to all who came to him. I saw a film of his visit to the United States. Those who came for his blessing formed a long line and he gave each one a long, sincere hug as they filed by. This, to me, is worth more than all the words in the bible.

A true teacher encourages students to find God within themselves, and does not foster clinging or dependence on the physical form. He or she will accept no honor, homage, or glory from the students. I have seen swamis given a garland of flowers by their students remove it immediately and place it on an altar, offering it to God. A real teacher avoids worldly power, ego or specialness. Hilda has said, time and time again, "You don't need to come to my classes, kids. If you really understood my message, you could just as easily stay home."*

By contrast, there are many organizations that lead students to believe that they will be lost or suffer the agonies of Hell if they leave the fold of the organization. Any teacher or group that says, "You cannot discover God without me or this organization," is not speaking Truth. When Jesus said, "No man cometh unto the Father but by Me," He was speaking of the "Me" with a capital M. In other words, He was speaking from the point of view of the Holy Spirit, the Christ, with which He was identified and One in consciousness. And the Holy Spirit is certainly not restricted to Christianity. It glows in the heart of every human being and lives within you and me right now.

The only goal of a true teacher is the advancement of the students and the celebration of Truth. Selfish or personal motivations are absent. I was once taking a kind of spiritual correspondance course, receiving monthly lessons from an organization led by a well-known teacher. Then I received in the mail this letter: "Dear student, please do not show anyone else these lessons or divulge their contents,

---

*My friend and professor, Dr. Alfred Gorman, a well-known author, consultant and expert in the field of organizational development, told me: "*A consultant is someone who borrows your watch to tell you what time it is.*"

because they are only for those who have paid for them. If anyone else wants these teachings, please give them our address and ask them to send us a check." That was the end of that correspondance course for me. As I see it, if someone really knows the Truth, they are eager to share it. This does not mean that they are opposed to money or that they reject it; it means that their foremost purpose is to teach the Truth, and they are confident enough in God's providence that they do not need to make any demands upon the students other than their own enlightenment.

Hilda explained it in this way: "The Truth, like clear light, if expressed by a pure teacher, will be seen without distortion, as if through clear glass. If a teacher has any impurity, such as hunger for power, or greed, or lust, the Truth will come through with a taint, as if through colored glass. We must learn to develop our God-given faculty of discrimination to feel the purity of a teacher, an organization, or a path."

If you have had a negative experience with a teacher who turned out to be less than enlightened, do not curse or hold the experience in remorse, but "take the best and leave the rest." Extract from the experience all that you can and be grateful for it. Even if a teacher spoke Truth that they did not live, you can take the words and discover their real meaning for yourself. In this way you have gotten much from the teacher, even though you would not now follow that person. If nothing else, you learned a valuable lesson in discrimination. You see the Truth a little — or a lot — more clearly by discovering what it was *not*.

Do not be bitter about being disillusioned about a person or group in the spiritual game. Just because someone may have spoken or taught falsely about God does not mean that God is false. It just means that the person did not really know God. I know someone who is very bitter about a group that he once surrendered to, which turned out not to be all that it made itself out to be. He now uses his experience as an excuse to denounce spirituality. We cannot look to outside people or groups to represent or give us God. We are obliged and responsible to find Him within our very Self. Then, and only then, are we free.

III

Do not worry about finding your teacher or Guru. If you are

sincere and really want God, your teacher will find you. I have seen this time and time again in my life and in the lives of those around me. We cannot plan how we are going to find a teacher. All you need to do is to make the most of whatever knowledge you already have, and (sometimes in the strangest and most unlikely way) you will be connected with one who can guide you.

One teacher found me in a traffic jam at a raunchy rock concert. Another found me working in a grocery store. And a friend of mine felt like she was at the end of her rope after a stormy break-up with a man, when the only job she could find was as a barmaid. In this bar she met someone who took her to a teacher that completely changed her life. James and John were fishermen and Matthew was a tax-gatherer, all just going about their business when Jesus found them.

We can even receive the grace of a God-teacher who is no longer living in a physical body. The first time I read the New Testament, the words seemed to jump right off the page into my heart, and I felt as if Jesus Christ Himself were speaking directly to me. In your meditation you can make contact with the vibration of any great teacher and receive their blessing just as if they were standing right before you in physical form. This is so because the spiritual path is free of form and not limited by time or space.

Be not anxious about *how* the teacher will come to you. Simply ask the Lord for guidance, do the best you can with what you know, be open to possibilities, and the teacher will be given. And you will be with a teacher for precisely the right amount of time in precisely the right way for your particular evolution. It is a wonderful and fascinating Plan — much bigger than we would expect or can understand.

IV

At some point it is necessary to go beyond the form of a teacher. There is a Buddhist instruction, *"If you meet the Buddha on the road, kill him."* This means that if you see any form which you believe to have more God or more Buddha in it than other forms, you must annihilate this thought from your consciousness. Herman Hesse's Steppenwolf meets a teacher who agrees to give him guidance if he will consent to follow her instructions fully. He agrees and proceeds to grow tremendously through his discipleship. One day she gives him a knife and orders, "Kill me!" He does so, but he is then filled with sorrow and guilt. When he later stands before the heavenly court,

Steppenwolf is found guilty — of not having a sense of humor about "killing the reflection of a woman with the reflection of a knife." He is sentenced to life on earth, to learn to laugh.

The same lesson was lived by Sri Ramakrishna, who was absorbed in the form of the Divine Mother. One day he realized that he would have to go beyond form to truly merge with God. So he took a piece of glass and jabbed it into his forehead, which represents the last strata of form. This was his way of releasing himself from the last attachment.

These stories symbolize the need, at the end of the spiritual path, to renounce all — including that which has brought us to the final point. As the sages instructed, "Give up your lust for growth" and "The last thing to go is God."

If we know how to look at life correctly, *all* of our experiences are our teachers. We must cease to see life as a random play of circumstances and begin to understand that the earth is a school, and all events the lessons. Contantly ask, "What can I learn from this experience? Why was it given to me? How can I use it to further my growth?" If you think in this way, all experiences will bring you closer to understanding yourself and the Truth.

Perhaps the purpose and work of the Teacher can be summarized in this story: One evening after Hilda's class, a young man came up to Hilda and told her, "Tonight I realized that God is within me and that I really do not need you or this class or any teacher or any class . . . It's all within!"

As she heard these words, Hilda's face lit up with a broad smile. She took the man's hand, shook it firmly, and told him, "Congratulations, kid . . . You got the whole idea of my class. I pronounce you graduated!"

"Those who teach in purity are few. Let the aspirant beware of those who claim to teach Truth and do not live it.

A student has the right to stand in judgement of the actions of one who claims to be a teacher. We do not speak of judgement of the soul, but of the reality of the teachings. Let the student discern between the truth that is spoken and Truth that is lived. Never surrender your soul to another person, but always align it with God. You may accept the guidance and instruction of one whom you feel is genuine, but let that decision be dictated by your Godly intuition.

If you would be a teacher, you must be unremitting in your dedication to Truth. You must found your life upon actions, and not upon words. You must give up all notions of teaching. At best, you may speak of your own experience. If you hearken unto these strict requirements, the Holy Spirit will fill you like an earthen vessel, and your life will be under continual guidance. This promise will be verified by your experience.

There is a hierarchy of education of which you are a part. This hierarchy has as its only purpose the uplifting of souls and the salvation of the world. The dedicated souls in this hierarchy are working steadily to shine Truth into the world. In these times of earth changes, Truth and Love are being given in great abundance. Blessed are you who would share in this noble work."

DISCRIMINATION

Discrimination is a lesson of spiritual growth that every single aspirant must master. The ability to distinguish between Truth and falsehood, even on the sublest level, is absolutely essential to one who would stand free of error and extricate the world from painful ignorance. Wisdom is the mark of the learned, but discrimination is the attribute of the masterful.

Real spiritual mastery boils down to knowing when to say "Yes" and when to say "No." We can make it all the way to God on just these two words and nothing more. The test is *when to use them*.

A friend of mine, Hal, owned and managed an Italian restaurant. When I would occasionally help out at the restaurant, I saw that he was irresponsible in the way he managed the business. Because Hal thought in terms of lack, he was very petty and critical of his employees, and he rarely gave encouragement or support. The business began to go downhill, and the worse things got, the less Hal was present, creating a vicious cycle of negation and failure, until the business was in the red. At that point, Hal went to a wealthy lawyer in the community and asked him for a large loan, presenting him with a grandiose scheme for expanding the restaurant and bringing in well-known entertainment.

As the lawyer was a friend of mine as well, he approached me and asked if I thought this would be a safe investment for him. As much as I wanted to see Hal succeed, I had to tell the lawyer the truth: I told him that I believed the business was failing, not as a result of circumstance, but of Hal's negative way of thinking. Because he was irresponsible, even if he did get a huge loan, it would probably slip through his fingers in a matter of time, just as Hal's original investment had dwindled. What Hal needed was not more money, but expanded managerial skills and consciousness.

Though I did not like stifling Hal's chances for success, I would have done a great disservice to the lawyer — and Hal — if I did not tell the truth. If he had gotten the money, he would have gotten himself into only deeper trouble. As the story turns out, the business closed and Hal got a salaried job with less supervisory responsibility, a position in which he is feeling positive and doing very well.

Being good or spiritual does not mean that we must always say "Yes" to everything. Sometimes it is spiritual to say "Yes" and sometimes it is spiritual to say "No." We have to decide which situations require which answers. Neem Karoli Baba told Ram Dass to "Love everyone, serve everyone, and remember God." "This," tells Ram Dass, "got me to thinking about what real service is all about; does it mean that I am supposed to do anything that anyone asks me to do? . . . No, it means responding uniquely to each request, according to the clearest intuition that I can feel."

The question of Hal's loan is a fairly obvious example of our need for discrimination. As we advance along the spiritual path, however, the tests and lessons become more subtle, and we have to dig deeper to find within ourself a more sensitive guide for correct action.

One night, for example, a student told Hilda that he had gone to a lecture by a certain organization whose leader spoke about many esoteric spiritual principles. "The only problem," he explained, "was that although everything the lecturer said was true, I did not feel Truth in the room, and I felt a sharp pain in my stomach." Hilda told him that the pain was in the energy center in his body that corresponded to power and that perhaps the teacher and the organization were more interested in power than in service. A few weeks later we learned from one of the students that left this organization that they had charged her a huge sum of money to allow her to teach their other students, who were also paying high prices for instruction.

The path is a razor's edge path, and if we are not careful we can give our trust to the wrong people. Let's face it: there are shams and flim-flam men in the spiritual game. Jesus said to "be as gentle as lambs, but as clever as serpents." We must think twice before surrendering to anyone's teachings. And it will do no good to say, "I will not surrender to anyone's teachings," because if a genuine teacher comes along, we cannot afford to miss the opportunity to accept their grace. So the only answer is to develop a keep sense of discrimination, to know who to be open to, and when.

There is yet a more subtle level at which we are required to practice discrimination: the inner plane, or the dream world. Even on a subconscious level we must choose. We may have a dream of a spiritual master coming to us and asking us to do something for him or her. Then, when we do it, we are overcome with an empty, almost nauseous feeling that we have been had. This means that our discrimination was not keen enough on this subtle level. I had a dream in which a certain master came to me and asked me to join a line of people who were happily filing into his temple. I had a gnawing suspicion, but I accepted the invitation. When I got inside, the people in there were writhing in pain and desperately trying to warn those on the outside not to enter. I had been had.

Yet, on another night I had a dream of the same master. This time it felt right to follow, and when I did, I was rewarded with a very beautiful and blissful experience.

We might say that in the first dream I was tuning to a force of charlatanry masquerading as the master. In the second case, I tuned in to the actual essence of the master. At a point as fine as this, we have no one to lean on but our own God-given sense of what is correct.

Do not be afraid to act on your discrimination. If something feels wrong or out of the flow to you, follow up your hunch and act with caution. Do not feel guilty or impolite about saying "No" to that which does not sit right with you. This is not judgement by the ego; it is the right and necessary identification of what is true. It is our responsibility to recognize error for what it is. We serve no one by believing pretentious words or participating in false affairs. The little boy who exposed the ruse of the Emperor's new clothes did a very great service to the townspeople and to the Emperor, as well.

Spiritual means the spirit in which an action is done. We can say "No" in a very loving way, and so serve the one who has asked something of us. If someone calls me up to try to sell me a magazine that I know I will not buy, I politely stop them before they finish their sales pitch, and in a loving way I say, "No thank you." I really do love them, even if I do not buy their magazine, and I like to think that they may feel happy that I did not hang up on them with a gruff "No!" ∗

It would be a waste of my time — and theirs, which they could be using on a more interested customer — for me to listen to their whole pitch.

As we grow, our ability to distinguish between what is right for us and what is wrong becomes finer and finer. I might be sitting in an office or waiting in a line at a supermarket, for example, and my eye will fall on some magazine. An inner voice says, "Leave it alone," but out of curiosity I pick it up, and upon paging through it I come upon some gory picture or story that I wish I had missed. On other occasions, I might see a magazine which doesn't seem especially interesting, yet the inner voice says, "Pick it up." When I do, I find just the article or information that I have been searching for, but just could not seem to find elsewhere.

Eventually we see that God is in everything, and there is nothing too small — or too big — to be unworthy of His Guidance. He will tell us which car salesman to trust, which charity to support, and how long to wait before we ask for a debt to be repaid. No act is too worldly for God, and no fork in the road is beyond our ability to make a correct choice.

Spiritual mastery begins on earth. Before we can enjoy Heavenly Bliss, we must conquer the marketplace. And that is precisely why we are here — to learn the difference between what is "right on" and what is right off. The mastery of discrimination is accomplished in traffic, at the staff meeting, and in giving the kids lunch. Since there are no traffic jams, board meetings, or luncheons in Heaven, here is our opportunity to master such challenges and gain control over our lives.

Real spiritual masters are sharp, exact, and firm in human interactions. They do not allow God's energy, with which they have been entrusted, to be misused against them. When some of Ramakrishna's young students came back from the store shortchanged, he told them, "Go back immediately and get the right change!" Hilda is very strict about "keeping it together" in the world. Once, when I bought her a package of bobby pins that she requested, she insisted on reimbursing me to the exact penny. She admonishes her students not to leave any possessions visible in parked cars, and she screens anyone who would give a talk at her classes. Though she can sit comfortably in the etheric realms of spiritual light, she does not miss one step in the worldly game. We must keep our head in the clouds and our feet on the ground. This is the path of the masters.

"Mark well the words in this lesson. They will be of crucial importance to you in the days to come. We would have you act in a manner befitting the masters that you are.

Fear not to weigh in your heart of hearts the words and actions of others. This is your right and your duty. The observation of righteousness is not the judgement of ego. Do not be afraid to realize a wolf for what it is; this is not negative judgement, but right seeing. We would rather have you see correctly than be prey to foolishness.

Error is often born of lack of confidence to make a stand for the Truth. The Master Himself drove the money mongers from the temple, and in so doing set an example for you to emulate.

Discrimination is the only real lesson in life. You are on earth because of previous errors in discrimination. Correct those errors, and you master the game of earth. Those in a position to teach are the ones who have refined their discriminative abilities to the point where they can recognize that which is of God. You, too, know what is real, but you have not acted on your understanding with sufficient consistency.

The fruits of your efforts, though now unseen, shall become more and more evident as the world comes to acknowledge the reality of God. Are you not already seeing your deepest intuitions confirmed? Continue on your path of right endeavor, and we assure you that all of your noble ambitions shall be borne out and manifest. Hail the goer!''

DECISION

To make a decision is to put the Will of God directly into action. Many of the problems in our lives are not a result of wrong choices, but of *lack of making a choice.* If we want to accelerate our personal evolution to higher consciousness, we must begin to make clear choices and to act on them.

When I started to make firm decisions, my life really began to take shape. I used to consider it spiritual or fashionable to be "spaced out." If I lost something or made a mistake, I would think, "Wow, I just can't seem to keep it together — I must be really high!" Actually, I was just disorganized. I now see that not keeping it together is not a mark of spiritual advancement, but mental sloppiness. Vagueness is not a quality of character that brings success or peace. It is a form of sloth and inertia. Hilda once said, "If God were vague, the planets would fall out of the heavens." But God is 100% precise and efficient; He cannot afford to be less. And when we act with precision and efficiency, we are living up to our selfhood as intelligent beings created in the image and likeness of a clear-minded God.

Spiritual masters practice decision and precision on every level. A student of Suzuki Roshi, a beautiful Zen master, told how the roshi would eat an apple in such a way that the core was left as a perfectly balanced sculpture. There would not be one bit of apple left to eat; no waste. Eating an apple was a meditation for the master. His meditation did not stop when he arose from *zazen.* His whole life was meditation, and meditation is clarity. If our lives do not reflect clarity, then we are not meditating correctly.

The stakes in the way we make decisions are high. If we decide with surety and resolution, we get what we decide for. If, on the other hand, we flounder in indecision and procrastination, we lose power. In such a case, we are like an ant in the middle of a highway, running back and forth between a granule of sugar and a piece of cake, unable to decide which one to take. Either one would be a fine choice, but he had better decide quickly, for a big Mack truck is barreling down the road. Because time is precious, we cannot afford to vacillate in our decisions. If we really want to create movement in our lives, we must be willing to take a sure step in one direction.

The impediment to decision making is *fear* of making the wrong choice or getting something we do not want. Often, however, a wrong choice is better than no choice, for then at least we would be certain of what is the right direction, and progress would be made.

When we do not know what choice to make, our best bet is to search our heart for the act that would be most in harmony with our most important ideals, and to act on that high standard. *If we act in the name of love, service, and good will, we cannot make a wrong decision.* God asks no more of us than to live up to the highest principles that we know. He does not hold us responsible for standards higher than those of which we are aware. We always know all we need to know to make any decision with which we are confronted. Take into account whatever you know about what is required for people to live on earth in harmony, and use that knowledge as the basis for your decision. Swami Sivananda taught that acts are judged not by their form, but by their *intention*. This idea has helped me enormously in my decision making. If you are unsure as to what course of action to take, summon your purest intention and let that be your benchmark.

If you do make a "wrong" decision, then be grateful for it. Turn a minus into a plus. A negative $(-)$ is half a positive $(+)$. Take the minus sign and add one stroke of vertical awareness to it, and you have a plus. Thank God for showing you the error that you have made, and resolve not to repeat it. This is very pleasing in His eyes. We have come on earth to learn. It is no sin to make a mistake. I am typing on corrasable paper. It is designed with compassion for typists like me. Life is, to a certain extent, corrasable. If you make an error, then admit it with firm resolve, do what you can to correct the mistake, and walk on. If you drive off the highway, it will do you no good to sit and bemoan your error. The only thing to do is to *turn back onto the highway and continue your journey.* The time spent in regret is only more time wasted. If you have to pay off some karma of a wrong decision, then pay it off like a master. Resisting your obligations will create only more karma. All of life is for learning.

Another rule of thumb for overcoming indecision is to listen to your inner voice. We need to be quiet enough to hear that guidance. If we are worried, anxious, or fearful, we will not be able to contact that voice of guidance. Our worry creates mental and emotional static that blocks our awareness of the right decision, an answer that is always working to make itself known to us. And practice following your hunches. You will find out which hunches come from your heart, and which come from your intellect. In this way, decison making will become easier and easier.

If you still cannot decide, then ask God to decide for you. Recently I wrestled for several days over whether or not to mail a certain letter. I was losing my strength and my clarity through this indecision. One night, I could take it no longer. I decided to get out of bed and sit down and pray until the answer came. I began to talk to God: "God, I do not see now what is the proper path to take. I just want to do what is right. I turn this one over to you." Then I began to thank God for the right decision. I did not know what it was, but I affirmed to myself that God very much wanted to show me what to do, and I tried to get the feeling of what it would be like if I had reached and acted on a satisfying decision. I just kept affirming, "Thank you, God, for the right decision . . . Thank you, God, for the right decision," over and over and over. After just a little while, there began to well up within me an awareness of the correct choice of action. It began to feel very right to mail that letter. The more I thanked God for the right decision, the righter this choice seemed to be. When I felt satisfied that this was the best path of action, I decided to mail the letter first thing in the morning. At the moment of that decision, my energy returned and I felt as if a huge cloud cover had been burnt away by the morning sun. A decision had been made.

We can use the routine experiences in our lives to practice the power of decision and precision. Arriving at the meeting on time, keeping our car in good condition, and carrying out an errand that we promised someone are good ways to mobilize decisive strength. The time of the meeting, the health of the car, and the nature of the errand are not nearly as important as our ability to make a commitment and stick to it. If we master little decisions, the big ones will come easy.

I will share with you a very powerful method that I have discovered for keeping my whole life in order: I keep my room clean. Our rooms are pictures of our consciousness. If you want to clean up your consciousness, then clean up your room. See if you have any cobwebs or "dustbunnies." If so, you have allowed indecision and inertia to creep into your temple. A very efficient and successful man I know said that the little balls of dust that accumulate in the corners of uncared-for rooms are manifestations of unconsciousness. I believe it. Sweep them away, and in so doing you sweep away your unconsciousness.

When a room is tidy and orderly, a vibration of power and harmony builds up in it, one which blesses everyone who walks into the room, by its reflection of Godly order. Hilda tells that when she entered Yogananda's retreat center, "You wouldn't believe how perfect was the vibration, kids! Everything was in its perfect place. I remember how the gold drapes were perfectly creased and how the blue carpet was immaculately vacuumed. It was like walking into clarity itself, and I felt as if I had just had a good meditation."

We have the same ability as Yogananda's devotees to make our homes and our rooms our *sanctum sanctorum* — a holy refuge. Such order is a tremendous support to our spiritual work. I can remember times when I walked into my house with the affairs of the day on my shoulders. The moment I walked into a clean room, I felt my troubles lifted off of me, as if gentle angel wings brushed off my shoulders. This blessing was not a result of chance, but *decision*.

Do not be so rigid in your decisions that you are unwilling to reverse them when necessary. We, like Ghandi, must hold Truth in higher esteem than unthinking obstinacy. Reversing a decision for a good reason is not the same as indecision. When we reverse a decision with reason, we have executed two strong choices. When we fail to decide and fall prey to wishy-washy lethargy, we have made no choice, and remain weak.

If you decide to wait, then do it with resolution, and not procrastination. Many decisions require a gestation period before they can be brought to birth. When you perceive such a necessity, decide to wait. This is not a sign of weakness, but wisdom.

For one week, practice being really decisive. It does not matter so much whether you say "Yes" or "No," as long as you do not say "maybe." Be crisp in your decisions. Answer questions, make orders in the marketplace, and if you are in a supervisory position, give directions with resolve. Be anything but vague. Banish fear through sincere and firm decisions. Do not waste one iota of your precious life-force on indecision. Do not give the rational mind anything to chew on. So chosen, your affairs will quickly fall into place.

In mastering the high art of decision, you will align your mind and your actions with all of the great masters of life who have used firm decision-making as a tool to release spiritual power for the good of the world. You will be joining the forces of Pericles, Moses, and Lincoln. These men stood firmly for their beliefs. They acted with resolve. I am sure that they were not without error. And I am sure, too, that they lived up to their mistakes like masters. Act with dignity and precision, and the power that made them great will uphold you in your aspiration.

Decide to make your life what you want it to be. No one else can decide for you, and certainly no one else can do it for you. Your decisions will line up life in the way that you choose it. The moment I make a decision — a firm one — the forces of the universe immediately set themselves in line to manifest that decision. *If desired events are not coming to pass in your life, it is because you have not firmly resolved what you want it to manifest.* Is this true, or untrue? Examine your circumstances carefully, and I believe you will agree that this is so. Your life is a picture of the decisions that you have made. If your life is in any way in conflict or confused, it is only because your decisions have been in conflict and confused. Declare your decision, and your life is certain to clear up. There is no slippage in the system of mind dynamics. What you think becomes reality. Think vague, and life will be vague. Think clearly, decide firmly, and act precisely, and your life will be a picture of surety. You will have made it so, by your willingness to decide.

"We would impart to you the wisdom of the Godly use of will. Your will has lain in atrophy. Man's Divine gift of co-creation through the Will of the Creator has not been fully utilized. It is now for you to master life through right use of your faculty of decision.

This is but an elementary lesson in the productive use of mind. Yet it is, for you, a necessary one. Master this task, and you take control of your life in cooperation with God.

The age to come is being founded on the intelligent and loving use of mental energies. Mankind will master the secrets of creation that now lie dormant in the unused realms of human potential. Your ability to enter this wonderous era depends on your development of concentration and resolve. Indeed, no further progress on the planet is possible until you have tempered your passions to use such powers for upliftment, and not destruction. Your resolution to harmonize with the Will for Good is a first requisite in the channeling of these faculties.

Ultimately there is but one decision that you need to make: the decision for God. All other decisions are in the service of this one. Do not underestimate the decisions that you must make, for your firm resolve in the smallest of these will unlock Heaven's gate before you. Decide, beloveds. Decide and grow strong."

SERVICE

Gotta serve somebody.
— Bob Dylan

Two robbers were crucified with Jesus. In the hour of their tribulation, one chided Jesus, "If you are the Son of God, then get us off these crosses!" Then the other robber rebuked, "We deserve to be here, but this man has done nothing wrong!" Later, Jesus promised this man, "Truly I say to you, today you shall be with me in Paradise."

Hilda described this incident as a model for selfless service in the world. The first criminal was so absorbed in his own pain that he could not see that it was the Christ at his side. The second, even while in his own suffering, compassionately saw that Jesus did not deserve to be there. The man "thought outward"; he turned his attention away from his own little self to feel the predicament of another. In this state of thoughtful kindness amid suffering, he was promised the Kingdom.

Each of us has our own cross to bear while there is much suffering in the world. If we aspire to serve others and to make some kind of contribution to humanity, we must first let go of our own self-pity, fear, and doubt. Like the first robber on the cross, there is a part of each of us that is preoccupied with itself, and which ironically mocks those whose love can most help us. At the same time, we also have within us a self — an aspect of our real nature — that has a deep compassion for the needs of others and desires to *give* rather than *get*. The reward of service is that when we turn our attention to help another, we forget our own misery, which was created and maintained only by our willingness to dote on it.

A friend of mine was in the hospital, and I was very worried about him. I allowed my energy to be depleted and I was feeling sorry for myself as well as for him. As God's clever plan would have it, during that time I was scheduled to give a workshop on "Positive Thinking" at a local library. As I left the hospital to do the workshop, I thought, "Now how am I going to do this workshop?! Here I am feeling so negative, and I'm supposed to go tell people how to be positive . . . a great example I am!" At that moment, I realized that my responsibility to the people who were coming to that workshop was more important than my need to feel sorry for myself. So I willfully decided to put aside my own woes and to go in there and give those people the best program I knew how to give. Otherwise, I would have felt like a real hypocrite. So I stopped worrying about myself, and thought about what I could give. And it turned out very well, indeed. My great surprise, however, was that by the time the workshop was over, I had lost my feelings of woe. I no longer felt troubled about my friend, and when I went to visit him the next day, he and I were both feeling much better. I had only to get my mind off my own little self.

I experienced an inspiring example of this kind of selfless thinking when I was spending an afternoon at a nursing home. This was at a Christmas party for the patients, and I was so happy to see them enjoying treats of cookies and candy. One woman, paralyzed, slow of speech, and in considerable pain, turned to me and asked, "Did you have anything to eat?" My heart flew open in a way that still fills me with a thrill of joy just to think of it. I was touched, not so much because she thought particularly of me, but because she was kind enough to care for the needs of another, even in the midst of her own suffering.

The prayer of St. Francis captures the essence of service:

> *O Divine Master,*
> *Grant that I may not so much seek to be consoled,*
>   *as to console;*
> *Not so much to be understood, as to understand;*
> *Not so much to be loved, as to love.*

Real service is given without any expectation of reward or

acknowledgement. In this attitude, we can never be disappointed and we will always feel fulfilled. If we feel irritated because we do not receive a "thank you" from someone for a kind act, then we did not do it out of a desire to give love; we did it to receive something, and this is not service; it is business. When we do not receive acknowledgement for a gift or an act, we should be grateful, for this means we did it for God. God sees all that we do, even if no one else does, and He will reward us more faithfully than anyone in the world ever could. "Be not like the hypocrites who say their prayers and do good acts to be noticed by others. Do your service in secret, and your Heavenly Father will reward you."

Because Jesus lived everything He taught, He demonstrated the importance of serving with humility by washing the feet of His disciples, teaching, "No servant is greater than His master." His whole life was a teaching in giving, as are the lives of all who love God, for those who know God know that the best way to serve God is to serve people.

One evening, for example, there was a guest speaker at Hilda's class. After the class, the woman asked, "Could you tell me where the ladies' room is?" Before the lady was even done asking, Hilda sprang from her chair and personally escorted the woman to the restroom, turned on the light for her, and made sure there was a fresh towel. My first thought was, "Hilda doesn't have to do that; she is a famous teacher with many students; she could have easily asked someone else to do it for her." But Hilda is great *because* she lives a life of selfless service. She treats all who come to her as if they were Christ Himself.

St. Francis well understood that we sometimes hesitate to give to others because we fear that if we do not meet our needs first, they will not be met. This is man's way of thinking. God's way is, as *A Course in Miracles* tells us, "To have all, give all to all." Hilda is also an inspiring example of this truth. As she spends nearly all of her time giving to others, her needs are miraculously met. Though she does not strive or ask for anything, the right people, money, and washing machines come to her exactly when she needs them, usually from people who are grateful for what she has done for them.

I remember, too, when I was debating whether or not to give a friend of mine a birthday present of a picture of mine that I loved. It was a delightful cartoon of a little smiling man being lifted by a heart up a steep mountain which he could not climb. The caption was "Love conquers all." Although this was one of my favorite possessions, I knew that my friend would really like it, and so I decided to give it as a present. The very next day, as a gesture of friendship, someone gave me an envelope. As I opened it, I found the *very same picture* as the one I had given the day before — and this one was even better: written on the back was a lovely poem from the one who gave it.

I saw and felt this same reverence for giving when I went to hear Swami Satchidananda speak. Among his first words were, "Thank you for the opportunity to serve you in my own small way." I was deeply touched by his humility. To the hundreds of people in the audience (or at least to me), he was doing us a favor by coming to speak to us. I felt indebted to him. From his loving point of view, though, we were doing him a service by allowing him to be there. He saw himself not as a great and important yogi, but as a servant of God. He sees life as a series of opportunities to serve.

Too often, we miss these opportunities because we believe that "work" is bad. We call our opportunities "obligations" or "chores" and we grumble through them when, with just a slight shift in perspective, they can become invitations to dance up the path to God. At my house, on a kitchen cabinet we had a list of jobs to be done, posted under the title "CHORES." A divine and loving guest crossed out the word "CHORES" and replaced it with "Blissful Karma Yoga" (knowing God through service). At another time, when I was at a Sivananda ashram kitchen, I saw posted a marvelous quote from the Master:

> *God realization does not begin in a cave high atop the Himalayas. It begins in the pots and pans of the kitchen. Treat all of your tasks, however small, as opportunities to see God and to serve Him. This is a sure way to Liberation.*

We do not need to be a Mother Theresa or a Moses to be liberated. We do not need to leave our family or job to give God's Love to all. We can begin exactly where we are, and we will find many, many opportunities to "think outward" and to serve. Every little thought and action, in fact, can be one of Divine service. If you are doing the laundry, you can fold each garment with a touch of love and a word of blessing. If you work as a secretary, you can answer the phone with kindness and availability. I feel so uplifted when someone answers my phone call with a pleasant "Hello?" You and I have the power to offer the same blessing every time we pick up the telephone — even if we are feeling tired or angry. All acts are opportunities to give love.

Hilda used to help out occasionally at a pizza shop in a tough neighborhood in New York City. Her ideal was to spread light and love. As she folded the pizza boxes, she would say a prayer over each one, such as "May the person who receives this be happy and blessed." Opportunities to give love are always waiting for us with outstretched arms, and God's promise becomes His gift when we are but willing to embrace them.

There are an infinite number of ways to serve. Each of the ways is equally important. Do not berate yourself because you are not a great doctor or social activist. Any service that we give is essential to the well being of all. I went to a hospital to visit a friend who sells used car parts. I was thinking how important are the doctors who were treating him. Then I realized that this man's job was equally as important as the doctors', for they need working automobiles to take them to the people they treat. Without his services, they could not perform theirs. It is a marvelous web of interdependence that unites us. All are equally dependent on each other for our work in the world, and we are all equally dependent on God, Who serves us through one another.

Sometimes we are not even aware of the importance of the service that we have rendered. There is a wonderful story about this called "It's A Wonderful Life." In the tale, James Stewart portrays a man who operates a private loan agency in a small town. He is compassionate and understanding, taking risks on loans for projects that he believes in. Through a quirk of fate, he stands to be put out of business, and everything in his life seems to go wrong at the same time. At his wits' end, he considers suicide. At that moment his guardian angel appears to show him what life in that town would have been like had he never been born. Without him, the projects and businesses he kindly supported were run down, degenerate institutions. The restaurant he financed was, in this vision, a sleezy bar; the movie house showed low-grade films; and people he had rescued were in the dregs of life. He sees how valuable his acts have been, though he realized it not. Finally he decides to live, and upon returning to his home, finds all the people he has helped awaiting him with a collection of just enough money to make good his losses.

Our work in the world is made easy when we share the load. The old adage, "Many hands, light work" is true. There is an expansion of the energy that we offer to another; they receive much more than we give. Taking ten or fifteen minutes out of my life to offer a helping hand to another is worth much more than ten or fifteen minutes to them. There is an essence of love that is added to time or energy rendered in service. It makes life satisfying for the giver and for the receiver. It inspires us to know a higher possibility for life than we have been taught to believe in. Loving kindness in the form of service is closer to the heart of God than any other act.

Serving others is a way of participating in the Grace of God. When we help another who is in difficulty, we are "taking on" some of his or her karma. We are becoming the man who helped Jesus carry His cross. I can think of no higher act that we can do in this world. Says Master Hilarion, "This is why the Christian teaching emphasizes above all else the commandment to serve one's brother in any way possible. For through this service it is possible not only to set aside one's own karmic burden, but to lift the load from the shoulders of another."*

Serving another, then, bears a double reward. Not only do we participate in the alleviation of his or her suffering, but we free ourself, as well. Sri Chinmoy, a teacher of the path of meditation, was once asked, "How can I feel the bliss of God?" His response was one word: "Serve."

Service is not always enjoyable and pleasant; sometimes it is demanding and repugnant to the senses. Meher Baba made pilgrimages to serve the sick and the destitute. He said, "True love is no game of the faint-hearted and the weak; it is born of strength and understanding." St. Francis understood this when he took on the task of caring for an ornery leper that no one else, even his fellow monks, could tolerate. As St. Francis washed the leper's body, the man's sores miraculously disappeared and he was healed in spirit as well as body. In order to truly serve, we must be willing to reach out to the unreachable; to tolerate the intolerable; and to love the unlovable. Then, and only then, can we understand the true meaning of selfless service.

When we are willing to serve in this way, we find the end of argument, strife, and discord in our lives. Practicing outward thinking

*Hilarion, THE NATURE OF REALITY, Marcus Books, 195 Randolph Rd., Toronto, Canada

brings freedom and joy beyond compare. The nature of argument is two people selfishly grabbing for themselves, like a tug of war. All the words and actions can be boiled down to "Me!" . . . countered by, "No, Me!" and so on, until both parties withdraw in painful isolation, or one person is willing to let go a little bit and give in to the other. Too often I want the other person to consider my needs more than I am willing to consider theirs. I have found that the quickest way for us to end any strife is to show our "opponent" that we are aware of his or her point of view. The moment he or she feels recognized, even in the slightest way, their wrath will subside, and resolution is then possible. When "*You* listen to *me*" becomes "*I* am willing to hear *you*," peace replaces discord. Jesus said, "Agree with your adversary quickly." In this way will harmony be where bitterness was.

The highest form of service is forgiveness. It is very difficult, from a human point of view, to forgive. Yet, to see the Light of God within a human being, no matter what their outer circumstance or appearance, is a deep act of love. In forgiving, we are affirming the true worth of a brother or sister who may have been spurned by a heartless world. We are serving him or her by recognizing the holiness within them, though the world would recognize only evil. All acts of charity or giving are valuable only inasmuch as they recognize the true dignity of those toward whom the contribution is directed. Any money or time given to another without recognizing their full equality, is as chaff in the wind, and serves only the mockery of ego. Pity or sorrow is never a worthy reason for charity, for it only reinforces the bondage of the giver and the recipient. Real charity is never a giving, but always a sharing. He who gives as a giver remains half; he who shares, knows wholeness.

No matter what our personal path to God, service is always a necessary step on the path. The meditator must arise from his pillow to share what he has seen within himself. The student of Truth must teach what he has learned, by living it. The lover of God must love the God in his brethren. Awakening is useless unless it awakens the world; wisdom is meaningless unless it is lived; and love is fruitless unless it is given. He who would be worthy of that which has been given to him must share it. Jesus told of the man who was forgiven his debt, but refused to forgive his debtor. The man incurred the wrath of God, and was thrown into a fiery furnace for it. When we take from the great bounty of God, but refuse to give it, we remain entrapped in the web of self. Sharing what we have received, spiritually and physically, is the true expression of brotherhood. When we give to all what God has given to us, God shall not diminish our supply, but only increase it.

When we perform an act of service and consecrate it in the name of Love, we align ourselves with all the selfless servants of humanity through whom the world has ever been blessed. When we reach out to another, we join Ghandi, Mother Theresa, St. Francis, and all of the devotees of loving kindness. The love and support of these masters wafts toward us as if they were standing by our very side in our act. If you do healing, teaching, cleaning, or any other form of service, call upon the servant of God who is dearest to your heart. Before I sing or teach a class, I say a little prayer asking God to support me in my work, and to work through me. I tell God that I want this work to be for Him and I ask Him to bless those who I am serving. It is my joy to tell you that God has not failed me. I have seen miraculous changes in the students and in myself. When we dedicate our acts to Light and Love, these powers stream through us, filling our activities with success and satisfaction. When we work for God, we cannot fail.

When you meditate, dedicate your upliftment to the upliftment of all humanity. Have the intention that you are not just meditating for yourself, but for the benefit of all. When I pray for others, I feel a peace come over me far in excess of what I receive when I pray for myself. At Hilda's meditation one evening, she directed, "Now pray for one other person in this room, and see what happens to the air." At that moment, the air became cool and pink, as if selfishness had been dissipated and replaced by selfless loving kindness. There seemed to be a network of golden threads reaching across the room, binding all in a fabric of Oneness. It was lovely beyond words.

We have within our very minds, hearts, and hands the power to heal and to transform the world. One kind word, look, or touch can make all the difference to a brother or sister in need of love. It is said that *"if everyone on earth loved each other, the earth would shine brighter than the sun."* If every one of us would do one little kind act for another person on just one day, I believe the earth would be redeemed instantly. It would release such a powerful energy of light and love that the forces of darkness, in the form of pollution, weapons, and hatred, would immediately disburse. Such a day would set into motion a snowball of service that could cleanse the earth of all the negative karma that has ever been accumulated, and release the spirit of hope and giving throughout the universe so that every planet in every galaxy would reap its benefit. "You may say I'm a dreamer, but I'm not the only one." If this indeed be a dream, then let us dream it together, for dreams are the stuff that life is made of.

"Children, understand well the meaning of service. Truly there is no greater hope in our hearts than for you to serve one another. You must now put your ideas into practical expression, for time is short and the need paramount. Though you understand the necessity of service, you must understand its urgency in this time of shadows. In a darkened room, a tiny candle casts a great beam.

As you enter the ranks of those who serve humankind, you awaken to the very purpose of those whose intention is the end of all suffering. Hold to your highest values in all of your endeavors. Set your mind on the Kingdom of Heaven, even while you act on earth; truly the two are One. You can come to know this only by raising all of your purposes to the most magnificent. Be not dissuaded by thoughts of mediocrity and mundane goals. Your goal is what it always has been: the expression of the Love of your Heavenly Father. Accept nothing less, for nothing else has any meaning.

We look on your work with support and anticipation, and we happily watch you unfold. Know that you are protected in any work that is consecrated. This is the law and this is our purpose. Assume this purpose for yourself, and no harm can befall you. Your path is marked. Walk it in mastery and light. We hail you in your conquest of all that is binding, and celebrate with you in your attainment of all that is glorious. The Peace of God is given unto thee. For this were you born, for this do you live, and toward this noble ideal are all of your efforts blessed."

Love

Hilda

AIM RIGHT FOR THE HEART

I saw a movie about Mother Theresa of Calcutta, the saintly woman who has devoted her life to helping the poor and the dying. At one of her centers for the destitute, I saw a man, perhaps a priest or a monk, holding in his arms a frail and weak man, possible starving or on the verge of death. The monk was looking into the dying man's eyes with a compassion that brought tears of joy to my eyes. He was telling him, "My dear brother, my dear, dear brother, I love you very very much." The monk just kept repeating these words, over and over again, offering the man greater love with each repetition. The dying one seemed too weak to respond in word or action, but his eyes were sparkling as if he were looking into the face of Christ Himself. At this moment in my life, I cannot imagine an expression of Love greater than this.

The feeling and expression of Love is the common need of all human beings. I have never met a person with a tough exterior who was not soft and sensitive underneath. One day, for example, I was at a children's zoo, where I saw a man become very loud and abusive over a discrepancy at the snack bar. A few minutes later, I saw the same man tenderly feeding a fawn. Behind the loud man was a soft little boy. This is the essence of the human being that I value, and it is the quality that I want to always remember.

I used to work on human relations workshops for teenagers, and the hearts of these kids were so beautiful. I shall never forget one boy, in trouble with school, not getting along well with his parents, perhaps had a brush or two with the law. He was very dear to me, for he allowed me to see the other side of his character. He was a good boy; he had just been knocked around by the world a bit. In one of our group sessions his tough facade was being challenged, and for the longest time (it seemed like forever), he just sat in silence. Then, as if the burden of the years of hiding was just too great for him to bear any longer, one lone, small, and so very important tear rolled down his cheek. The illusion of hardness was dissolved.

Experiences like these have led me to where I no longer believe in anyone's "tough" act. When I see a tough guy, I see a scared little child. When I can talk to that inner person; when I can acknowledge the human being behind the armor; when I can symbolically say, "I know you're in there and I love you," I feel that I have made real and worthwhile contact with a soul, and contact with souls is what life, for me, is all about.

Dr. Leo Buscaglia was moved to create a college course called "Love" when several years ago he established what he thought was a close rapport with one of his students. To his surprise, this young lady was absent from class for a few weeks, although she had been attending regularly before then. He inquired on campus as to her well-being and he was told that, tragically, she had jumped off a cliff. This caused Dr. Buscaglia to deeply reconsider what education is all about. "I began to think," he explained, "that for fifteen years this young lady had received thousands of hours of information about history, science, and English. I wondered, though, that if someone had taught her or given her even a little bit of love, she might not have left this world alone, in despair."

I saw a video tape of Dr. Buscaglia's lecture called "What Is Essential Is Invisible to the Eye." Though thousands of people sat in the audience, his sincerity and genuineness set a tone as personal as the most intimate conversation between two old friends. The faces in the audience were beaming with joy, for what he was telling them was true — and they knew it. He had learned to aim right for the heart.

Bringing such a love into tangible expression is the Divine challenge that beckons to all of us. Patricia Sun was once about twenty minutes into a lecture when a man in the audience raised his hand and blurted, "I came in late; could you please tell me what happened?" I thought this was rather rude, considering there were several thousand people in the audience. Patricia looked at him gently, told him, "I love you; that's what happened," and returned to her talk.

Patricia could say this because she knew the secret of aiming for the heart: *When we ask for anything, we are asking for love.* All of our actions are skillful or unskillful attempts to feel love. The meanest person in the world craves the feeling of love just as much as you and I do, perhaps even more so; but he or she is simply going about getting it in a wrong, or unskillful way. Such a person believes that love can be manipulated, when it can only be won. This belief creates tough facades and disruptive actions. *The most powerful way to short circuit such negative acts is to deal directly on the level of giving love.* It is the seeking of love that is the hidden motive behind all questions and disruptions, and the giving of love that satisfies them.

Jesus knew that all human separation is a disguised form of trying to feel loved, and this is the why he taught to "love your enemies as yourself." He knew that *people act unlovable because they believe they are unlovable.* He understood that one who cries out for love in such a way has been dealt severe blows in life. Said Longfellow, "If we could read the secret history of our enemies, we should find in each man's life, sorrow and suffering to disarm all hostility." And Jesus knew that when we love such a person, we awaken in him his ability to love himself.

Hilda was once confronted by a tough guy in New York City. "I'm William, the king!" he arrogantly proclaimed. Hilda looked him in the eye with deep compassion and softly told him, "I know a greater King, William." Immediately the man broke down and began to weep, for Hilda had touched a long-concealed memory of tenderness and gentleness in this seemingly hardened man.

That memory bank is not unique to William the King who thought he was king. That deep well of innocence belongs to you and me, as well. We *are* more alike than we are different. The words and actions that would hurt or help me are pretty much those that would affect you in the same way. The big lie of life is that we are unaware of what hurts and what heals, and the great Truth is that we are all basically the same.

Yet, too often we speak unthinkingly, with sarcasms, innuendoes, barbs, and banter, acting as if the other guy would be able to take a joke that we, ourselves, could not. I can think of too many jests that I have made without consideration for the feelings of my brothers and sisters, which are really my feelings, as well. The adolescent years in our culture are replete with this kind of biting humor, and for that reason I feel that it behooves us to give our teenagers all the love and support we know how to give. We can overcome negativity with love.

We must never underestimate the healing potential of any act of kindness that we do, however small. Years ago, I received a telephone call from a friend who was going through a difficult time with her parents. She told me her story, and I, having no idea what to tell her, simply listened and quietly loved her. We lost contact with each other after that. Then, years later, I received a letter from her, telling me how grateful she was for all that I had done for her during her trouble. She said that our telephone conversation helped her tremendously in clearing up an extremely difficult relationship, and it was a turning point in her life.

I was amazed! I hardly even remembered the conversation, and when I did, I recalled that all I did was to open my heart and listen without judgement. Yet, somehow, this was just what she needed to transform her situation. The fruits of thoughtfulness sometimes remain hidden until the moment is ripe.

The language of the heart does not demand complexity. Its power lies in quiet simplicity. A friend of mine was struggling through a rigorous Zen meditation retreat. He was fighting his way through the cold, long hours of meditation and hurting knees. He didn't think he could make it to the end. Though he said nothing, a friend at the retreat approached him and silently placed a gentle, reassuring hand on his shoulder, as if to say, "I know what you're going through; I know you can make it; I am with you." "At that moment," my friend tells, "in that simple little touch, more love and understanding was communicated to me than could have been put in any amount of words. That small act of understanding gave me more than enough energy to continue and finish. I shall never forget that one thoughtful touch."

This account confirmed to me that the good intention that we invest in our acts far outshines the outer forms. Rabbi Shlomo Carlebach tells a beautiful story about the Jewish holiday of Purim. On this holiday there is a custom to give fruit and pastries to friends. One Purim evening, three friends found themselves with just one orange among them. One of them took the orange and lovingly gave it to another with a full blessing. The second took the orange, the love, and the blessing, added to it his own kind intention, and passed it on to the third. By this time, the orange was brilliant with light. The love from the sharing was so deep that the three friends decided to pass the orange around again, with more blessings. This went on all night, and by dawn the men, the orange, and the room were overflowing with the purest golden Love.

The noble challenge of our lives is to reach out, to act, and to live for what we know is real, even if that reality is not apparent to our senses. This is the only real faith. The path with heart is walked by those who know the Truth of Love, and are willing to ignore the separations that would discourage others from breaking down the lonely towers that have been constructed about our hearts. When we find the hearts of our sisters and brothers, we discover our own.

"We love you because we are fully aware of your holiness. You are now ready to join us in our happy vision. You are prepared to release forever your mistaken notions of foulness and baseness as the nature of man. You have realized that your nature is blessed by the Light of the world, because you now know yourself to be the Light of the world. You have come to accept your original and abiding goodness, and in this knowledge are you free to nourish it within the consciousness of your brethren by blessing them and loving them.

You have been given the way to heal yourself, your brethren, and your planet. Would you choose now to accept it? In its use is the end of all suffering and the release of the downtrodden. This task is not beyond your capacity. It is your only task. It is your purpose for incarnation and your reason for being. Were there not unconsciousness to rectify, your existence as an entity would hold no purpose.

Go forth, Children of Light. Healing is the gift that you offer to the world. You have everything that you need to transform the earth into paradise. The world is waiting for your love. Do not wait for the world to love you, for that is the great mistake of the world, the very thought which stands between pain and happiness. Give your love fearlessly, and darkness shall flee like the shadow that it is. You are marked by the Light in your heart."

TRANSFORMING RELATIONSHIPS

There is no more fruitful avenue of spiritual growth than that of transforming painful relationships into rewarding ones. In our relations with other persons, we are actually looking at the dynamics of our inner self, in a form we can see in the outer world. When we heal our relationships we heal ourselves.

Many psychologists tell us that problems exist between people when there is a lack of communication. This is true, but we need to discover why communication is not flowing. Lack of communication is really a lack of feeling *communion*. When we see other people as separate or alienated from ourselves, we slice up the universe into limited chunks, and in so doing, we erect prison bars around our heart. When we realize our unity with others, when we feel *with* them instead of *at odds* with them, the joy of our being together comes naturally.

An existential author said, "Hell is other people." He was correct, but not in the way that he meant it. I would add two quotation marks to his sentence to make it accurate: Hell is "other people." Put another way, hell is *thoughts of other-ness*. When we believe, "I am in here, in my own separate existence, and there are 'other people' in their separate existence," we set the scene for the experience of a hellish life, for we have denied the truth of our oneness with all people, with all life, and with God. When Jesus was asked, "What is the greatest commandment of all?" He answered, "God is One." If hell is "other people," Heaven is *One People*.

If I could boil down what I believe is the key to healing in relationships, it would be *forgiveness*. As I see more and more how forgiveness works, it is clear to me that the power of forgiveness is far greater than any tool or weapon known to man. Forgiveness is letting go of ideas of sin, guilt, and evil. *When we forgive another, we free not only them, but ourselves, as well.* Anger, bitterness, and resentment take their toll on he or she who would hold onto such negation. When we let go of judgements and bitterness, we remove from our shoulders and hearts a heavy load of pain. If I find myself holding onto any resentment, I must let it go, for my own good. God will not punish us in the afterlife for our bitterness, for we have already punished ourselves through lost love and aliveness.

When Jesus said, "Love your enemies, do good to those who spitefully use you, and bless those that curse you," He was not just uttering spiritual platitudes. He was giving a scientific formula for resolving painful human relationships and bringing about inner and outer peace. He knew the healing power of Love. He knew that people want to feel united and whole. And He knew that seeing others in the light of forgiveness is the only way to complete our Love.

The pharisees were aghast at Jesus' acceptance of the adulterous woman. "Your sins are forgiven," He told her; "Go and sin no more." They cried, "Blasphemy! No man has the power to pronounce forgiveness! Only God can forgive!" In a way, they were correct, but not in the way that they believed.

No man has the power to pardon someone else's sin, because in Reality there *has never been any sin*. There have been plenty of *thoughts* of sin, which is what the pharisees held, in their readiness to condemn. Jesus, however, was one in consciousness with God; He saw the situation from a Godly point of view, and in *God* consciousness *all* is God, and there is no place for sin. Jesus was not undoing or changing anything that the woman had done. All he did was to look at the Chastity of her soul and tell her the Truth that he could have spoken with equal authority to anyone, saint or sinner: "Your sins are forgiven."

Jesus was looking at the inner perfection, the sinless Light within the woman. This is what we need to do, as well, to heal our relationships. We must focus on the purity and the perfection of those against whom we are prone to hold judgement. Forgiveness of sins is not a special boon reserved for Jesus Christ or for priests, judges, or anyone else. We are *all* equally endowed Children of the Most High.

Jesus also said, "Greater things than I, shall ye do."

Outer harmony in relationships is a manifestation of harmony and acceptance within ourselves. If we hold any ill will or animosity toward anyone, it will be reflected in our outer interaction with them. If we are to bring a troubled relationship into peacefulness, we must first find serenity and the vision of good intention within our own consciousness.

I had a startling experience that demonstrated this to me. One evening I attended a lecture on the power of positive thinking. The speaker gave us this exercise: "Close your eyes and let the face of someone who you are not getting along with, pop into your mind." Immediately, the image of a woman who lived next door to me came into my mental view. I squirmed to think of her.

When I and several of my friends had moved into a large house, our neighbor Mrs. Ryan began to feel threatened. This was a fairly conservative neighborhood, and here were five young men with beards moving in next door. We heard that she attempted to pass a petition around the neighborhood to have us ejected on the premise that we were a gang of undercover terrorists. (Meanwhile, we were a bunch of meditating vegetarians.) She then found many opportunities to create situations about which she could complain, and she literally built a fence between our houses. I reacted and felt pretty uncomfortable with her, as well. When this lecturer suggested to take the image of someone we didn't like, I had no trouble picking her.

"Now," he guided us, "imagine this person standing a few feet away from you." ("Oh, no!" I thought.) "Take a few deep breaths and relax until you feel a little more comfortable with their face." Reluctantly, I did so. "Now, walk up to the person and take their hands." ("I can't do that!" I thought. "She'll probably run away screaming, even in my imagination!") But I did it anyway. "Now I want you, in your mental picture, to embrace this person, look them in the eyes, and tell them 'I love you.' " Well, by that time I had surrendered to the exercise, and I carried out his instructions. I was able to let go of some of my animosity toward Mrs. Ryan, and I actually felt better about her.

He then told us: "This is a very powerful method for resolving troubled relationships. If you practice this for five minutes a day for three weeks, one of two things will happen: your relationship with this person will clear up, or they will leave your life." (Either of those alternatives sounded fine to me.)

319

To be quite honest, I didn't practice the exercise again, but something remarkable did happen. A few days later, one of my roommates was picking tomatoes in the garden when Mrs. Ryan called to him.

"Mark, can I please have a word with you?"

"Oh no!" he thought, "What now?"

"Mark, I bet you think I'm going to complain about something, don't you?"

"Oh, no," he replied, "what makes you say that?" (He was a good actor — and in this case, a liar as well.)

"Well, you know, Mark, I've been thinking that I haven't been a very good neighbor." (Mark almost fainted.) ". . . and I'd just like to say that I'm sorry if I've given you fellows a hard time."

By now Mark was engaged in some serious reality testing. Mrs. Ryan went on:

"I know you boys (some of us "boys" were thirty years old) are really nice fellows, and I want to be your friend."

If Mark and I did not believe in miracles before then, we became immediate converts. Mark gave her some tomatoes, and our relationship with her improved after that time. As it turned out, Mrs. Ryan was actually a very nice lady, and we were very nice "boys," but I had to *see* her lovability — accept her goodness — before I could experience it.

The lesson, or the miracle, with Mrs. Ryan encouraged me to try this method of inner clearing again and again. It has worked every time. Whenever I feel any conflict between myself and another person, I seek to work it out first *within myself.* I visualize the person, send them much love and light, and I feel what it would feel like if they were my friend. This technique has helped to transform many of my relationships, and I recommend it to you with the greatest confidence.

Relationships are lessons in tangible form that we need for our personal growth. If we are holding any unconsciousness about a character trait, or some prejudice or judgement about any kind of action, someone who does the thing that we don't like will be drawn to us so that we may learn to let go and to love. *The quickest way to free yourself of someone who does something that irritates you is to love and accept them with their trait.* The more you fight it, the more prominent it will become. When you let go of your resistance, the person may or may not leave your life, but if you have truly released them it will not matter.

This places relationships in an entirely new light — one of challenge and promise. Persons that are hard to accept cease to be nuisances and become opportunities for us to practice understanding and forgiveness. When we experience any negative reaction to another person, we have a precious chance to reprogram our emotional computer. Someone once complained to Hilda, "I can't stand to visit my parents; I have to watch them eat meat!" Hilda's advice: "If I were in that situation, I'd go and sit down next to the one that had the biggest piece of meat and when the meat was being passed around for seconds, I'd offer them some more. I'd make myself sit there until I was relaxed and happy and I felt a lot of love for that person."

In India, Satya Sai Baba sometimes blesses a proposed marriage by saying, "Very happy, very happy!" When one of his followers agrees, "Yes, Baba, I'm sure they will be happy from the start!" he sometimes corrects, "Happy from the start? That is not what I said! They will rub each other's ego down, like the best sandpaper! Then they will *really* be happy!"

What, then, is marriage all about? What makes some marriages successful, and others fail? How do we know if our intended marriage will work? How can we save a marriage that is not working? Why is the divorce rate so high? These are questions that many of us have wrestled with, questions which have too often been answered through pain and hardship. I would like to share with you some of my observations on relationships.

We might say that our motivations for entering into marriage or a relationship can be distilled to two basic dynamic attitudes: "I am going to get something from this person," or "I am going to share with this person." The first attitude leads only to pain; the second, to joy. The first is seeking to get; the second, to expand. Sharing works, taking doesn't.

The question is: How *whole* do I feel in this relationship? Do I feel complete and full and enough *without* this person? Can I enter into this relationship without expecting to receive something from my partner that will make me *more* complete? Can I maintain the integrity of my own individual creativity, *with* my partner? If we can sustain our awareness as full beings, and enter into a marriage as an overflowing expression of the celebration of life, then the marriage will

321

probably work.

If, on the other hand, I marry to "lean out" on someone who will fill a gap within me that I feel I cannot fill myself, then I am in for big disappointment. If I love you because you say you love me, or because you will have sex with me, or because you agree with my way of looking at life, or because you have a character trait that I feel I am lacking, this is not love, but a business arrangement based on lack. In depending on you to fulfill my needs, I am affirming my weakness and establishing a marriage on marshlands. As Jesus said, "A house built upon sand cannot stand." The divorce rate affirms this parable.

If the relationship is inaugurated on the foundation of celebration and overflow, we will receive many of the things that others marry in order to get, but they come as *gifts* and *joys*, and *not* as a *payoff*. I see many marriages around me and I see the relationships in which I have been involved, and it is clear to me that the reasons for which we are taught to marry and the myths about romantic marriage are more illusory than they are real.

Eric Butterworth describes the two different types of relationships in a very neat way: In one relationship we are hypnotized, staring moodily into each other's eyes; in the other, we stand together, hand in hand, looking out the window onto the great panorama of life. In the first, we have made gods of each other; in the second, we rejoice together in acknowledging the One God. In the first, we have narrowed down our source of happiness to one little person; in the second, we remain open to the fulfillment that all of life can offer to us.

The relationships that I have seen work are those in which the partners seek to serve and support each other with encouragement and confidence; where the partners refrain from making demands upon each other; and where the individual creativity of each person is honored and encouraged. More important, the relationships that have God at their center, or that have at least some kind of commitment to a higher purpose than to fulfill each other's fantasies, are the ones that are the strongest. People with individual spiritual foundations create marriages with strong spiritual foundations. Anything that is dedicated to the ideals of Godliness, works.

Can we heal a relationship that has not been based on these ideals? Yes, we certainly can. In fact, many of the strongest and most rewarding relationships are those that have been *transformed*. As we begin to allow God into our lives, we find the strength and the wisdom to create peace and harmony where there once seemed to be none. We discover new ways to give love, and, to our happy surprise, the love and the freedom that we give another to grow and expand are return-ed to us many times over.

If we truly want to enjoy fulfilling relationships in marriage, with our children, or in the office, we must be willing to be big enough to give love *before* we receive it. We must not allow our actions or at-titudes toward others to depend on theirs toward us. We must have the faith to see a possibility for goodness in another, though they recognize it not themselves.

Someone put it in a lovely poetic form:

> *They drew a circle that kept me out,*
> *But I and God were bound to win.*
> *We drew a circle that kept them in.*

Jesus said it this way: "You have been told, 'an eye for an eye, and a tooth for a tooth.' I tell you to forgive." Someone asked Him, "Master, how many times shall we forgive — seven?" "Nay," He answered — "seventy times seven." In other words, just keep right on forgiving.

I would like to conclude these thoughts on relationships with a promise of the unlimited possibilities for positive change through forgiveness. I want to tell you that it is possible to heal a troubled rela-tionship even with someone who has passed on. This is possible because all such healing is a result of *inner* forgiveness and *spiritual* love. Relationships are lessons in inner growth. If we can grow to a point where, were the other person still alive, we would be in har-mony with them, we have learned the lesson of the relationship, and it is complete.

My dad and I did not have very good communication in our rela-tionship. We loved each other in a family kind of way, but we were not intimate, like friends. In my adolescent years, I was sometimes disrespectful toward him, and I did not give him as much honor or understanding as I would now like to have given him.

In the years following his passing, I did a lot of growing up. As I learned the importance of respect and understanding, I shuddered to think how uncourteous I had been to my dad. In my heart, I wished to apologize to him, and to tell him of my love and appreciation for him.

One night he came to me in a dream. In this dream, I met him at a party, and he was radiant and peaceful. While he was overweight and reclusive in life, at this party he was slim and friendly. When we greeted, he told me that he was doing fine, and I was very happy to see how joyous he was. I felt, too, that he now had his own life to live. We parted in friendship and mutual respect for each other's path. I awoke from the dream with a deep sense of resolution and peacefulness about my father and myself. I believe that our relationship was healed, even after he left this life.

This experience and the others like it have served as my lessons in what is necessary to transform relationships. As I have learned more about how to love, forgive, and find goodness in myself and others, I have discovered that forgiveness is a gift from God that always heals. I know that it can heal our relationships, our lives, and our world. In so doing shall it mend our broken hopes, return to us our forgotten dreams, and bestow upon us the miracle of Grace. Fulfilling relationships, I have found, are not too good to be true. They are good enough to be true.

"Your purpose on earth is to make peace. As you have discovered this purpose, the power to heal relationships comes to rest in your hands.

You hold the entire universe within yourself. Take all into your arms, and all persons and things reveal themselves to be the expression of God's Love for you, which is really your Love for Him. Where Love is, the purpose of life is understood. Where there is no love, there is nothing.

We implore you to raise each precious moment of relationship up to the altar of the Most High. Hold your fellows in holy respect, and speak to all as you would speak to the holiest angel. Chide not yourself for your errors, but correct them. Were you to forgive your brethren but not yourself, you would remain in error. In Truth, the forgiveness of your brethren and yourself are one and the same.

You have been cleansed by the Blessing of your Heavenly Beloved. Your soul rests satisfied as you stand, bathed in purity, clad in the white robes of forgiveness, before the chair of your Father, who quietly acknowledges your Holy Presence. This day is cause for great celebration, for this is the reunion for which you have borne the tribulation of earth. Your life has led you to the reward of loving kindness — a blessing that you have always deserved by virtue of your Heritage. Our hands are outstretched to take yours, as you step across the threshold of your new life. Your efforts are completed through Grace."

FILLING UP AND SPILLING OVER

Filling up and spilling over,
It's an endless waterfall,
Filling up and spilling over,
Over all.
> — Cris Williamson, "Waterfall"

One bright spring morning, I stepped outside the restaurant where I was working, for a breath of fresh air and sunshine. As I closed the door behind me, a man that I had not seen before approached me with a radiant smile and exclaimed, "Gosh, it's a beautiful day, isn't it?"

"It certainly is!" I happily agreed.

"You know, my friend," he went on, "I just want to tell you how happy I am since I allowed God into my life!"

I was a little surprised that he spoke so intimately to me and I was, in fact, a little leery that he was about to go into a sermon or invite me to a meeting or ask for a donation. But there was something genuine about him, and so I loaned him my ear.

"I used to be miserable," he explained. "I had so many worries and poor health, my business was floundering, and I just did not like life. Then, one day, I realized how wonderful and magnificent is God! I saw, as if for the first time, the splendor of His creation! He made the trees, the birds, and the flowers! And what's more, I realized that He really loves me!"

As I listened to his delightful story, my doubts disappeared, my heart opened, and I began to feel and flow with him.

"Since that splendid moment," he continued, "my life has been miracle after miracle. I wake up in the morning and I look forward to each new day. I have many wonderful friends, and my work is satisfying. I just love life, and I am so grateful that God is so good to me!"

He put his hand on my shoulder, looked me squarely in the eye, and told me, "I just want you to know that I love you, and to say, 'God bless you.' "

With that, my mysterious friend turned and walked (or floated) on down the street. No sermons. No meetings. Nothing asked in return. Just "filling up and spilling over."

Thrilled over such a miraculous encounter, I ran into the store to tell my coworker, who I knew would want to meet this extraordinary man. She immediately dropped what she was doing, ran out the door, and sought to find him. But he was nowhere to be found. It was a small town. He could not have gone very far. She searched all the streets, yet he seemed to have disappeared. Perhaps he was an angel.

Spiritual awakening is spread by *overflow*. We cannot force another into higher consciousness. We are all like flower buds — we must open and bloom at our own rate, catalyzed by the warmth of the sun. The best way to support another person in their growth is to love them. They will feel so free and easy in our presence that their blocks to growth will just melt away. No amount of preaching, teaching, or pressuring will speed up their evolution, and it may even retard it. We may share, offer ideas, and invite if we feel to do so, yet this reaching out must be offered lightly, with an open hand, so that our friend feels completely free to accept our invitation or decline it. That's just the way sharing God has got to be. God must be chosen.

No one has ever been browbeaten into God, but many have been inspired, impressed, and enthused. We must teach not so much with our words, but by our example. If we would like a spouse, a friend, or a child to "get" what we have gotten, they must *catch it* from us. If we simply live the values that we hold dearest in our heart, there is a good chance that our friends will notice the positive changes in our life. They will respond to the light in our faces, and the peace in our eyes will awaken peace within them. One day they may say to us, "You look so happy lately — what have you been doing?" This is our opportunity to share, if we like — we have been asked.

There are many paths to the top of the mountain, where we all meet as One, without religion, name, or form. There is no need — and no use — to clutch at or attempt to proselytize potential converts to whatever cause we hold dear. If our cause is worthwhile, it will inspire on its own merit. ("Those that are mine will know me," said Jesus.) There is no truth in the idea that the more people that belong to an organization or a group, the better or truer it is. Truth cannot be measured by a number of devotees; it is a qualitative experience in the heart of each aspirant.

The Truth does not need anyone or any organization to sell it. The Truth sells itself by transforming the inner and outer lives of those that it touches. The Truth needs no marketing, packaging, or promotion. It needs only to be *lived*. People who live Truth usually have many people attracted to them without any advertising or soliciting. One characteristic of a cult is that members are coerced to join and restricted from leaving. The students of a teacher of Truth are free to come and go as their hearts guide them.

Jesus Christ, for example, was so full that His Truth has spilled over for two thousand years, to billions of people. It is staggering to me how one man could live and teach in a remote land for three short years, and in His Name millions of churches have been erected all over the world, incalculable healings have taken place, and the lives of so many human beings have been transformed and uplifted. Jesus brought a force of forgiveness to the earth that has reverberated throughout the entire universe which we, as a race, have yet to understand or put into practice.

Jesus was not the only great one. Moses, Buddha, Mary, Krishna, Mohammed, St. Theresa, Lao Tse, and many, many others have served as messengers of Light. Though they each had a slightly different style of teaching, they are all one in teaching the Truth of One God, One Life, and One Love. On this they all agree.

The best and only way to teach is by sharing. My life is a lesson for me and for the world, and so is yours. My experience is an illustration of God's Truth in expression. My "failures" are as educational as my successes. Each of our feelings, problems and insights are here for the upliftment of all humanity. When one person grows, all of humanity grows. When one of us conquers a personal limitation, we conquer the limitations of all. Every one of us is cleansing the universe of error. When we live in Truth, our thoughts and actions send out ripples that awaken the awareness of Truth in all living things. Our life is a sacrifice — not in martyrdom — but in service. When one person suffers, he or she is ending the suffering of all living beings. When we know God, we are bringing all of creation closer to God. In this way, we are truly instruments of God's Peace. This Peace would She share with all, through each.

"Your awareness of God is the healing you offer to your brethren. The Light you see is a gift given to be shared. What God gives to you belongs to you, and through you it belongs to all.

Those who live the Truth can never lose it. If you feel diminished in rejection, you face only your learned insecurity. Do not expect to be accepted by those that see you as a part of an old world. When your faith gains the firmness of a rock, resistance can find no place in your experience. Stand for the Truth, and those that love Truth will stand by your side.

Your creative words and simple deeds are shining stars in a dismal night. We charge you with glorifying the Truth in a world that hates Truth, and we ask you to live for Love in a world that flees from Light. You yourself have chosen this work, and we hail you for so commiting your acts. The days to come shall challenge you to your mettle, but through the Holy Spirit, that selfsame Spirit to Whom you have dedicated your life, you shall emerge unscathed. This is our dauntless promise to you.

Go forth, Children of Light, as did the original disciples and as all who truly love God must do, and ignite the fire of Truth by living it. Be true to yourself, for only in such simple honesty is Peace confirmed. The Light of the world shines through your faces and your hearts, and blesses through your hands. You are the song that I sing to the world."

THE POWER OF APPRECIATION

Appreciation and blessing are one and the same. We sometimes say, "Let's bless the food now," or "Bless you," or "May this house be blessed." Actually, we have no power to make anything more Holy than it already is. *Everything is already completely blessed,* and all the prayers in the world could not make it more blessed. We certainly could not imbue a loaf of bread or a person with more God than already lives within them. What we can do, however, is to *see,* or appreciate the God-infused blessedness in the person or object, guaranteed by the Light that lights the world.

If we are not seeing that Light, it is not because it is not there — it is because we are not looking at it. I was once feeling annoyed at a good friend of mine over a little matter — he owed me a small amount of money. I allowed my resentment to obscure my vision of him, and I was judging him more than I was loving him. When I realized this, I decided "No! Love is more important to me than a few dollars. I will not throw him out of my heart." I then began to think of all the qualities about him that I appreciated. He is a very strong, good-natured, and sensitive man. He is extremely compassionate and generous. As I thought more about his good qualities, I realized how much I really did love him and I felt so grateful to have him as a friend. Compared to the importance of his friendship to me, this small debt seemed miniscule. I traded my irritation for appreciation, and that made all the difference. (And he paid the debt, as well.)

When we appreciate someone or something, we are blessing them in the most powerful way. We are acknowledging their Divine origin.

THE DRAGON DOESN'T LIVE HERE ANYMORE

We are giving thanks for a gift from God. Appreciation is a form of prayer. If you are uncomfortable with traditional forms of prayer, just start appreciating the things in your life, and this gratefulness will be more pleasing in the eyes of God than a ritual that has no meaning for you.

There is an old song that has ever-new meaning:

> *Count your blessings,*
> *Count them one by one.*
> *Count your blessings,*
> *See what God has done.*

Every year around Thanksgiving, I take a piece of paper and make a list of all in my life for which I am grateful. I start with the basics, the things that we sometimes take for granted, like food, shelter, and clothing. Actually, we should "take them for granted," for, like the lilies of the field, we are in the loving care of a nurturing Divine Mother who gladly takes it upon Herself to meet all of our needs. Too often, however, we overlook these gifts without appreciation, and our thoughts of lack push abundance out of our experience. When we consciously focus on the good in our lives — such as through a list like this — we unite our mind with the power of appreciation, and we make ourselves available to receive the blessings that God is always offering.

On my list I include my friends and the loving and caring things that anyone has done for me, especially the "little" things, like a bright smile or a prompt reply to a letter. There are so many miracles that we can find when we are willing to acknowledge them. A few weeks ago, for example, I received a phone call from a man in my town who has the same name as me. Because my telephone number was not listed in the directory, he was receiving calls from my friends and coworkers trying to get in touch with me. What I appreciated so much was that he was extremely kind and pleasant in asking me to make my number more available to my friends. He didn't have to be so congenial. Someone else might have gotten irritated about this unnecessary nuisance. When I apologized to him for his inconvenience, he said, "Well, that's O.K. — we Alan Cohens have got to stick together, you know!" He didn't even know me, and yet he was willing to stick together with me. I thought that was pretty grand.

Next on my list I write down the hardships and challenges that have made me strong as I have had to overcome them. Perhaps these should be first on the list of appreciations, for these are the gifts that have brought me closer to God, and I can think of no greater blessing than knowing the Source of all blessings.

My thanksgiving list concludes with any abilities or skills that God gave me to be creative and expressive, and through which I can make some kind of contribution to the world. As I finish writing, I am always amazed at the length of the list, and I always feel a little foolish at not having recognized the abundance in my life.

The people who are successful are those who are grateful for everything they have. Those who complain, whine, or fight life cannot in this consciousness be successful, for in their negation they lose their creative energy and cut themselves off from any possibilities of abundance that are flowing their way. Giving thanks for what we do have always opens up the door for more to come, and ungratefulness always closes it.

I like to start and end my day with thoughts of praise and appreciation. I look in the mirror in the morning, and no matter how I feel or look, I say (out loud) "Wow! A new day! I'm so grateful to be alive and healthy! Something wonderful is going to happen to me today! I believe in miracles! There are limitless possibilities for me! I know that God is working *with* me. Just think how many opportunities there will be to love! Thank you, God, for this new day!"

Now, if anyone who didn't know me just happened to walk by the door at that moment, they might think I was a little flaky, but I don't care. I think we have to be a little unusual to make it in life. The world is inside out. That which the world approves of is insane. So, if I ever find myself doing anything a little crazy like this, I know I must be on the right track.

I like to end the day in the same way, with a gentler tone. As I lie in bed before going to sleep, I quietly look over my day and think of the blessings that have been given to me. If I made any foolish blunders, I give thanks that I became aware of them, and I am grateful that I will be less likely to repeat the same mistake. I like to live in a realm of thanksgiving.

The more we appreciate, the more we will find to appreciate. "To him that hath, more shall be given." This can work both ways. Just as blessing a situation brings freedom, cursing it brings bondage. The more we rail against a problem in our lives, the more pain it will bring us. Cursing a person or event is denying the God that lives within them, and until we recognize the inner Light there, the situation will remain a curse to us. Just as it is not in our power to really add blessing to anything, neither is it in our power to curse anything. All we can do in condemning anything is to uphold and increase our own sense of separation and loneliness, which is the sole root of our desire to curse anything. Lack of appreciation is simply a matter of limited seeing, like looking at a crack in the ceiling of the Sistine Chapel. We do not need to create anything new; we need only to see the whole picture of what we already have.

Another old song goes:

> You got to AC-CENT-CHU-ATE THE POSITIVE
> Elim-my-nate the negative
> Latch on to the affirmative
> Don't mess with Mister In Between
> You've got to spread joy up to the maximum
> Bring gloom down to the minimum
> Have faith . . .

The song contains the secret of happiness. We *can* control the amount of happiness in our lives, simply by training our minds to focus on that which is good, beautiful, and true. We do not need to fight or curse that which is not good. All we need to do is to accentuate the positive, and the negative will shrivel up and waste away from lack of attention.

More than anything else, we must appreciate ourselves. Swami Muktananda said, "The biggest error we can make is to not love our Self." God made each of us with the intention to bless the world through us. We can make a supremely valuable contribution to the universe simply by appreciating our holiness and seeing all as blessed. The more we bless life, the more life will bless us, for that is The Plan, The Great Idea for which all creation sprang into existence. As we sanctify our lives through our own gratefulness, the illusion of lack vanishes like the morning mist, and our cup runs over with thanksgiving enough to share a million times over.

"All is fully blessed. Your growth is but an adjustment of consciousness, a change in your perception of the Source of your life. The first petal of spiritual awakening is wonder. This is the beginning of the acceptance of your Heritage.

All things are born of the holy spark of God. In such realization is your release from the burdens of your own creation, ghostly concepts which you vainly attempted to prove. You relieve yourself from your fabricated expectations when you see that God has an Expectation for you which far outshines your small idea of what you can do with Love.

There is a certain popularity in words and expressions of derision. This is the very error that denies bliss to the hearts of those who cry out for it. Think clearly about the effect of your words. Such contemplation will reveal to you your ministry, which is your power to heal and to bless through supportive words and acts. You are entrusted with the answers to your brothers' prayers. Deliver blessings through your kindness, and you serve in the way of the Divine.

As your sense of appreciation expands, great wonders are made known to you. Miracles cease to maintain the cloak of mystery that enshrouded them, for it is only in the fear of Love that you made a rarity of what you admitted as miraculous. The spiritual master does not seek in exotic lands for the demonstration of the miraculous, but welcomes the simple aspects of life as marvelous. Be childlike in your enjoyment of what is given to you, and the Kingdom of Heaven welcomes you as its happy prodigal."

IF I HAD MY LIFE TO LIVE OVER

Nadine Stair — 85 years old
Louisville, Kentucky

I'd dare make more mustakes next time.
  I'd relax, I would limber up, I would be sillier
than I have been this trip.
  I would take fewer things seriously.
I would take more chances.
  I would take more trips.
I would climb more mountains, swim more rivers,
  I would eat more ice cream and less beans.
I would perhaps have more actual troubles but,
  I'd have fewer imaginary ones.

You see, I'm one of these people who live sensibly
  and sanely hour after hour,
day after day, oh, I've had my moments and if
  I had it to do over again,
I'd rather have more of them.
  In fact, I'd try to have nothing else.
Just moments, one after another instead of living so
  many years ahead of each day.
I've been one of those persons who never goes
  anywhere without a thermometer,
a hot water bottle, a raincoat, a parachute.
  If I had to do it over again
I would travel lighter than I have.

If I had my life to live over, I would start barefoot
  earlier in the Spring and stay that way
later in the Fall.
  I would go to more dances.
I would ride more merry-go-rounds.
  I would pick more daisies.

DANCIN' UP THE PATH

The first time I saw Swami Satchidananda, I learned what spirituality is about. The scene was very subdued. On the stage there was a couch, a microphone, and an array of beautiful flowers. A group of his devotees, wearing white, led the audience in chanting. When news of the swami's arrival came, a great hush fell over the audience. As he entered the room, all silently rose to their feet. Every eye in the room was fixed on the poised figure in the flowing robe. The swami politely bowed, and those around him respectfully returned the bow. As he took his place on the couch, not a whisper could be heard. He crossed his legs in full lotus position, closed his eyes, took a deep breath, and prepared to speak. It was a very serious moment.

"This microphone looks like a big cigar in my mouth!" were his first words, and that was the end of the seriousness. The audience roared with laughter that released the subtle tension of an idea that spirituality is supposed to be stuffy. The audience had been grave; the swami was full of fun. "I have never met a holy person that was not joyous and happy," Hilda has told us many times. Too often, we believe that to be spiritual is to be serious, somber, and even maudlin. Yes, the spiritual path requires of us seriousness of purpose, discipline, and sometimes sternness, but these attributes must always be combined with lightness, fun, and celebration.

Enlightenment does not only mean to see the light, but to *take it light*. Enlightened people take life lightly. Light is the opposite of dark, but it is also the opposite of "heavy." If we see life as a heavy burden, a load, an obligation, we are not looking at it from an enlightened point

339

of view. Jesus said, "Come to me, all who labor and are heavy burdened, and I shall give you rest. My yoke is easy, and my burden is
light."

I just know that Jesus was not a sad sack. I thrill to every movie
or play that portrays the life of the Master. Jesus is, however, too
often shown as such a serious character, stern and foreboding. I don't
believe that Jesus could have really been so grave, or else He would
have scared all of His disciples away. I believe that He won His
followers to Him by His light-heartedness and His love. Yes, I'm sure
He was very serious at times, but I am also certain that most of the
time He was joyful, radiant, happy, delightful, and delighted. I would
stake all that I feel about Jesus on this picture of Him. I know that He
laughed with his disciples, that He had a sense of humor, and that His
whole life was *not* a crucifixion. He loved little children, and He
taught, "You are the Light of the world." I do not believe that He could
teach the Light of the world without emanating the Light of the world.
I love the statues of Him where He is alive and beautiful and standing
with arms open in forgiving love. This is the Jesus that we need to
know more of; it is the Jesus of the garden, as well as the cross. Life
will hand us our share of crosses. We do not need to build any more
for ourselves by making ourselves miserable because we have
somehow learned to equate spirituality with agony. The sign of real
spirituality is joy. As we learn how to accept and express joy, we find
we have fewer crosses to bear.

Many people are familiar with the story of Norman Cousins. Dr.
Cousins is a medical doctor and former editor of *Saturday Review.* He
was diagnosed as having a rare degenerative disease of the spine,
which his doctors called irreversible and gave him no chance for
recovery. Dr. Cousins was not, however, prepared to accept their
prognosis. He understood the power of thought. He reasoned that *if
negative thinking causes disease, then positive thoughts should be able
to dissolve it.* So Dr. Cousins borrowed a movie projector, rented
some old Marx Brothers and Candid Camera films, and invited his
friends to his hospital room to join him for some light entertainment.
Here is Dr. Cousins' story of what then happened:

> *We pulled down the blinds and turned on the machine . . .*
> *It worked. I made the joyous discovery that ten minutes of*
> *genuine belly laughter had an anesthetic effect and would*

give me at least two hours of pain-free sleep. When the
pain-killing effect of the laughter wore off, we would
switch on the motion picture projector again, and, not in-
frequently, it would lead to another pain-free sleep inter-
val. *

After a few days, Dr. Cousins was required to leave the hospital because the laughter from his room was disturbing the other patients. So he checked out of the hospital and into a hotel, where he continued his laughter therapy and took large doses of vitamin C, found primarily in citrus fruits, which absorb a great amount of light (as in en*light*enment). His account continues:

By the end of the eighth day I was able to move my thumbs
without pain . . . it seemed to me that the gravel-like
nodules on my neck and the backs of my hands were
beginning to shrink. There was no doubt in my mind that I
was going to make it back all the way. I could function,
and the feeling was indescribably beautiful. *

Dr. Cousins discovered — for all of us — the healing power of laughter. This medicine was given to Alan Watts by an old Zen master who prescribed a very unusual form of meditation: "You stand up, place your hands on your hips, and begin to laugh. Start with a few 'ha-ha's,' then add a few 'he-he's,' and before long, the 'ho-ho's' will be coming of themselves." At first, the laughter seems phony and forced, but as you stay with it, it becomes real — and uproarious. Use of this meditation is especially indicated for dull groups. It is also a very practical way to start the day. I know a man who, upon awakening each morning, walks directly to the mirror, places one hand on a hip, points the other at the image of himself, and begins to laugh as hard as he can. (It certainly is more fun than looking in the mirror and groaning.)

In the Tarot cards, there is an especially intriguing image of *The Fool*. This is a picture of a young man with a flower in his hand, skipping along gaily, about to dance over the edge of a cliff. There is some

---

*Norman Cousins, *Anatomy of an Illness as Perceived by the Patient*, W.W. Norton & Co., 1979.

controversy, I am told, as to whether this is the first card in the deck, or the last — whether it represents a form of wisdom, or ignorance.

Perhaps it is both. Surely we must keep our feet on the ground and take care to be cautious in a treacherous world. On the other hand, there is an element of Divine foolishness in many spiritual masters. From a worldly point of view, some of the great saints, like Joan of Arc, St. Francis, and Sri Ramakrishna (in India) were considered insane. But their madness was not unto the devil, but *God*. In *Brother Sun, Sister Moon*, St. Clare tells St. Francis, "They say you are mad because you would rather romp through the fields and sit among the flowers than be a slave to business, as they are; but I think that it is *they* who are mad, and not you."

The Tarot card may represent our need to dance up the path of life, even though the body and our worldly attachments are destined for death. We never really know when the edge of the cliff is approaching, so we might as well enjoy a few flowers while we can.

The world does not know how to enjoy itself because it does not really know what are the ingredients for happiness. If it did, the world would be happy, and (if you have read the newspapers lately) you can see that the world is not a very happy place. It follows, then, that if we want to feel joy, we are going to have to find it in some other way than the world is trying to get it.

Song and celebration are written off by the serious-minded as foolishness, but they are gifts from God, given to heal feelings of aloneness and separation. It is impossible to sing and be miserable at the same time. Without song and celebration, life is a bore and a drudgery. With it, we can dance. It doesn't matter so much *what* we celebrate, but that we *do* celebrate. (There is an old joke about a man who quit being an atheist because there weren't enough holidays.) If we allow our minds and hearts to be open, we can celebrate all the holidays of all the religions. We can enjoy the light on Christmas, on Hannukah, and on Krishna's birthday, as well. God is grand enough to take it *all* in. When we sing along with it all, we join the Godly chorus and infuse the Voice of God into a dismal world.

If we find ourselves lost in the world of pressures, stress, and insecurity, the best method to find our way home is to "ease on down the road." I went to an astounding series of lectures by a very astute and successful chiropractor, on "Maintaining Good Health." The first lecture was on proper exercise and care of the spine. The second was on good nutrition. The third, which he described as the most important, was on positive thinking. He told that, after he had completed his education on all the proper health practices, he went to work in a clinic in New York City. There he found as patients a number of old men who had, from his perspective, horrendous health habits. They smoked cigarettes, ate lots of junk food, and drank liquor. To his surprise, they were in remarkably good health. He saw that, though they did not take care of their bodies, they had a very relaxed and easy-going attitude toward life. They lived from day to day and let nothing bother them. In short, they took life easy. This, perhaps, balanced out or even overrode their poor health habits. Though they will eventually have to reconcile their mistreatment of their bodies, they have caught on to one of the keys to joyous living: *taking it easy.*

A man who picked me up when I was hitchiking told me of a study that was done on the relationship between diet, frame of mind, and health. A group of hard-core health food devotees and a group of junk food eaters were tested for the amount of vitamins and nutrients in their blood. It turned out that the health food enthusiasts registered *fewer* nutrients in their blood than the "junkies." I believe that this, if it is so, is because the stress and worry about eating the right foods probably robs the body of more nutrients than the foods put in. If someone adheres to a diet or any regimen *fanatically*, afraid of losing health or life with bad foods, he is likely to suffer more from the fear than he would from the food. I am not advocating junk foods over health foods; I strive to keep a nutritious diet. It is important, however, to know the effect of an easy and relaxed attitude in life and to remember that the spirit is always more important than the form.

Life is too short and too insane to take it very seriously. Yogananda said that "This world is just a big mental institution." If we learn to see the people around us — and ourselves — as mental cases, we can laugh at the world and ourselves. Think, for example, of the things that people believe are important, like toothpaste that gives you sex appeal and blue jeans that cost twice the price because a name is printed on the hip pocket; think of the state of world politics, in which an unelected brother of a president is paid millions of dollars by a foreign government to wield influence which the president can't control; and think of the silly things that you and I have become upset about (when I was a child, I was ejected from the audience of *The Merry Mailman* TV show when I went into a hysterical fit because I thought the clown on the show had stolen my father's hat). Surely we are all a little crazy. I don't think that we would be here if we were not. How, then, can we take ourselves so seriously?

I believe that if we cannot find a way to laugh about a situation, we have not seen it in a big enough perspective. We need to be able to laugh at ourselves and our problems. Sometimes our difficulties even disappear when we laugh at them. And even if they don't, we will at least have had a good laugh.

My old friend Jim and I would spend many hours trying to figure out the meaning of life. One day we got onto the question of "What is laughter about, anyway?"

"All laughter," Jim told me, "is a reflection of *The Cosmic Absurdity*."

"Wow — The Cosmic Absurdity! . . . What's that?" I wondered. It sure sounded fascinating, whatever it was.

"The Cosmic Absurdity is this," he explained. "If you really think about it, all of life is absurd. There is no meaning to anything. When you realize the foolishness that our lives are based on, all we can really do is laugh." To tell you the truth, I didn't really understand what he was talking about, but it sounded absurd, and so we just laughed.

Wisdom and humor hold thrones of equal stature in Heaven's court. More often than we would realize, there is no difference between the two. There is an old story about a man who goes to a doctor and says, "Doctor, every time I raise my arm like this, it hurts!" The doctor thinks for a moment, and prescribes, "So don't raise your arm like that!" The source of this parable is under controversy. Some say it is an ancient Zen koan and others argue that it is a Henny Youngman joke. It could be either. Or both. Or neither.

What good is life without laughter? Those who know God know how to laugh at life. Swami Vishnudevananda is a fine example of living in fun. At a potentially serious conference on the coming tribulation in the world, the swami sat on the edge of the stage and heckled the other speakers with loving wisecracks. His humor was not directed at any person, but at the foolishness of life itself. There was talk of earthquakes and floods and devastation, and the swami laughed his way through all of it, even though he was one of the speakers. When it was his turn to speak, he heckled himself as much as the others. He was blessed with the rare ability to not take himself seriously.

It is said that it takes only about seven muscles to smile but fifty or more to frown. It seems to me that God makes it easy for us to do what She wants us to do. I think She likes to see us smiling, because we like to see each other smiling, and She gets to enjoy life when Her children do.

The story is told of Rabbi Nachman of Bratslav, a pious and revered Hasidic sage. During a time of great oppression of the Jewish people, his students came to him, distraught. "Rabbi," they queried, "are we permitted to say the holiday prayers of rejoicing and thanksgiving during this dark time? How can we rejoice when our people are so maligned?"

The rabbi lit up with a wise smile. "Ah!" he exclaimed, "This is the time when we most need to rejoice! It is easy to celebrate God in the easy times, but when the blows of life are severe, our song must ring out twice as loud!"

> *Dance, dance, wherever you may be*
> *For "I am the Lord of the Dance," said He*
> *I'll lead you all wherever you may be*
> *I'll lead you all in the Dance with me*
> — *"THE LORD OF THE DANCE"*

"*Children of Light*, pay attention to what we call you, for in your name is the key to your liberation.

We delight in your joyousness. *Listen* well to the laughter of children at play, for these little ones are close to the heart of *God*, and they play at the very feet of the *Master*. *Would* you remain wailing at the gate while *He*, with open arms, bids you enter? *The* wonders of the garden await you. *Step* through the gate of roses into the home of your heart.

Were you to go through one day, yea, even one hour, in song and celebration, your too-long held woes would melt like ice before the sun. *You* do not realize with what tenacity you cling to your self-created misery. *You* clutch at it as if it were a prized possession, a pearl of great price. *You* believe that you enjoy it, but inwardly you know that this cannot be the way for you. *Your* learned will for sorrow is replaced by *His* will for your joy.

You best serve *God* with all of your heart. *God's* real nature is happiness. *Serve Him* by expressing joyousness, and your reward is the awakening that your joy is *His*."

LOVE IS THE
GREATEST OF ALL

If, when I leave this mad world, I am required to give an accounting for my acts in this life, there is only one question that I am concerned about answering: "Did you love?" If I can earnestly answer "Yes," then I shall consider my time well spent and my purpose in living fulfilled.

Years ago, while in the seemingly mundane act of walking up a back stairway in a college building, I realized that there is no power in the universe greater than Love, and no act more important than loving. I was thinking about what it is that enables great people to achieve excellence in their art. As I pondered, it became clear to me that anyone can become anything he or she sets their heart on being. I just knew that any master orator, musician, or photographer has become proficient only through commitment and practice. As I realized in that very special moment that I, too, could see the fulfillment of my deepest wish, I asked myself, "What would I like to make a stand for in this lifetime?" The answer came immediately and clearly, in a firm but gentle whisper: *Love*. How happy I felt to know that if I determined it to be so, my dream of Love could actually come true!

Love is the ideal and the dream of every person who lives, for in Love were our souls conceived, and in Love is our Destiny to express. We are fulfilled when we are in Love, and somehow empty without it. It is the very purpose of our being alive, and the idea God held in Mind when we sprang from the celestial womb.

Though billions of words have been written about Love, not one of them — or all of them — could fully capture Love. Love is infinite, and like a mountain spring that bubbles up from an unending source, it fills all hearts and hands that open themselves to accept It. Love is always alive in our hearts, expressing Itself in ways that we do not understand. Love is always eager to share and expand Itself to bless all who desire Its radiant Presence. Meher Baba said,

> *Love has to spring spontaneously from within. It is in no way amenable to any form of inner or outer force. Love and coercion can never go together; but though Love cannot be forced on anyone, It can be awakened in him through Love itself. Love is essentially self-communicative. Those who do not have It catch It from those who have It. True Love is unconquerable and irresistable; and It goes on gathering power and spreading Itself, until eventually It transforms everyone whom It touches.*

Love is not limited to any age, place, name, color, or experience, and yet Love lives equally within all of these. Love is completely free of any kind of restriction. The oldest person is as sensitive to the life of Love as any young lover, for Love is ever new. The hardest heart is opened instantly through the magic of a loving word or touch. Love is more vital to us than food. There are saints and yogis who live for many years with little or no food, yet their hearts are full to overflowing with Love, and they are fully nourished. We may consume the finest delicacies, yet, if we have not Love, it is as though we were dead.

Love and giving are as inseparable as the lily and its fragrance. It is impossible to love without giving, for giving is the very nature of Love. Neither can we truly give without Love. Sai Baba said that "all acts of service are meaningless unless they are given with Love." When we discover the miracle of Love, we cannot stop ourselves from giving — nor do we want to stop. It is obvious to the lover that Love only increases when It is given.

All Love is Divine. Let it never be said that physical or romantic Love is less than God's Love, for ideas cannot be apart from their source. Even when Love takes an object, It is holy, for Love is Love, and It is uncompromising in Its commitment to Its own purpose. As the first two leaves of a flower, which later drop away, help the stem rise out of the soil, conditional Love is a herald of the unlimited Love to come. With Love we learn forgiveness, and with forgiveness, compassion. We come to understand that Love remains constant through the evolution of Its expression.

The Christ beseeched us, "Love God with all your heart, with all your soul, and with all your strength; this is the greatest teaching of all." Of course it is. God is in everything and *is* everything. When we love all people and all things, we love God. And when we simply love God, all things reveal themselves to embody His Holy Presence.

Love is the true healing force of the universe. When we love another person, we see their wholeness, and when this wholeness is kindled in our thoughts and fanned with our good intention, it awakens their own knowledge of their Divine heritage of completeness.

I saw a healing that I want to always remember as a symbol of the unsurpassable power of Love. The man I am thinking of was nervous, withdrawn, and fearful. A group of people surrounded him, gently rested their hands on him, and quietly gave him healing Love. I saw that man go through the most dramatic transformation I have ever seen. I could literally see the lines and the dark spots leave his face. He began to breathe heavily, and I felt like I was having the privilege of witnessing a birth. The light that began to shine from his face was so bright that everyone in the room could hardly believe that it was the same man they saw a few minutes earlier. He looked as if he had lost about fifteen years of age in just a few minutes. If someone had thrown away their crutches or walked away from a wheelchair, I do not think it would have been as powerful as the transformation I saw in this man. It was a healing of the inner man — of the soul — a healing available to every human being. Such is the miracle of healing Love.

Love cannot be bought, sold, or reduced to any kind of commodity. We can sell our bodies, our possessions, our thoughts, and our work, but Love is ever free of ownership. It simply shines without concern for who or what It touches. The sun shines equally on the morning glory and on the weed. We may attempt to make a business of Love by saying, "I will love you if you will love me," but this is a distortion of the all-encompassing way that real Love unfolds. The happy Law of Life is that "If I love you, you will love me." And yet we cannot love another for the sake of receiving their Love in exchange. Love in exchange is a guilt bargain, and we only rob our own self in futile barter. Love given freely is the only Love that can satisfy, and we only magnify our joy in so loving. Some draw an artificial distinction between Love and power. I say that power is a ray of light from the star of Love. How much energy we have at our beckoning when we are in Love! Suddenly we are able to travel great distances, forsake sleep, and offer mighty acts of selfless service and giving! We are prepared to sacrifice our own desires for the sake of the beloved, and we are willing to overlook the imperfections and faults of the beloved. Love *is* blind, and blessedly so. Love is not blind to the Truth; It simply overlooks the unimportant aspects of personality that we usually, mistakenly, call "truth."

Who can fathom the mystery of Love? Certainly not I. To attempt to intellectually dissect the miracle of Love is to pull apart the threads that are woven into the very fabric of our existence. I do not care if I ever understand Love. I only know that I love, and if I never do anything else, I shall be fulfilled.

Sri Ramakrishna told that more than anything else, God loves to love. "Though a wealthy man with a large estate has many rooms in which he may dwell, he has one favorite sitting room in which he delights in being. The Lord loves to dwell in the chamber of the heart of man."

If we feel we have been hurt or disappointed in Love, we have been given a gift and a blessing. We receive a redeeming grace in disillusionment, for illusion is a tyrant and Truth a redeemer. The outcome of disillusionment is the Vision of Truth, and in Truth shines a Peace far greater than the world could give. In our suffering we may be tempted to believe that we have been forsaken by, or exiled from Love. Take heart, beloveds; Love could no more turn Its back on us than the sun deny itself to the treetops, or the ocean refuse to accept the rivers. No, beloveds, Love is as certain as Life and as constant as the mother's heartbeat to the babe in the womb.

No person or experience could offer us more Love than we already possess within our very own hearts, a Love that is eternally and irrevocably ours. Let us not wait for Love to come to us. Love comes to us only when we love. We can awaken our hearts in an instant by turning our thoughts toward our ideal, our Beloved. To look for Love is to offer our hand to a mirage. Who could give us more than we already are? Who could edify that which was created whole? Who could teach Love to Love?

Love finally reveals Itself to be the Holy Spirit, which we mystified by our belief in the mysterious. One has described the Holy Spirit of Love thus: "We cry out, 'Where can I find the Holy Spirit? . . . Tell me where to go, what to do!' Meanwhile, the Holy Spirit is pouring to us and through us, waiting only for our quiet acceptance to reveal Itself." Instead of mourning, "I want Love," we need only to affirm "I love."

Thus could Kabir say, "I laugh when I hear that the fish in the water is thirsty!" So, we stand initiated at the altar of the Temple of the Living Heart, ready to assume our charge as ministers of Love and Light to a world that begs for communion because it does not realize itself to be the body of God. As the purple mantle comes to rest on our shoulders, we, like Love Itself, must bow to our very Self in humble acknowledgement of the simple truth that what we sought is Who We Are.

"My Love for you, my own Children, is infinite. You could never be outside the fullness of my Love and the cradle of my loving arms. There is nothing that you could ever do that could cause you to lose my Love. I am eternally committed to loving you fully, without condition or expectation. This is my greatest, and my only, joy.

I am your Divine Mother. Your pain is my pain. Would that I could remove all of your sufferings from your shoulders and bear them, gladly, upon mine. But you are in the midst of a glorious adventure, a Divine journey in search of Truth, which shall reveal to you more freedom than I could offer you by removing your hardships.

Learn your lessons quickly and well, my beloved Children. I shall watch over you with guidance and protection as you wend your way home to my open arms. My heart is brimming with pride as I watch you grow in the knowledge of your own Perfection. My Love for you is so great that I can hardly bear the waiting for your homecoming. Yet shall I bear it, in confidence and strength.

In moments of trial, remember these words: My Love is ever with thee. Feel them in your heart and nurture them with your trust in my Presence. Call upon me when you need me. Do not feel unworthy to summon my help. You are precious to me in a way that you do not now comprehend. Trust that you will succeed in the innermost dream of your heart — the dream of the fullness of Love, which is my very dream for you."

The Future

NORMAL BUT NOT NATURAL

If you do not change direction, you may end up where you are heading.

— Lao Tse

Humanity, as a mass, has strayed so far from the path of Light that, for the most part, we have forgotten what the Truth is. We have become so steeped in ignorance that Reality and illusion have become reversed in our order of thinking. We have accepted hatred, pain, and separation as ways of life, and we have given up hope for fulfillment. We have adapted, accommodated, and adjusted for so long to the warped values of worldly life that we see visions of contentment, harmony, and peace as pipe dreams. We have become very, very lost.

Ignorance has not been cast upon us like a net, but has gradually crept into the fibre of our awareness like the smog around our cities that began as a subliminal veil, and grew into a monstrous cancer that enshrouds our livelihoods. We have gotten used to too much. Crime, evil, and prejudice are accepted as a matter of course. Horrendous reports on the six o'clock news fail to move us because we have heard them so often. Of necessity, we have become callous and withdrawn. Though we have adopted a posture that assumes that this is just the way life is supposed to be, there remains a faint, gnawing whimper deep in our gut, persistently reminding us that we were made for much more, for we *are* much more. Yet we would cover over that still, small voice with the habituation that has dulled us to our sense of Truth.

I cannot believe that this is the way God intended for us to live. It seems senseless to me that a Creator would bring forth a creation for an end of such suffering and separation. The world as we see it cannot be His Will. Yes, everything is His Will when seen from the highest perspective, but we cannot afford to accept that which we must realize to be in error. We cannot say "Yes" to a world in agony. We must recognize its need for healing.

I recently heard a lecturer on world hunger state that all of the hungry people in the world could be fed for seventeen billion dollars a year. The United States currently spends seventeen billion dollars on "defense" expenditures every *two weeks*. Our values are confused and our priorities inverted. Bribery, corruption, and dishonesty are no longer shocking, and they are accepted as a matter of course. When Richard Nixon was ejected from office in 1974, many of his defenders argued that "Nixon was no worse than most politicians — he was just unfortunate enough to get caught." And in a more recent government scandal, when several politicians were videotaped accepted large amounts of bribe money, their defense was that the government was guilty of "setting them up" for the bribe, and that their conviction should be overturned because the government was deceptive in its methods. Who of clear mind could accept this plea? What honest man could be "set up" for a bribe? Our sense of integrity has been dulled.

There is one more example of misdirected thinking that leads me to believe that we have become lost as a culture, as a civilization, and as Children of God. I recently heard that there is now a formal organization, with a title like "Children's Sexual Liberation," with the purpose of legitimizing and defending those who would molest children. The rational mind has become confused, and it attempts to uphold error in the name of Freedom. Something is wrong.

The recognition of delusion is a necessary step to the awakening to Truth. It takes honesty and courage to admit that we have strayed from the path. But it is a necessary admission. I must stand before God each night and see whether I have lived up to my highest ideals. Sometimes I do and too often I do not. But it is necessary for me to recognize both circumstances. I must ask God to show me what I am doing wrong, that I may correct it. Usually I do not like to hear it, but when I do, I am grateful.

We must scrutinize, with a clear mind, how we were really meant to live, as individuals and as the family of humankind. We may not like having to change, but a change of direction toward the Truth always brings a deep sense of peace within our heart, a fulfillment far deeper than the surface desires that seem to be satisfied with untruth. As Patricia Sun said, "The Truth feels good." Our deepest instincts always tell us when we have touched Truth. It feels like home, like a completion, like, "Of course."

Truth is the most natural thing that there is, but in the world it is the most foreign. Because the values of the world are upside down, light is a stranger, and the darkness welcomed. It is very easy to be normal. The world will love you and support you in your normality, for the world loves its own. Those who gravitate to negativity, gossip, and innuendo have a sure place in society; they shall never beg for company with which to commiserate. The marketplace of common affairs is built on complaints, criticisms, and guilt.

One who chooses the God-path faces loneliness and derision. He cannot expect or hope for understanding from the world. It will seem to accept him with a polite smile, but secretly mock and slander him behind closed doors. Friends and relatives will support him in word but not in thought. The devotee of Truth must be great enough to take the world into his heart though the world would cast him out of its own. Truth must love sin in a way that sin cannot understand Truth. This is because the lover of Light can see the Christ in all, while one who lives in darkness sees only veiled reflections of confused images.

Every human being is a Child of God. Some live their Godliness, while others hold it in potential as it lies dormant until awakened. The world of error, the normal world, is a husk of a seed of Divine possibility, patiently waiting to be released. The natural is hidden within the normal, though the two do not now seem to be one in expression on earth. We must feel the constriction of the husk before we can break through it. We must see the *dead end* sign on the street we are traveling before we can turn about to correct our course. The awareness of error is the impetus for transformation. Those who would harp on error have not yet seen it in full, for an error truly recognized is a correction set in motion. The only result of real understanding is change.

Eventually, all that is natural will become the normal; ideal and practice shall be one. This is the glorious vision held by all of the prophets of Truth. Until then we must tread the path of learning to distinguish between peace of mind and feverish dreams. The universe will not tolerate illusion, for untruth runs against the grain of all creation. Why would God have created Truth, were it not to be lived? Untruth exists only to be corrected. The unnatural that is accepted as the norm can continue to be perpetrated only until it is exposed. The world will then grasp for another illusion to mollify itself. Illusion, like a strain of bacteria that gains resistance to an antibiotic, reinforces itself in increasingly gross intensity until the forces of Light and darkness are divided by a chasm that clearly defines their difference. At that point, there can be no misunderstanding of the distinction.

At that point — the point at which we now find our evolution as a civilization — illusion has been exaggerated to a ridiculous degree, and the voice of sanity must be heard. The raving of insanity has revealed itself by its farcical grossness. The only remaining choice is Truth. At that moment, and only at that moment, can Truth and normality merge in expression on the earth plane. This is the meaning of the Age of Aquarius.

Join me in a vision of a world in which the Good Life is expressed as it was intended from the beginning. I see a world in which there is no dichotomy between what is idealized and what is condoned, where the will of men and the Will of God are One Will. In this new, bright world, nature is honored and revered as a loving friend, and not a threat. Here, there is nothing to conquer, for all forces are realized to be Holy, harmoniously working for mutual good. The foot that was turned astray is once again set firmly on the path of wholeness, and all who walk this path shine with the Love that the world has ignored, but could never be forgotten.

''The ways of the world are not those of God. The world loves darkness and would have its children believe that the darkness is the Light. Popular opinion is not to be the standard by which the Child of God may guide a Holy Life.

We know your difficulty in discerning between accepted belief and God's Truth. In the beginning stages of spiritual development, the aspirant may be sorely tried to distinguish between Truth and fantasy. While we understand the nature of this challenge, we tell you that it is fully necessary to know and to surrender to the voice of Truth that reverberates within your soul like a guiding star over a dark sea. We assure you that as decisions for the Light are made, the faculty of discrimination shall become very sharp, and the marriage of the intellect and the intuition is sanctified.

Hold firm, soldiers of Truth, to that which you cherish as dear. You may be tested and scorned, but the Angel of Valor protects you in your campaign. She looks over your shoulder in gentle support of your decision for God. Bear your loneliness bravely, and comrades of like purpose shall join you when you most need them.

The Truth is your only refuge. Pay homage to the words of no man, but reserve your worship for the Holy Spirit alone. You may be pressed to relinquish your ideals for the sake of the world, but you will find solace and renewal in the life of your heart's deepest bidding.

Be vigilant. Fear not to look at the world with clear seeing. Those who fail to regard signs of illness are required to pay the price of irresponsibility. Relinquish not your view of perfection, and never fail to execute right action in accord with widsom.

Children of the Most High, make integrity your banner and your bastion. Those of integrity are few, and the smallest act of right conscience shines in the darkness more than you know. Our hearts leap to consider those who live a life for God amid the mire of foulness. Be one of these. In so accepting this noble charge, you stand at the rudder of the destiny of mankind. Please do not underestimate your ability to save the world through your vision of morality. Choose rightly, and legions of angels and invisible brethren fly to your support. Choose wrongly, and you stand alone in a lost world.''

COMMUNICATION, COMMUNION, AND COMMUNITY

I

One of my favorite stories is that of the earthworm who pops his head out of the soil and sees a gorgeous earthworm just a few inches from him. Overtaken by the other worm's beauty, he tells her, "I love you . . . Will you marry me?" The other worm smiles and answers, "Don't be silly; how could I marry you? I'm your other half!"

We stand, now, on the threshold of a new evolutionary step in the unfoldment of humankind. The keynote of this step is the new understanding of an ancient truth: *We are One.* Behind our nationalities, colors of skin, cultures, lifestyles, and histories, we are One. It is this unity, this common bond, that will be the hallmark of a new age on earth.

During the past few decades, we have seen the rays of light of this new age beginning to make clear our next step, like the first faint glimmerings of dawn on the eastern horizon. These initial heartbeats of the child to be born to all have taken the form of sharing, joining together, and the affirmation of our collective unity as one family of human beings. Those who have heard the call of the conch, have let go of old, taught patterns of separateness and hiding, and stepped into the freedom of sharing. If there is any hope for mankind, it is in the sense of community that is rapidly maturing on the planet.

Humanity is now at a critical turning point. The dynamics of our choice are the same as they always have been, but the stakes, now, are very high. Our choice is this: *Unite, or die.* We must learn to cooperate. We must learn to accept. We must build our world on the foundation of God, and not upon separateness.

361

The question is: How big can we expand our idea of "Us?" How much can we widen our idea of who is equal to us? Who are we willing to take into our family?

As little egos, each of us once lived in a cold and limited world, revolving around "me." "Me" was not really satisfying, but it was all we knew. As our sense of self matured, we expanded to include our physical family, such as mom and dad, brother and sister, and later husband or wife in our sense of "Us." Everybody else was "Them," and "They" were always out to get "Us." Perhaps "They" were people of another color, another country, or another political idea. One thing was for sure, however: "They" were different than "Us," and "We" had to watch out for "Them." It was O.K. to share, accept, and be intimate with "Us," but certainly not "Them."

As we grew and the world forced "Us" to come into contact with "Them," experience revealed that some of "Them" were really not so bad. When that happened, we expanded our idea of who was "Us," until, as there became more and more of "Us" and less and less of "Them," we realized that *there really was no "Them" after all*, and in fact, *there never was*. It was all a mistake. As soon as we understood that everyone is "Us," we were ready for the next step in human evolution.

This is the threshold at which humankind now stands. Fantastically rapid developments in technology, communication, and transportation have allowed human beings, in a very short time, to make almost intimate contact with one another in a way that has revealed everyone in the world to be alike, and not different. We can no longer hide behind the facade of naiveté, for we now live on a very small planet, and our civilization has become, as Buckminster Fuller describes it, a "planetary village."

Since humanity has now been shown to be one great family, the task before us is: How quickly can we own up to our oneness with all people? When we know something to be true, we are held accountable for that knowledge in a way that we were not responsible in ignorance. Now that we know we are One, God expects us to live as One. The responsibility of that knowledge is very great, indeed.

All of the great spiritual masters and teachers throughout the ages have led us to this point. They have all along been giving us the principles of the life of unity that we are now ready to live. As we can now see, the Bible, the Koran, the Bhagavat Gita, and all the other writings of Truth have *not* been in conflict, and neither have the

COMMUNICATION, COMMUNION, AND COMMUNITY

religions that stand with them. It was only the small-mindedness of men that misconstrued similarities as differences and found separation where only harmony existed. We can see, as well, that while the outer expressions of the world's religions have been slightly different, their *essence* has always been the same. They have all been trying to tell us that there is One God, that man, in real nature, is Divine, and that Love is the key to man's unity with God.

It is this very unity that is reflected in our newly acknowledged family of man. We must now meet all people in the place where labels have no power to separate. This is not a physical location, but a realm in the heart, a space where it is obvious that we are not fragmented, but whole.

Our new awareness is really a powerful energy of a new consciousness — *planetary consciousness*. We have begun to realize that our actions affect all people everywhere, and that the earth and all of her inhabitants are really one great living, breathing organism. This consciousness is a major breakthrough for our planet — and it is our only hope for survival. We will survive only through our common identity, through our acknowledgement of our mutual Selfhood. The highest good of each of us is the highest good of all; my success is the achievement of all, my pain is the hurt of all, and humanity's well-being is one with my own. Patricia Sun said, "How can I be happy if there is someone who isn't happy?"

II

As conscious beings, we cannot afford to stop the growth of our awareness at planetary consciousness. We must constantly go beyond all ideas of limitation. If we now believe that earth is "Us" and everything else is "Them," we have not really understood the lesson of spiritual unity. We must open our consciousness to accept all in the universe as One.

I was fascinated to see how *Close Encounters of the Third Kind* has had a marked effect on our culture. Soon after its release, the themes and symbols of the motion picture were popularized in many forms. Children's games using sound and light became common; there was an advertisement for a religious retreat: "Have a close encounter with Judaism"; and I even saw a billboard showing a county bank rising up at the end of a long road to the stars. I believe this movie was so popular, far and away beyond any other U.F.O. movie, because it artfully portrayed "aliens" as *benevolent*. Although their form was very different then ours, these beings from outer space were portrayed as gentle, loving, and peaceful beings. They were "Us."

By contrast, most of the flying saucer movies I saw as a child showed aliens as power hungry monsters who came to conquer the earth with death rays, either for the sheer terror of it or because their planet was about to blow up, and they wanted to take over ours.

This beautiful *Close Encounters* movie, though, had communication and sharing as its theme. The "aliens" returned intact all of those persons that they had taken away; the people who saw the U.F.O.'s were drawn to them in a positive way; and the movie concluded with a most uplifting exchange of peaceful wishes between earthlings and the spacelings. A friend of mine who has been involved with a religious organization for a long time confessed to me, "Seeing that movie was probably the most profound spiritual experience of my life."

I believe that this movie symbolized a very significant expansion of our consciousness — we accepted non-earthlings as our friends, and not as our enemies. To me, the film represented yet another step in the growth of mankind: *universal consciousness*. In it, we took our brothers in "outer space" — or at least the possibility that they are there — into our circle of "Usness" — into inner space. In a way, we accepted that we are one with all life everywhere.

This time on earth is about putting into action our new understanding of our place in the cosmos. It is about practicing living in Oneness with all people. It is about bringing together the forces we hold in our hands, ones which could ultimately destroy us, but, if used wisely, can unite us. From the point of view of the person who thinks in terms of the past, it is a painful breakdown of the familiar. From the viewpoint of the aspiring soul, it is the herald of a new and better life, one of drawing together and sharing. It is a promise of friendship, mutual support, and community. It is the end of a "Them" which never existed, and the affirmation of an "Us" that has always been.

"The door to your Destiny is now opened before you. You now have the key to your new life: Oneness. Bring all of your efforts together to work for unity. Take every opportunity to affirm togetherness, family, and community. None of you can move any more rapidly than all of you, for now that you understand your unity as a family, you accept the joy and the suffering of all humanity as your own.

We who mark your way along the mountain path, would now direct you to a plateau as a gathering point. Unify your people. Draw together your factions. Scrutinize any residues of limitation that continue to bind you. Evaluate all of your plans and actions in terms of unity. You can proceed no further until you learn to move as a whole.

The recent political, monetary, and cultural events have forced you to gather together to share. It has become very advantageous to share living quarters, transportation, fuel, and food. Do you believe these events are accidental? Do not foolishly accept them as happenstance. The lessons of the world are now directed toward coming together. You have become accustomed to living in isolation and separation. We speak not of physical barriers, but spiritual ones. Separation exists not in the physical world, but in the mind. The lessons of this time are given to correct these false notions of boundaries.

Accept your membership in the community of souls. You are not apart from others, nor could you ever be. You are very much One being. Act united, feel integrated, and practice Oneness, for Union is the Truth that heals you."

LOOK, DADDY, THE WORLD IS TOGETHER!

A young father was beginning to feel a little annoyed with his five-year old son, who was asking him endless questions while he was trying to read the evening newspaper. Seizing on a scheme to buy him some quiet time, dad found a picture of the earth in the newspaper, cut it out, tore it into little pieces, and gave it to the child to reassemble as a jigsaw puzzle.

To the father's astonishment, the child was back minutes later with the picture perfectly intact.

"Look, Daddy, the world is back together!" the child exclaimed.

The father was amazed at how quickly the boy had finished. "How did you do it so fast?" he asked.

"It was easy! First, I couldn't fit the picture of the earth together. Then I looked on the other side of the pieces, and there were pictures of the parts of a man. It was much easier to put the man together, so that's what I did. And when the man came together, so did the earth!"

All of humanity's guides through the ages have taught exactly this truth. "If you want to bring about peace in the world," they tell us, "first bring about peace within yourself" . . . "Don't worry about reforming the world; reform yourself! . . . "The peace that you would have others find must first be found in your own heart."

While we have lofty ideals for social reform and world change, our real purpose in life is to work on ourselves. This at first may seem selfish or uncharitable, but it is honest, and in the long run we will make more of a contribution to society when we are clear than when we are in any way confused. Unless we are gelled and whole in our own consciousness, we are not in a position to serve. The greatest service we can offer to others is to purify, sanctify, and know our own Self. Then, and only then, are we in the proper position to give. Until then, we are taking.

This does not mean that we are to run off to a cave and meditate until we are realized. Our work on ourselves may involve a great deal of social service. We can be nurses, teachers, and therapists, but we must always bear in mind that we are really using these avenues to expand our own consciousness. Serving others with all our heart does not contradict working on ourselves; to the contrary, it supports it. Until the end, we must remember to use everything we do as a vehicle for our own awakening.

The Master Jesus said, "How can you say to another, 'Let me take a speck out of your eye!' when you have a bigger one in your own? Hypocrite! First remove the speck from your own eye, and then you will be able to remove that of your brother." There are many teachers, leaders and therapists who teach what they have not yet mastered. If a student learns from such a one, it is the student's grace, and not the teacher's guidance.

Does this mean that one must be a fully realized spiritual master before one can teach or offer service? No, not at all. If we waited for everyone to be perfect before anyone could teach, we would have a long wait indeed. It is sufficient to teach what we know and have directly experienced. In this case, teaching is really a sharing, a comparing of notes. It is as if we are all working together on a huge jigsaw puzzle. As you find the place for your piece, you make it easier for me to see the pattern and the place for mine. You might even find a piece that I can use. Teaching is sharing. We have nothing to teach each other, but much to share.

If each of us lives up to our highest ideals, we will be giving the best teaching there is. The most powerful teachings that I have received have come through my ignoring what people say and observing what they do. Words are the last and most superflous elements of teaching. Real change comes only through example. One night, after Hilda had worked hard to give a strong and meaningful class, I and some friends went down to Ammal's Pizza Shop (a front for an orphanage) for a snack. I had heard many lectures on selfless service, but when I saw Hilda there wiping down the counter, after she had already given so much, I immediately understood what loving service is all about and in that moment I wanted to do it, too.

If we want to get another person — or the world — to do something, we must *do it first*. If we want people around us not to fight, we must be peaceful ourself. If we want our kids to clean up their room, we must be willing to keep our own room clean. And if we want the government to not make radioactive nuclear reactors, we cannot afford to radiate poisonous waves of angry emotional reaction. Those that we seek to change will be affected by what we are *doing* in such a way that they will experience that there is a better way than the way that they have been trying. Our friends in conflict may be inspired by our peaceful example, and the good feelings that they experience in our presence will encourage them to be that way, too. And even if they do not change, our job is to be peaceful anyway, so there is really no question about what we need to do. We need to live what we want to see.

There is an important Buddhist scripture which contains many high and lucid truths. The very first sentence of the aphorisms is the author's admission that "The only purpose of this writing is the clarification of my own understanding." The delightful paradox is that as the author focused his own understanding, all those who read the work gain the benefit of his newfound clarity.

In this writing, I have come to see exactly what the Buddhist meant. As I have worked to put these ideas onto paper, I have learned much. I have been forced to look at what I believe is true and to see how much I am living what I believe in. I must wrestle with what I am willing to be responsible for telling you. And, over the months of editing and revising the book, I feel that I have actually been editing and revising *my own consciousness.* No matter who else or how many other people read this book, I know one person who has gotten a great deal from it — me. It is not so much the words that I have learned from, but the *process* of participating in its birth. And if you gain something from my experience as well, that is a nice fringe benefit.

When we love ourselves, we are bringing love to the world. When we master our own lives, we are bringing mastery and harmony to all people. It is said that "it is easier to conquer a city than to conquer one's self." Find tranquility within yourself, and the world around you will become tranquil. Each of us is a force field that creates and shapes all that is around us. One thought of love from the center of your mind spreads like ripples throughout the universe and touches everything, everywhere, with love. We are all connected to everything. Each of your thoughts and actions has a profound effect on all. I cannot underestimate my relationship with the whole of creation, for I am deeply connected with all that I see.

It has also been said that "you only see yourself." If, then, we want to see a new world in a new and beautiful way, we must first cultivate love and beauty within *ourselves*. If we send thoughts of anger and bitterness to those who pollute the earth with smoke and chemicals, we are poisoning the atmosphere with our thoughts. Hating anyone has never done anyone any good, and it certainly has not brought any more peace to the world. The only things that can bring peace to the world are thoughts, feelings, and actions of peace. To think is to create. If we think hatred, hatred shall be manifested in the form of new bullets and bombs. Hilda has said that every thought of anger produces one new physical bullet. When we see an insane arms race, we are seeing the results of our collective consciousness, and we can hold no political or military strategists to blame. They are simply acting out our thoughts of fear and competition, expressed in a world of our own creation, for which we must stand responsible.

If we are to truly change the world, we must give it new thoughts to be manifested — thoughts of the world as we would like to see it. We must fill our minds and hearts with ideas and feelings of harmony and celebration. One person quietly sitting for a few minutes a day and meditating or praying for world peace has an effect on the world greater than those who angrily protest and criticize those who make war. Someone who runs down the street cursing those who fight, is in effect sending out a set of vibrations that bring about only more war. As it is said, *"Don't curse the darkness — light a candle."*

Each of us can light our own candle, in our own way. We may feel that we have little power to change the destiny of the world, but it is through individuals that the world is changed. One little burning match can start a forest fire. Jesus had his ministry for only three years. Ghandi was only one man, and his humble actions transformed the lives of millions. You do not need to be a Jesus or a Ghandi to change the world. You do not need to be famous or honored. You need only to be *you*. As a cab driver, or a housewife, or a prisoner, or a tailor, you can bless the world fully. I know an old German tailor who, in his simple joy and happiness, contributed immensely to my own life, though he knows it not. From a worldly point of view, there is nothing outstanding about him. He is not well known, highly educated, or wealthy. He just shines. Whenever I see him, his eyes light up, my heart awakens, we embrace each other, we call each other Yiddish names, and for one moment, one very special moment, time stops. There we are, just the two of us, in friendship, in eternity. I have learned from him that greatness is not of the world, but of the heart. He has less prestige, money, and political influence than most of those who are in "positions that can change the world," but he has done more to change it for the better, perhaps, than they have done. In the eyes of his customers, he may be just an old German tailor, but to me he is a saint.

There are many evangelists who would save the world. I believe that real evangelism starts with one's own self. Before I can offer others salvation, I must have found it myself. Instead of eradicating sinners from the world, I must first eradicate anger, pettiness, and bigotry from my self. Before I can build a huge cathedral to the Lord, I must first consecrate the temple of my own body and soul. Before I can preach, I must practice. *A Course in Miracles* asks us, "Can the world be saved if you are not?"

The miracle is that each of us really *can* save the world. Indeed, we must, for what else of value is there to be done? Since there is no order of difficulty in miracles, our desire to save the world must be within our reach. And since the task of our physically maneuvering the world and its people into harmony is unthinkable, there must be some other way.

That way is the way of the Spirit, the way of God, the way of Love, which is not confined to time or to space. When we align our hearts and minds with the intentions of Godly Love, we are joining the forces of that power, indeed the only power that can redeem humankind. We have found the only avenue of action that can have any real effect. We have aligned our intentions with Him whose intention is salvation. In attempting to change the world according to the ways of the world, we cannot succeed. In working to bring Light to the world according to the way of Light, we cannot fail. Our will has become His Will. When we discover that only peace begets peace, we have understood the principle of salvation for all people, and the only real answer to the problems of the world. It is true that "unless you are a part of the solution, you are a part of the problem." No man can serve two masters. No man can serve peace while living in discord. And no man can sustain chaos if he is absorbed in harmony.

Absorb yourself, then, in the highest peace that you know, and believe that God, in making this promise to Abraham, who lived for the One God, is making it directly to you: "A great nation shall I make of thee." Believe that from your simple, quiet thoughts and actions will spring forth a new era of peace on the earth. Believe that *the destiny of all mankind is in your very hands*, for so it is. Believe that you have been put on earth for a purpose, and as you fulfill your purpose, all the people in the world are redeemed. If you believe that it would take a miracle for your life to bring about peace on earth, then believe in miracles, because God sure does.

"When you know the Truth that sets you free, you are free of the burden of saving the world. Indeed, the task of saving the world can never be your burden, for it is the intention of the Creator, and that which is His intention can never be difficult.

Your frustration in attempting to change the world is born only of personal ego, and no salvation can ever come through the limited self. In seeking to reform others, you are dealing only with the projections of your own self, which can never be mastered while you see yourself as another. Release all others from the burden of your projections, and you release yourself from the burden of world salvation.

Only when you realize the outer world to be a reflection of your inner self can you make real progress in fulfilling the destiny of peace on earth. There can be no peace on earth until you know the Peace of Heaven. The Kingdom of Heaven, in which Peace must always reign, is within.

Look into your hearts, Children, and there shall you find the solutions to all problems. Indeed, there is but one solution to all problems, and that is the recognition of your eternal and irrevocable oneness with God. Know your kinship with the Creator of all things, and all things shall reveal themselves to be your own creations. At this moment, and only at this moment, peace in the world is restored, for only in this moment do you realize that it has never been lost. Know your Heritage as Sons and Daughters of Peace, and Peace must certainly come to you, instantaneously and forever."

THE KEY TO THE FUTURE

We hear many prophecies and predictions about the events that will occur in the coming years. Many of them foretell vast changes in the form that our lifestyles will take. We are told that we will have to make sacrifices and that we will see the collapse of many of the institutions and ways of life with which we are now comfortable. We are given even more foreboding pictures of food shortages, civil unrest, and disastrous changes in the land forms of the earth, including that of a shift of the earth's axis. We are told with striking consistency that we are on the doorstep of Armageddon and the end times.

Frankly, I do not know whether or how many of these predictions are true. It is amazing to me, though, that so many prophets, traditions, scientists, and psychics agree on the same things. Many of the ancient prophecies, such as that of the Hopi Indians, the Buddhists, and the book of Revelations are being fulfilled with uncanny accuracy. I have also heard these warnings from spiritual masters whose guidance and advice I trust. As their insights are correct on nearly all other accounts, I have little reason to believe that they would err on this matter. To underscore the predictions, the trend of human events, with its race hatred, separatism, and weapons craze seems to be magnifying to an unprecedented degree. One swami said that "We are like a person soundly sleeping in a bed, with a deadly snake slowly winding its way toward us." I do not really know what the future holds, but I take these warnings seriously.

One thing seems clear, though, which I, and I believe you as well, can see in the present. There is great suffering in the world. Most people are living in a sort of sleepwalking state of ignorance. As a race, we have strayed very far from the path of a Godly life that was intended for us to live in fulfillment and peace. Immorality and fear are rampant. I say this without judgement. It is a fact. I cannot believe that this is the way human beings were meant to live.

Werner Erhard put it very neatly: "We hear many prophecies of catastrophe and doom," he noted, "but it seems to me that the worst thing that could happen would be for things to stay the way they are." I am inclined to agree.

Our Mother Earth has been raped, plundered, and desecrated. I drive on the New Jersey Turnpike, and the air is foul. We must buy our water in plastic bottles that are shipped from hundreds or thousands of miles away. Factories in Detroit pollute the air with deadly acids that have rendered useless the water in Adirondack lakes a thousand miles away, and the fish are dead. When the fish die, the animals that eat fish die, and the entire balance of life on the planet is upset. The trees in New Zealand are dying from pollution from America. Nuclear power plants are allowed to spew deadly radiation into our water, land, and air, and the people of one of the few remaining unspoilt states in our nation — Maine — have voted to allow nuclear plants to continue operation. Greed for power and money has taken precedence over love for life and the right to live and breathe. How long can we convince ourselves that things on earth are O.K., when our planet is hurting so badly? "None are so blind as those who would not see."

When the seers explain the changes to come as a necessary cleansing of a toxic civilization and earth, it is not difficult to believe. Sadly, it makes sense. Any organism gorged with noxious substances would revolt in self-survival. If this is what Mother Earth needs to do, then I cannot blame her.

On the bright side, we are told that these transformations will bring about a new era of peace and unity on earth. As the darkest hour is just before dawn, we are bound to see a return to a life in which people of good will live in harmony and brotherhood. If this is difficult to believe, then it is all the more indication of the sad state of affairs to which we have fallen — one in which we cannot even conceive of people living in harmony. Yet we are told that the millenium and the rapture and a thousand years of peace are at hand.

We are already seeing the signs of a new age beginning to bud. Over the past fifteen or twenty years, there has been a tremendous proliferation of spiritual movements on the planet. Millions of people have been drawn to the study of meditation, ancient spiritual traditions, healing, and the ways of living in harmony with the natural order of the earth. Communities with the high spiritual ideals of love, sharing, and service have sprung up all around the planet. There is an increasing interest in returning to the simpler things of life. Many are forsaking "status" jobs to return to working with the land and studying how to harness the ever-renewable power of the sun. Some would say, perhaps, that these are faddists or escapists, but I believe that these are the pioneers of a new way of living, a way that will bring fulfillment instead of heartache.

Some say that if we change our ways and voluntarily re-form our ways of living with each other and with the earth, these painful purges will not be necessary. Others say that it is too late, and we will have to weather these unprecedented upheavals. Perhaps our civilization can renew itself without these difficult changes, but so far life on earth seems to be getting worse, and not better. It would be wonderful if civilization as it is adopted a new lifestyle of love and sharing, but, quite frankly, that does not seem imminent.

The question then becomes: How are we to relate to these changes? What can our response be? How can we prepare? The beauty of the answer is that it is the same answer to every question ever asked by any person at any time in civilization. What we need to do to weather these changes is exactly what we need to do if none of these changes ever occurs. We need to live our lives in harmony with the Spirit. We need to love. We need to be strong and compassionate. We need to remember who we are — Children of a Loving God. We need to serve and respect each other and our home, the earth. We need to let go of negative ways of thinking, speaking, and acting, and to replace them with laughter, mutual support, and truth. We need to practice what we were advised, in love, to do, two thousand years ago, and thousands of years before that:

Love God with all your being, and Love one another as yourself.

If there are earthquakes and economic collapse, Love and Faith will be the only standards that carry us through. And if there is never one more earthquake and the economy is very healthy, these same principles are the only ones that will make us happy.

The Truth is eternal. How to live is eternal. Yes, the forms that life takes may change, but the principles that make life work are constant. Love is as powerful and important as it ever has been and ever will be. Awareness of God is the only foundation that has ever made any life worthwhile, and so shall it always remain.

"The Truth stands invincible, untouchable by the frail whims of passing events. The only key to living is the acknowledgement and expression of God. So it was for your first ancestors, and so shall it be until the end of time.

We tell you with the deepest assurance that you are loved, you are protected, and you are cared for. Where else could you be, but under the benevolent protection of the Divine Mother? Let go of your worries, your anxieties, your unworthiness. Look carefully, Children, at the lives of those who radiate the shining Light of Love. Their worries have been dissolved in the infinite ocean of God's eternal Love. Cast away your doubts, and count yourself among the Holy and the Pure, for so you are.

You are privileged to participate in the transformation of consciousness on the planet earth. Such a position is very auspicious indeed. You are a part of the unfoldment of the Destiny of mankind. You shall bear witness to the long-awaited emergence of Truth from its cocoon. The occasion of your birth is a joyful and glorious one. You have chosen to step forward into the Light.

Go forth then, and live the message of Light and Love and Peace. You are an emmisary of God. He will work through you to create a future which will bring with it the end of all human suffering. From the deepest sincerity of our being, we tell you that there can be no greater privilege than this. This is the most cherishable and glorious Destiny at any time in all the universe."

The Promise

"Sons and Daughters of the Living God:

You are created in the image and likeness of the God that you love, and it is your only Destiny to know yourself to be one with the Spirit that eternally dwells within the entire universe.

Holy art thou in the sight of the Father of all things, and splendid is the Truth of your Beauty. Children of Light, the wonder of your Self shines with an effulgence far more brilliant than mortal eyes can behold, and it is our great privilege to share with you the awakening of your soul to the magnificence of your own Godly nature.

It is now for you to take your future, and yea, the future of all humanity into your heart and your hands, and mark a path of Light as a blessing to all. You are entrusted with the ability to heal the world. Let every thought, breath, word, and deed be consecrated unto Divine purpose. So shall your reason for living be fulfilled and your dream of Love realized.

Beloved ones, always remember your Holiness. We bid thee walk the path of service, and love one another as you would be loved. Give what you would receive, and offer support and encouragement to all. Ignore shortcomings, acknowledge strength, and bless all with your holy thoughts.

Have unrelenting faith in the great power of Love. No matter what travails or adversities befall you, faith in God will carry you through all challenges. This is our promise and our pledge, unassailable and invincible, guaranteed by the Truth of God's Reality and His eternal Love for you.

Our Love and our Blessings are now given to thee. Our greatest joy is for you to accept Love in Its fullness. Go forth in splendor; go forth in courage; go forth in confidence. Be the Light of the world, for that is what you are. Live in Love, grow in strength, and sing the Song of Freedom that was written for you aeons ago at the moment of your birth, the very song that you are now ready to once again claim as your very own.

Go forth, Divine Ones, Holy Ones, Blessed Ones. May Love live forever in your Heart, and in the Name of the Living God, may the world be Blessed through you.''

By Alan Cohen
BOOKS

The Healing of the Planet Earth
A golden gift of empowering ideas, an excellent guidebook to give you the courage to release all fear and allow yourself to be lifted naturally to the next stage of personal and planetary transformation. Introduction by Barbara Marx Hubbard, with magnificent photographs by Awakening Heart Productions.

The Dragon Doesn't Live Here Anymore
A bestselling book of encouragement and joyful self-discovery. This warm, open-hearted, and inspiring journey through spiritual growth sheds loving light on self-acceptance, healing, and the power of positive living. A steppingstone and companion to many hearts.

Rising In Love
A touching guide to healing our relationships in the light of love. In a personal, comfortable, and captivating way, Alan offers important, practical insights on how to create fulfilling relationships by believing in ourselves and those we love.

Companions of the Heart
An attractive hard cover volume of the above three popular books. This collection is perfect for those who love to read and re-read these inspiring ideas and to offer as a gift to friends.

The Peace That You Seek
A deeply inspiring and moving collection of channelled messages of guidance, offered as gifts to the Children of Light on the threshold of a New Age. These messages offer great strength, wisdom and caring, shared to serve as healing reminders of the wonder that shines within us. A special gift for the spirit.

Have You Hugged A Monster Today?
A delightful story that teaches how to discover the hearts of the meanest monsters and make friends with the friendless. Shared through clever, laughable cartoons and captions, this is an entertaining course in human relations for children of all ages. Illustrations by Keith Kelly.

Setting the Seen
A series of fascinating guided visualizations for deep relaxation and stress management. Written with instructions for use by teachers, counselors and those in the healing profession, this is a practical guide to physical, emotional and spiritual tranquility. (Companion to cassette *Peace*)

CASSETTE TAPES

Peace
A soothing tapestry of guided images, excellent for meditation, relaxation and personal growth. Useful for spiritual growth, awakening creativity and mental clarity. Alan Cohen's voice blends with Steven Halpern's music to create a deep harmony of being that will touch you in a most important way.

Deep Relaxation
A one-hour program of exercises to relax, renew and reinvigorate. Excellent for those who would like to practice yoga at home; this tape guides the listener through a basic series of yoga postures, guided deep relaxation, breathing exercises and meditation. Gentle background music by Dr. Steven Halpern.

Miracle Mountain
A live recording of one of Alan's workshops, in which he invites the participants to become themselves and celebrate their own strength. These tapes capture the essence of Alan's teachings, including many powerfully inspiring moments. Themes include: keys to healing, loving relationships and believing in ourselves. Tapes include songs and music, guided meditations, group interactions and joyous laughter.

I Believe in You
An orchestral journey of self-affirmation, including inspiring, empowering songs by the popular minstrel, Stephen Longfellow Fiske, and a marvelously uplifting guided meditation by Alan. A very moving and practical gift to encourage healing for yourself or others.

★ ★

Personal Orders:

For a free catalog of Alan Cohen's books, tapes and workshop schedule, write to:

Alan Cohen Publications and Workshops
P.O. Box 5658, Somerset, New Jersey 08875

Bookstore Orders:

New Leaf
5425 Tulane Drive S.W.
Atlanta, Georgia 30310-2323

(1-800) 241-3829
toll-free number for stores only